WW2 Codebreaking
EVENTS AND ORGANISATIONS

This book is dedicated to Betty Hollingberry (née Vowles). Betty worked at Outstation Eastcote as a Wren during the Second World War, operating Bombe codebreaking machines. She reached her centenary in 2023, receiving her telegram from King Charles III.

WW2 Codebreaking
EVENTS AND ORGANISATIONS
A WARTIME GLOSSARY

RONALD KOORM

Pen & Sword
MILITARY
AN IMPRINT OF PEN & SWORD BOOKS LTD.
YORKSHIRE · PHILADELPHIA

First published in Great Britain in 2025 by
PEN AND SWORD MILITARY
An imprint of
Pen & Sword Books Limited
Yorkshire – Philadelphia

Copyright © Ronald Koorm, 2025

ISBN 978 1 39905 344 0

The right of Ronald Koorm to be identified as Author of this work has been asserted by him in accordance with the Copyright, Designs and Patents Act 1988.

A CIP catalogue record for this book is available from the British Library.

All rights reserved. No part of this book may be reproduced, transmitted, downloaded, decompiled or reverse engineered in any form or by any means, electronic or mechanical including photocopying, recording or by any information storage and retrieval system, without permission from the Publisher in writing. NO AI TRAINING: Without in any way limiting the Author's and Publisher's exclusive rights under copyright, any use of this publication to "train" generative artificial intelligence (AI) technologies to generate text is expressly prohibited. The Author and Publisher reserve all rights to license uses of this work for generative AI training and development of machine learning language models.

Typeset in Times New Roman 10/12 by
SJmagic DESIGN SERVICES, India.
Printed and bound in the UK by CPI Group (UK) Ltd.

The Publisher's authorised representative in the EU for product safety is Authorised Rep Compliance Ltd., Ground Floor, 71 Lower Baggot Street, Dublin D02 P593, Ireland. www.arccompliance.com

For a complete list of Pen & Sword titles please contact
PEN & SWORD BOOKS LIMITED
George House, Units 12 & 13, Beevor Street, Off Pontefract Road,
Barnsley, South Yorkshire, S71 1HN, England
E-mail: enquiries@pen-and-sword.co.uk
Website: www.pen-and-sword.co.uk

or

PEN AND SWORD BOOKS
1950 Lawrence Rd, Havertown, PA 19083, USA
E-mail: uspen-and-sword@casematepublishers.com
Website: www.penandswordbooks.com

Contents

Introduction vi

Events.. 1
Links, Events and Sequencing 130
Commentary on Events.. 140
Organisations 160
Commentary on Organisations.. 188
Questions and Answers 194

Abbreviations... 199
Terms and Names... 201
Acknowledgements.. 208
Bibliography 210
Author's Note... 218
List of Events 220
Endnotes... 226
Index 234

Introduction

This part of the glossary on wartime codebreaking and intelligence revolves around events and organisations that form part of the military and associated history of the twentieth century. The first volume in the series was subtitled *People and Places*, and it is the case that there will be some overlap across the two books. It is natural to assume that people involved in codebreaking or intelligence in the past would be involved to varying degrees in events, and be part of various organisations, which may be mentioned here.

This is an opportunity for us to explore and analyse some of those events and the establishments that developed over time with relevance to intelligence, encoding messages, and in codebreaking too. Just as organisations such as the BBC are very different today compared with when they started in the mid-1930s, we might track the development and metamorphosis of organisations such as GC&CS[1] and GCHQ, of listening stations, and those that managed them, of clandestine intelligence organisations, those that designed, built, and tested encoding and codebreaking equipment, and others. Then there are the 'events' which influenced war and politics in history, relevant to codebreaking. Some of these events might be seen as minor, some more significant, but all would make a difference along the road of communication of secret messages and intelligence, and of ways to crack those codes using a variety of methods and skills. The text reflects the international scene during the last century, as many of the events and indeed the organisations would be based in, and across Europe, America, Asia, Africa, and the Far East. It did not all happen in Great Britain but, of course, a good proportion of it took place here, with a wide cross-section of skilled and semi-skilled personnel working across multiple establishments. Many would evolve over time, sections become spilt off, expanded, merged with other organisations, dissolved, created with new specialist personnel, and so on. Some would develop further into modern military or pseudo-military defence departments and enter the world of data analysis, computing, anti-terrorist activities, etc.

The relevance to the twenty-first century here is significant, with war in Europe at the time of writing, uncertainty as to how NATO and the EU will react in the future to increasing threats from Russia and its allies, and the need for up-to-date intelligence in order to be one step ahead of the enemy at all times. We are living in the world of drones, pilotless aircraft, artificial intelligence becoming more advanced each day, those who have your data being in a position of immense

INTRODUCTION

power, and the need to protect nations from cyber crime, hackers, and actions against the state.

Knowledge is everything. Understanding how your opponent thinks and plans their strategy is essential, and not always easy to assess. Reflecting on twentieth-century history on this subject can sometimes give us a better understanding of what worked, and what didn't, all those years ago. It is the case that the technology has changed, for sure, since the Second World War, but that the approach to gathering and analysing intelligence is as relevant today as it was all those years ago.

We rely on data protection legislation today to protect individuals, as well as passwords, fingerprint codes, eye scanners, and other methods. But this has become a game of cat and mouse, whereby the other side is finding more ways to circumvent the security systems and obtain their intelligence by clandestine means, irrespective of the cost. Possession of 'data' is not enough; it is the selection, filtering, analysis, and scrutiny of that data that gives organisations and states real power, if they have the systems and skilled personnel to do so. Find out the weaknesses in the other side's military equipment, manpower, software, or order of battle and that can be a huge advantage when waging a future campaign to gain land, power, and political influence.

One of the great Allied successes in the Second World War was in concealing from the enemy what they were doing with the intercepted Axis radio communication and non-Morse[2] messages. The Axis powers had no clue that the Allies had the *Bombe*, *Robinson*, *Colossus*, and *Tunny* codebreaking machines to attack the Nazi encoding systems. Those systems meant the Allies could process many more encoded messages to find the settings that were the key to reading the individual messages. They weren't created overnight. They required teamwork on a massive scale, then highly specialised men and women to develop them, test them, modify them, and operate them. The United States and the Poles also contributed to this process. Let us not forget the Nazis also developed complex encoding systems and improved them over time. There were delays in breaking the message settings at times, and consequently, acute frustration. Just because you were proficient at mathematics, did not mean you could automatically break into the codes. Cribs or clues would be required, and some luck also. But codebreakers were used to bouncing ideas off one another, and if someone got stuck on a problem, there would be others to approach it from perhaps a different angle.

Using this glossary

This glossary volume utilises time, via appropriate dates, to sequence the events that were relevant to codebreaking. An 'event' may be considered as an action or occurrence at a time in history that is worthy of inclusion within the glossary, having a relevance to either codebreaking, be a support to codebreaking, or be intelligence-based. While the body of this glossary revolves around the Second World War, there are a number of different events and activities listed here that are both pre-war and post-war. This is to assist the reader in understanding better how things evolved in intelligence and codebreaking over time. The Government Code and Cipher School, or GC&CS, was established originally many years before the start of the Second World War. However, one can track the evolution of that organisation here, to a degree, and it being further established at Bletchley Park in 1939. Encoding machines such as Enigma didn't just happen. They had to be invented, designed, trialled, modified, and evolved to improve security and operational efficiency. The same is true for other encoding and encrypting machines, and indeed for developing both new codebreaking systems and machines. The glossary outlines events that were relevant to some of those developments.

The events listed were carefully identified, selected, and sequenced broadly in time/date order for this glossary. Some may be considered as minor events in the bigger picture of things, but all helped influence the progress of the war or pre-war and post-war activities and development. For example, the introduction of Post Office engineer Tommy Flowers to Max Newman by Alan Turing at Bletchley Park had consequences that arguably became pivotal in the outcome of the Second World War, although it might be considered by some as a minor event by itself. The reader can always refer to the author's first book in the glossary series, *People and Places*, for further information. Against each event listed is a note or comment marked 'significance'. This is the author's comment on the significance of the text inserted against the item, to put the item into better context. This may particularly assist readers who may not be so familiar with the wide range of occurrences that impacted on intelligence and codebreaking during wartime or close to it. Of course, there is opinion expressed under this part, and some academics might consider there were other aspects of the event that had significance and impact on relevant persons, countries, organisations, or other events. The subject matter is not always black and white, and there are plenty of shades of grey in interpretation too. Note that while this glossary principally revolves around the period of the Second World War, there was also a need for a pre-war and post-war listing of events, to enable better appreciation of how things evolved over time. Note that there is a listing of the events at the back of the book, in the same sequence as written in the events chapter.

Where dates are in brackets adjacent to the bold text of an event, that is understood to be the year, or approximate year for the date of that event. Those events without years inserted at the heading in brackets imply that the event may have covered more than one year or a wider period of time, or that the date for the event was unclear or unavailable without further research.

A chapter is included titled 'Links, Events and Sequencing'. This is included to provide a relatively quick reference in bullet point form, to explain certain issues that could be more easily understood in that format. For example, the development over time of the WRNS, or Wrens, who had such an impact on codebreaking and other activities during wartime. It can be studied in purely text form, or alternatively in the bullet point list, with various dates provided. At the end of each numbered section is a list of relevant links pertinent to the text, outlined in words, which can be used to explore further, either using the index, entries within the glossary

INTRODUCTION

volumes, or other sources of information. A commentary on events is the author selecting certain items and discussing them, some in more detail, or to give a somewhat broader overview.

The organisations section is in alphabetical order, and there are plenty of abbreviations for those, with an explanatory section at the end of the book. Although the glossary revolves principally around the Second World War, there are some exceptions to this, where pre-war and post-war events and organisations may be of interest to the reader. Some dates are very specific, others more general. Although the glossary is about codebreaking, it expands further than this, into areas of spying, espionage, deception, and trickery even. One should remember that codebreaking is but a means towards an end objective; to provide an advantage to the codebreakers, to allow it to win battles and eventually the war itself. It was but a tool in the arsenal of communication, albeit an important one. Without it one is largely blind as to what the enemy is planning, and when. Not having the correct intelligence at the right time can result in catastrophic circumstances, and with major losses of men and land area.

The research that I carried out over several years surprised me in many ways as to what I eventually discovered. There were various coincidences, and links between unlikely people, places, organisations, or events. There was the intense race for the Allies to develop complex, new systems, methods, organisations, and equipment to crack the enemy codes in good time. The need to maintain the utmost secrecy of the operations to avoid letting the cat out of the bag and giving the enemy a warning of what they were doing. Yet, some of the enemy had ideas very similar to the Allied engineers, but were in the end let down by Adolf Hitler, who did not always listen to his advisors. One can only really make significant progress with the appropriate support technically, as well as with the manpower, resources, and finance to move the project forward. The Allies were better at this than the enemy, but it would never be an easy ride.

The reader will be able to appreciate that many organisations relevant to the entries in this glossary started small, with a handful of people, then developed over time to become substantial and influential departments supporting the war effort. The interaction between them was not always efficient, but it is quite remarkable how well they worked together as a whole, in practice. Many would go on later to support post-war industry, scientific laboratories, and technical innovations. Sadly, not that many of the true innovators were recognised post-war for their contribution to codebreaking, although some were. Alan Turing, of course, came to an early, and premature death. The country really could not afford to lose someone like Turing, as they only come along infrequently to help change modern society with ground-breaking technical achievements. He was only properly appreciated some years after he passed away. There are several blue plaques commemorating him on different sites and I have listed these in the glossary.

GCHQ is the United Kingdom's leading intelligence agency, protecting the country from terrorism, cyber crime, and enemies of the state. It shares selected intelligence information with other allied agencies around the world. It is only by linking these organisations together and sharing information and data that effective progress can be made in an ever-complex and threatening world. Yet, the enormous GCHQ complex in Cheltenham developed slowly over time just over a hundred years ago, from a handful of specialists just after the First World War had ended. The systems and equipment used by GCHQ now would have truly amazed those in the early twentieth century, with use of complex algorithms and computers, telecommunications linking satellites and interpreted by more computers, A.I., and by humans too. Bletchley Park held a conference on the implications and impact of artificial intelligence in November 2023, an A.I. Safety Summit, with many international organisations represented. Bletchley was the precursor of the modern GCHQ. Yet, GCHQ would be less effective if it did not link up to the United States equivalent, the NSA, and European security agencies, to get the bigger picture. We rely on them, and they rely on us, to a degree. Where this will end is anyone's guess. But we need GCHQ just as much as we need modern tanks, missiles, men, women, and equipment of the armed services, to counter the evolving enemy threats. This glossary and other volumes associated with it in the series of books should give a better understanding of the evolution of GC&CS to GCHQ, together with the people, places, events, systems, organisations, and the activities that made it happen.

Finally, this glossary volume commences in the pre-war period, and finishes several years after the end of the Second World War, but the main body of information is centred around the war.

Events

BTM awarded Hollerith licence (1908)

Hollerith was an American company, and the British Tabulating Machine Company in England was awarded a licence in 1908 to manufacture and market Hollerith tabulating machines to sell across the British Empire. This was the same year that Winston Churchill married, and honeymooned in Eastcote, Middlesex, adjacent to the open fields that would eventually house and operate many codebreaking Bombes, which were built by BTM.[1] Hollerith machines were electrically powered to sort and process punched cards with data. They had many different uses, including census processing. Bletchley Park management could see advantages in utilising this equipment in conjunction with the collection of mass intelligence via Morse code intercepts from enemy Enigma machines. Prior to the Second World War, BTM would develop the Rolling Total Tabulator, a British invention and independent of Hollerith. However, due to the pressures of war and the codebreaking Bombe production, they still relied on the use of Hollerith machines for punched card processing.

Significance: The opportunity for BTM to market abroad as well as in the UK, in the area of punched card tabulating machines. This would prove to be a double-edged sword for BTM in the longer term. BTM really wanted to be independent in the sale and rental of manufactured equipment, and this was later proved to be possible with their developments and inventions. BTM would go on to manufacture codebreaking machines in the Second World War, and would provide Hollerith machines to others for data processing.

Scarborough provides intelligence base and supporting GCHQ (1912)

The Royal Navy set up a wireless telegraphy unit in the Scarborough area in 1912, in Yorkshire, England. It became a Signals Intelligence or SIGINT unit and was relocated to Irton Moor in Yorkshire in 1943. The unit came close to closure in 1932 but was reprieved in 1935. During wartime, it intercepted German Naval and Naval Air radio communication as a key listening station, or Y-station. There are reports it also managed Direction-Finding (D/F) for a substantial area, to locate radio transmissions. Civilians mainly operated the base with some servicemen and women, including several WRNS personnel. The SIGINT civilians would be known as part of the Admiralty Civilian Shore Wireless Service, abbreviated as ACSWS. There was a transfer of this division to GCHQ in 1965 and it then formed the CSO, or Composite Signals Organisation. It was then known as CSOS Irton Moor. Now known as GCHQ Scarborough since July 2001, it provides an important support role to the GCHQ at Cheltenham, in terms of helping to identify threats to the state and counter-threats. The origins of the site make it the longest continuous signals intelligence location in the world, according to GCHQ.

Significance: Scarborough has a long history in intelligence and listening via radio and Morse code. That it still provides a support service, albeit in different times, is testimony to the skilled personnel who have worked there.

Deciphering the Zimmerman Telegram (1917)

The Zimmerman telegram was significant in the First World War as the contents triggered the United States of America into entering the conflict. It was a secret encoded communication in January 1917 between the German Foreign Minister, Arthur Zimmerman, and the German Embassy in Mexico, offering recapture of certain United States land and territory in exchange for Mexico joining Germany in the war. The states of Texas, Arizona, and part of New Mexico would be part of the deal. Mexico was in a state of civil war at the time. The recipient of the telegram was the German ambassador, H. Von Eckhardt. The telegram was manually deciphered in England by codebreakers within Room 40 of the Admiralty, and the predecessors of Bletchley Park. While the decoded message from the Germans was eventually shown to the senior staff at the US government, Britain's codebreakers were reluctant to advise that it was they who managed to decipher the message, so that part was kept confidential. By early March, the German foreign minister had confirmed the telegram was genuine. The knowledge gained via this telegram forced the hand of the United States government to enter the war against Germany and its allies. It demonstrated that understanding codes and ciphers and being able to break them using various methods (manual codebreaking at the time) could be invaluable intelligence for those in power.

Significance: The recognition that decoding intercepted coded messages in detail could reveal intelligence was sufficient to have major consequences. The Zimmerman Telegram is seen as extremely important in codebreaking history, even though it occurred within the First World War.

Scherbius patents the Enigma machine (1918)

Although the Dutch were also working on designing rotor-based encoding machines around the same time as Arthur Scherbius, it was Scherbius who would be quick off the mark to take out patents on his new Enigma encoding machine, beating the Dutch. However, various patents were granted to the Dutch, and most of these were acquired eventually by him over time, strengthening his position in the marketplace for intellectual property of the Enigma and modified versions. He would file for patents in 1918 for Enigma, with applications granted in Great Britain in 1927. Two years later, Scherbius would die a premature death in a tragic accident.[2] But the development of the Enigma codebreaking machine would still advance technologically and be built in quantities of tens of thousands for the German war machine and Nazi infrastructure.

Significance: The beginning of a journey to make the Enigma machine protected in respect of intellectual property. It is unclear if Scherbius fully understood the potential of the Enigma at the time of his invention, and at the time of applying for patents. However, he had considered that it may have a useful part in the German military if he could gain sufficient interest.

BTM Established in Letchworth, Hertfordshire (1920)

It would be around 1908 when the American company granted a licence to BTM in London to market Hollerith machines and equipment throughout the British Empire.[3] Profitability increased when BTM started manufacturing its own machines. By 1920, BTM, or the British Tabulating Company Limited, would establish itself in the city of Letchworth as a production factory and a new base for operations. It would also start manufacturing its own machines, and not just re-selling or hiring out American Hollerith products, which would be part of a licensing deal. The Hollerith machines were used for sorting and processing punched cards, an early version of data processing. Prior to this, BTM had been formed in 1902 as the Tabulator Company Limited. Around another twenty years would pass before BTM won the Government contract for the building of the Turing–Welchman codebreaking Bombe machines. BTM had also been successful in designing and building the Rolling Total Tabulator, a machine that gave it some independence from Hollerith. The American host company eventually became IBM, International Business Machines, and BTM post-war became ICT, and later ICL.

Significance: Letchworth would be geographically some distance from London, with less expensive land and building costs, and with room for possible expansion of the factory and BTM site. This would become important in the wartime years when Bombe codebreaking machine production was carried out in relatively large quantities.

Enigma displayed to the public at an exhibition (1923)

Arthur Scherbius, the inventor of the Enigma machine, displayed it to the public for the first time at an exhibition for postal services in 1923. This would be almost twenty years before the start of the Second World War. It was sold as a commercial business machine, initially for banks and finance houses so that secret and confidential messages could be sent back and forth between them. The sales literature would claim the Enigma machine codes were unbreakable. The rotor wheels could be removed and inserted in different sequences, which increased the permutations of the settings of Enigma.[4] The rotor wheels would be kept in a neat, hinged wooden box. The original Enigma was bulky, heavy, and not particularly user-friendly to operate. It was also quite expensive. Scherbius would work on improving Enigma and reducing the physical weight as well as the cost of the machine, making it more affordable.[5] While the initial Enigma design printed on a sheet of paper like a typewriter, later models evolved to use glow lamp indicators, so that printing was unnecessary, reducing the mechanism's complexity. Users had to write down the letters that were illuminated and triggered by pressing the keys, with some considerable force. It would be 1924 for this version to be made (i.e., Glowlamp type), and at a substantially reduced cost too. It would be available for £1,000 Reichsmarks, and about one-eighth the cost of the printing Enigma version. It would weigh substantially less than the original and make it far easier to transport.

It would be some years before the German military and others expressed interest in it for sending and receiving messages, when public purchases of the encoding machine would be prohibited. The Imperial German Navy would sign a contract with the company in 1925, and an army version was produced in 1928. Scherbius and Ritter would be the company to manufacture it, although that would change later, and machines were made eventually by other firms under licence. By the start of the war, Germany would be using Enigma extensively as an encoding tool, by the armed services, the Italians, Swiss and the German Railways. Newer versions would become more challenging for the enemy to break into the Enigma message settings.

Significance: The testing of the market by Scherbius, and publicising the potential of the Enigma encoding machine. Initially, it would be a security machine for finance houses, banks, and similar commercial enterprises. To aid profitability it had to have a much wider use, which took time, and the military had a use for it.

Enigma machines sold to general public initially (1923)

In the early years of the Enigma design, the machine was openly sold to the public by Scherbius, the designer. It was advertised for financial institutions, banks, and finance houses. This was so they could send confidential messages and communication about their funds and clients' money over great distances. The advertising literature stated Enigma was unbreakable as an encoding machine. This offer to banks, etc., continued for a time until the German military eventually realised its potential and used it for themselves. The military stipulated that it should no longer be available to the public and it was then promptly withdrawn. Britain had acquired an Enigma before they were withdrawn from sale.

Significance: The availability of Enigma to the general public showed the commercial aspect of the designer and production company. It would be later that the Enigma was restricted to the military and a few other specialist customers, such as the German Railways, the Swiss, and the Italians.

Steckerboard added to Enigma (1926/1930)

A plugboard, or steckerboard, would be a modification to the Enigma machine to increase the permutations of settings. The plugboard was like a miniature telephone exchange with short electrical cables where the operator would plug in cables to sockets at the front of the machine, based on the code book instructions. Not every letter would have a cable or plugged in connection, however.[6]

It was the case that not every Enigma model would incorporate the plugboard, but most would as development of the machine variants progressed. By 1930, well before the war commenced, the plugboard was installed into army machines. In practice, only ten pairs of letters were connected or stickered, leaving six sockets unconnected when set up. That would still increase the permutations of the cipher system significantly. The timber case for the Enigma machine would have a front-hinged flap to be able to access the plugboard by the operator.

Significance: The added security in the Enigma design would make penetrating the Enigma cipher machine much more difficult, increasing the permutations of the message settings considerably.

Scherbius acquires Dutch codebreaking machine patents (1927)

Arthur Scherbius, the inventor of the Enigma machine, acquired important Dutch patents on rotary-based encoding machines prior to his death. Although some reports indicated that the Dutch had the basis of a machine similar to Enigma in terms of the principles of the design, they were slow to apply for and obtain patents. With the acquired Dutch patents, Scherbius and his company would be in a strong position in terms of intellectual property for future developments, and to resist potential legal challenges over his invention. Scherbius died tragically in 1929, but would acquire Dutch patents via H. Koch in 1927, and others prior to his death. Scherbius' original patent was filed on 23 February 1918, and there would be numerous other patents issued and granted via him, also via those designing encoding machines in the Netherlands. Some of these patents would be relatively minor 'tweaks' supplementing earlier patents. Experts will continue to debate and disagree who was the first with rotary-based encoding machine patents, but overall Scherbius appears to be in a strong position in this respect. Early rotary machine designs were, however, also developed by Dutch naval officers as far back as 1915.[7] However, they did not work as the Enigma machine operated, and the patents granted provided a perspective on the legalities of design and intellectual property at the time.

Significance: Scherbius understood the history of rotary-based encoding machines and in acquiring the Dutch patents ensured that his Enigma was protected from being copied by others.

Poles discover an Enigma at a railway station (1928)

The opportunity to examine a new encoding device would be advantageous to a government or nation looking to find ways to break enemy ciphers. Such an opportunity occurred at a Warsaw railway station in 1928 when a mysterious crate and package turned up en route from Germany to the German embassy in Warsaw. Section BS4 was the Polish cipher section, which dealt with German intelligence and ciphers. The police opened it and called in Section BS4 cryptographers, who took measurements and details over the weekend before carefully repacking it. It was an Enigma machine, and apparently unused. They had little time, as the customer was anxious that the package would continue to travel on its journey so it could receive the goods. Polish customs had no authority to open diplomatic parcels or crates, and stated the package had clearly not yet arrived when being questioned by German representatives, which was untrue. The Poles could ill afford to give the game away in that they had opened the package and seen what goods were inside. The information gathered would be useful for understanding the Enigma layout and wiring. The following Monday the crate was passed to the German embassy resealed, as though nothing untoward had happened. The commercial availability of Enigma was one thing, but the interest of the Poles would be principally in the wiring and configuration of the army Enigma, and secret service versions of Enigma. It was a step in the right direction, but Enigma would still be modified again and again over time. Small steps would be taken in the discoveries made, but the changes to Enigma and the protocols adopted by the Enigma operators would make consistent codebreaking a real challenge, with failures and frustration along the way.

Significance: An opportunity for Polish codebreakers to inspect an Enigma machine in detail, and to obtain useful information in a relatively short time period. That the Germans did not suspect the Enigma had been tampered with was essential to the clandestine operation.

Arthur Scherbius is killed in a tragic accident (1929)

In 1929, Arthur Scherbius, inventor of the Enigma machine, died in a horse and carriage accident at the age of 50. However, the production and development of Enigma would continue with other skilled engineers and designers in Germany leading the way. Scherbius, sadly, would never see the impact of his invention, which would become significant in the Second World War for secret communication by the Axis powers. He would never be aware of the amount of resources in terms of men, women, equipment and time that would need to be allocated by the Allies in order to break the Enigma settings and read the secret enemy messages.

The company's senior engineer, W. Korn, would take the reins in terms of leading Enigma design and modification, including applying for additional patents over the years. The company would change its name on the eve of the war to Helseeth and Rinke.

Significance: The inventor of the Enigma died at a time when the Enigma was starting to influence organisations, and would need planning by others and a robust marketing strategy to succeed.

AVA company start making copies of Enigma machines (1930)

Due to the work carried out by three Polish students led by Marian Rejewski, the AVA Radio manufacturing company based in Warsaw started to manufacture components to duplicate the Enigma machine, or a version of it. Some of these finished products complete with manuals of instructions were given to the French and the British in July 1939, when a meeting was held in Pyry at a cryptographic facility. The machines would be sent from Poland by sea for safety and security. There was much demand to have duplicates of the Enigma for experimentation and help with finding Enigma keys to break. Due to the need for extreme secrecy, the work was done in two parts. Some parts were manufactured in a General Staff building in Warsaw. Noisier work involving heavy machinery would be done at the AVA factory after most of the staff had gone home, except for four AVA partners and an assistant who could be trusted. A prototype replica had been built in 1930, taking around six months to complete, although the wiring was more of a challenge for some time. By August 1939 around seventy replica Enigma machines had been built by the AVA company in Poland. Germany would invade the country in early September 1939.

Significance: The secrecy of this operation in making Enigma copies by AVA would help in codebreaking by the Poles and others.

French obtain Enigma secrets from a German traitor (1931)

A frustrated and disgruntled German working in the army cryptographic headquarters offered the French technical details and settings of the Enigma encoding machine, including valuable code books, in return for payment. The offer was made by Hans Thilo Schmidt to General Gustave Bertrand of the French Army in 1931. This offer was then accepted by the general. In effect, Schmidt would become a traitor to his country for money and to finance his extravagant lifestyle. He was given a code name, Asché. His French contact would be 'Rex'. The deal would be like finding gold dust in the pursuance of cracking the Enigma ciphers. This information was then shared with the British, who had experts working in codebreaking, but little progress was made. It would be in 1932 that the information was shared with Poles, including Marian Rejewski, who, with colleagues, managed to break the Enigma ciphers. The information supplied to the Poles made the difference in analysing the permutations and finding the way through to break the code. Schmidt was eventually betrayed by Rex, when Rex was picked up by the German Gestapo and interrogated. Schmidt was arrested and killed in 1943. The impeccable pedigree of Schmidt included his brother, who would become one of the most trusted leaders of the 2nd Panzer Army under Adolf Hitler. It is almost inconceivable that someone so senior would have a close relative who betrayed Hitler in the 1930s purely for money.

Significance: Schmidt's sale of secrets about the Enigma machine would provide a way to decode the machine for the Allies, and that information could be shared between interested parties. It was seen as an important turning point in the Allies' favour. The development of the Enigma and improvements made would mean the information acquired would be of limited use in the longer term.

The Poles crack the Enigma code (1932)

A spot of luck in 1932 had seen the French handed important documents relating to the Enigma machine by disillusioned German civilian Hans Thilo Schmidt. These were passed to the Poles, who were able to decipher Enigma using mathematics and logic together with the new information. Although the Germans changed Enigma's design and systems over time, the Poles stayed one step ahead and managed to frequently crack the ciphers.

By the start of the Second World War they were reading almost all Nazi Enigma messages. The team of three cryptographic experts would escape across to France soon after Poland was invaded, to continue their codebreaking activities. Information would be communicated to both the French and British, which saved Bletchley Park and its codebreakers a great deal of time.

Significance: The cracking of Enigma by the Poles showed it could be done, even if the Enigma would be further developed and security increased later.

Post Office Research Engineering Station Opens (1933)

The PORES in Dollis Hill, north London, opened for research as part of the GPO in 1933, but principally as the engineering arm of the organisation. It would investigate materials, components, systems and build specialist equipment relevant to telephones, exchanges, teleprinters and other equipment, and provide an engineering support role to the Post Office on technical matters of communication. This was a large site and building with various laboratories. It would become famous for the engineer Tommy Flowers, who studied at night school and later designed and built the first semi-programmable computer, which was the Colossus codebreaking machine during the war. This machine would help change the course of the war and arguably shorten it due to the codebreaking at Bletchley Park of advanced enemy encoding machines.

Significance: The site would host many engineers who would lead and eventually become the later privatised organisation British Telecom post-war, through a metamorphosis of technology over many years. BT would take the engineering arm of the Post Office and develop it for the latter part of the twentieth century and beyond.[8]

Typex machines developed by the British (1934)

Wing Commander O.G. Lywood of the RAF took on board the idea of developing a cipher machine for use by the armed services and British Government including the Foreign Office. This was to be the RAF Type X machine, which was a variation of the Nazi Enigma encoding machine. Time could be saved by examining an existing cipher machine and then adapting it. The principle of having a cipher machine for the armed services and the Government was tabled as far back as 1926 via an inter-departmental cypher committee. The initial Typex Mk 1 machines were delivered in 1937, with Mark 2 versions in 1938. The Mark 2 weighed 54kg and needed an electrical supply, so it was not portable, unlike the Enigma machine. Output production of the machines was slow initially, but eventually it was to be used across a variety of stations and sites including abroad, by the Allies. Indeed, so useful was Typex, that versions were produced post-war up to Version Mark 23, when cooperation with the Americans established that a machine that could benefit both nations would be extremely useful. To give an idea of the quantities of production, a simple table is set out below:

1938	350 machines contracted for
June 1940	500 machines
End 1942	2,300 machines
December 1943	4,078 machines
May 1944	5,016 machines
Mid 1945	11,000 machines

The Royal Navy ordered 630 Typex machines in 1939, but much of the early production had to be distributed across a wide variety of sites so the Navy had to be patient until production increased. Bletchley Park relied heavily on Typex machines as the final stage of decoding the Nazi messages once the Enigma settings were broken.

Significance: An extremely important development in codebreaking systems. It made sense to take an existing cipher machine and redesign it to make it work even more efficiently. This took time, however, as evidenced by the numerous versions that were produced. It is curious that GC&CS did not develop the Typex, leaving that to others with the facilities and skills.[9]

Factories licensed to build the Enigma (1935)

German factories would eventually be licensed to build the Enigma machine, in order to cope with the increased demand. This occurred largely after the death of the inventor, Arthur Scherbius. The need for such encoding machines was great, not only from the German armed forces but also the German railways, the Swiss, Italians, and some other nations. It is thought that around 100,000 of these machines were built, although the exact number cannot be verified. Firms producing Enigma included Gewerkschaft Securitas, Konski & Kruger of Berlin, and Geyer in Nuremberg. Many different variations and versions were built over time and the security of the design was improved with innovation, making it much harder to penetrate the Enigma cipher system. Numerous patents were applied for in respect of the development of the Enigma machine and granted across the world, including in Britain.

Significance: The licensing to various factories had to be arranged in order to make the quantities of Enigma required based upon the demand.

US passes The Neutrality Acts (1935–1937)

Three separate neutrality acts would be passed by the United States between 1935 and 1937. When Churchill, Britain's Prime Minister, requested assistance from the Americans for military equipment in 1940, he was rebuffed by the President because of the Acts, which tied Roosevelt's hands. The situation would not change for Churchill until Pearl Harbor and war being declared on the USA by both Germany and Japan. The lifting of the Neutrality Acts would be a blessing for Churchill and the British people in a time of great uncertainty.

Significance: These Acts would put Great Britain in a difficult position both politically and practically during the early part of the war.

Enigma in the Spanish Civil War (1936–39)

The Spanish Civil War spanned the period 1936 to 1939 and was an opportunity for Hitler to support the Spanish Nationalists and General Franco, and to try out new military techniques pending a much larger conflict later on. Franco purchased ten Enigma machines in 1936, but these were quickly transferred to the Spanish military. They would be in the A to K series. Some later had steckerboards, or plugboards, at the front. Enigma machines would be used by the Spanish, Italians and the Germans for communication and secretly sending and receiving military instructions. Two machines are in the Spanish Army Museum in Toledo, being referenced/numbered A17316S and A1252. One unit that would utilise the machines was the German Condor Legion Intercept Unit, a military support detachment.

Significance: The Enigma encoding machine could be used in a wide range of conflicts, and could be tested 'in the field' to iron out any problems and to make improvements for the Nazis.

EVENTS

GPO introduces the scrambler telephone (1937)

In 1937, the General Post Office introduced a scrambler telephone system based on a 300 series telephone handset. The intended use was for the Government and the military. Early models were unreliable and could only deter a casual eavesdropper. The scrambler unit was positioned under a desk and connected to a telephone, with 'SECRET' and 'NORMAL' buttons on the front. When one pressed 'SECRET' and the other end recipient did the same, the scrambler electronics would come into play. However, the electronics were valve-based and consequently had to warm up before becoming effective to generate noise and avoid eavesdropping of the conversation. King George VI used such a device, but HM Queen Elizabeth II told GCHQ that the King became very frustrated waiting for the equipment to warm up and was unimpressed. A chosen frequency would be inverted and generate noise to anyone who tried to listen to the private conversation. The scrambler part of the circuit was known as the 'privacy unit', and was built by the Telephone Manufacturing Company or TMC, and by Plessey. As the war progressed, the units became much more reliable in use and effective. Churchill used them but also used the SIGSALY equipment, which was a completely separate and highly complex voice encoding system using PCM technology and recorded noise on record-playing equipment, designed by the Americans, and installed in the basement of Selfridges. It would be linked and wired into the Cabinet War rooms in Westminster as well as to the American Embassy in Grosvenor Square.

The Science Museum in London possess a scrambler telephone and privacy unit, the system being called the 'Secraphone'. Their unit is circa 1941, and is referenced as '2004-184 Privacy set 6AA (GPTN) Diagram SA5061'. The telephones have a dial with text stating 'Telephone Calls are not secret'. The same advice could be applied to modern-day social media, perhaps, and even many emails that may be less than secure.

Significance: The recognition that there was a real need for confidential conversations by telephone to be secure, as they may be used by military personnel or by politicians for communication. Some scrambler phones would be basic, others more refined over time, and hence much more secure.

The Poles build the Bomba machine (1938)

It was 1938 in the Polish cipher bureau when Polish mathematician Marian Rejewski designed the first electro-mechanical codebreaking machine. This was the Bomba or Bomb, incorporating a series of six rotors, many cogs and wheels and driven by an electric motor. It would attack the German Enigma encoding machine ciphers. Rejewski would meet up with two other colleagues and mathematicians to help innovate in the specialist area of cryptological ciphers, and with the objective of breaking them. Germany would invade Poland the following year, but the three specialists would escape to France and later Algiers, working against the Nazis and breaking codes. British codebreaking machines built later would be quite different to the Bomba in terms of design and construction, but it can be stated clearly that the Poles were the first to design and build such a machine. The Polish mathematicians who worked on this machine and who made considerable progress in decoding were Marian Rejewski, Henryk Zygalski, and Jerzy Rozycki. They would go down in history as pioneers in the building of early codebreaking machines.[10]

Significance: The understanding by Polish cryptographers and mathematicians that building a machine to crack Enigma may reduce the permutations of the message settings sufficiently to make a difference in saving valuable time.

Enigma rotors increase in quantity (1938)

Initially the Enigma wheel rotors were limited to three from a selection of around five. As time progressed the number of rotors increased to eight, and this increased substantially the permutations for the settings of the Enigma machine. The rotors would be kept in a hinged wooden box and selected according to code books. It was essential that both sender and receiver of the message had the same rotors in exactly the same sequence and adjusted to the correct position for transmission and reception. The rotor wheels were given roman numerals such as I, II, III, IV, V, etc. There would also be reflector rotor wheels affecting the output. The operators would initially work on three-wheel Enigmas but there would also be more advanced four-wheel rotor models for improved security. Thus, as an example, the Nazi Enigma code book may instruct selecting rotor numbers IV, II, III, I, in a sequence to be selected and installed. There would be differences between some of the German armed services in their Enigma machines, and setting them up. It would be late 1938 when the German Army would use an Enigma with two additional rotors, IV and V. There are six rotor wheel orders possible with just three rotors, but considerably more with five rotors. These calculate through to form much-increased permutations of the settings.

Significance: The rotor increase was one method of increasing security in the use of Enigma, in conjunction with applying strict rules, protocols and instructions for Enigma operators, within code books as to which rotors to select and the settings of them.

Bletchley Park acquired and purchased (1938)

The site of Bletchley Park in Buckinghamshire, England, was purchased by Admiral Sir Hugh Sinclair, the head of the MI6 security service, in 1938 for the sum of £6,000. It is reported he used his own funds at the time to acquire the estate. It would be known as the Government Code and Cipher School, or GC&CS, and included some 58 acres of land. For the estate sale in July 1937, it was originally offered with 581 acres including the mansion, grounds, parklands, and the Bletchley Home Farm. Factory sites close to the railway would also be advertised. A building contractor purchased large parts of the original site prior to Sinclair's purchase of the mansion, lake and surrounding grounds for GC&CS in May 1938. By 1939, and even prior to the start of the Second World War, it was a crucial headquarters for British codebreakers to try and break the enemy codes, particularly those using the German Enigma encoding machine, which was built in the thousands, and used by all of the enemy armed services to varying degrees. The original mansion house in the grounds was built for Sir Samuel H. Leon in 1883. Bletchley Park would grow over the war years to house several thousand people in a variety of roles from codebreakers, linguists, to administration and typists, and become famous for its many huts allocated for different tasks across the site in codebreaking and analysis. One of the unique aspects of Bletchley as an operational base was that staff would be a mixture of military personnel and civilians. It would be expanded, new huts built and changed over time to adapt to the needs of the headquarters, and the specialist personnel that worked within it. It would remain top secret during wartime, and even after it had closed post-war.

Significance: The acquisition of a site that could be developed into a major headquarters for codes, ciphers, and intelligence gathering over time. Sinclair would have no idea how large and significant Bletchley Park would become, or the extent of the role it would play in wartime. GC&CS at Bletchley was indeed a school for learning and for trying out new systems and techniques. A type of post-graduate university for many.

Churchill addresses Parliament upon becoming Prime Minister (1939)

The elevation of Churchill to become Prime Minister of the United Kingdom during wartime was a gamble, as he was not the first choice of some members of the Government or his political party. A coalition would be organised to work together for a common aim. His first speech as Prime Minister would set out his objectives to defend the nation against Nazi oppression, even though Lord Halifax and some others wished for a peaceful negotiation with Hitler to avoid war. Churchill would go on to use all his tools and expertise to defend Britain, and would help to bring back around 300,000 encircled British soldiers from Dunkirk through his suggestion to use small civilian boats to cross the Channel. He would have a good understanding of the need for accurate and up to date intelligence, and would go on to support Bletchley Park to have the resources they needed for codebreaking activities. Most importantly, he would obtain the support of HM King George VI after some initial concerns.

Molotov–Ribbentrop Pact signed (1939)

This was a non-aggression pact, signed in Moscow on 23 August 1939, between Nazi Germany and Russia, to give a degree of assurance and stability to both countries at a time of uncertainty in Europe. The treaty was signed by the Foreign Ministers of both nations, Joachim von Ribbentrop and Vyacheslav Molotov. There would be a secret protocol as part of the treaty, outlining borders and 'spheres of influence' of Germany and Russia. As part of the deal, Russia was secretly permitted to access the Baltic States for themselves, and it seems that neither Churchill nor Roosevelt opposed that when it later occurred. The agreement also empowered Russia to support Nazi Germany in any invasion of Poland, which would happen in early September 1939, but with Stalin delaying the Polish attack by Russian forces until almost three weeks afterwards. It is interesting that whilst Britain declared war on Nazi Germany for the Polish invasion, they did not declare war on Russia. The Non-Aggression Pact was effectively torn up when the Nazis invaded Russia in Operation Barbarossa on 22 June 1941. Hitler had made a major mistake in his strategy, and would never control Russia or its people. Attacking Russia would be his undoing, and the beginning of the end of the Third Reich. Some of his generals were reluctant to attack, but were overruled.

Significance: The signing of such treaties would buy Germany time, before their true intentions were exposed. Russia would be keen to keep the peace and had no intention of attacking Germany. Hitler had other ideas as regards attacking Russia.

Denniston leads Bletchley Park (1939)

As the founder and head of the Government Code and Cipher School from 1919, Alastair Denniston would be in overall charge of Bletchley Park. Commander Denniston would be the head of GC&CS at least until 1942, when Commander Travis took over.

Significance: The selection of an experienced codebreaker and one who understood the key priorities in developing a team. Others, including Commander Travis, would build on that with their own personalities influencing the personnel and organisation.

Bletchley Park becomes GC&CS (1939)

The establishment of Bletchley Park in 1939, led by Alastair Denniston, made it the Government Code and Cipher School or GC&CS. This was a development from earlier codebreaking historical sites including at Watergate House in The Strand. GC&CS began in 1919 and encompassed twenty-eight clerical employees and twenty-four cryptologic staff, plus assistants. It would develop into a large codebreaking and cipher analysis undertaking, using a wide range of skilled staff, from mathematicians to linguists, from classicists to cryptographers. It would become the headquarters of such operations, working for the British Government, until it closed down at the end of the war. The site would make important links across the world, to share key information and work closely with allies in wartime. Bletchley would rely on the

Y-Stations and sometimes from reports via double agents to make progress in the codebreaking of enemy messages. The methods and systems used by Bletchley would be fine-tuned and developed over time, with some use of machines to gain speed in data processing. However, it would be incorrect and misleading to assume that machines resolved all the codebreaking problems, and were the sole reason of success during wartime. Machines were nothing more than a tool or an auxiliary aid, to support the personnel who had the skills to decode message settings and enemy messages. The analogy might be manual methods versus using computers to solve a problem. Manual methods will, with skilled staff, still arrive at the solution, albeit probably slower than if a computer had been programmed to resolve the problem. In practice, people are needed to work together with machines to work efficiently, and to have the necessary skills and knowledge to identify where errors and anomalies can occur. The development of Bletchley Park as GC&CS was in a time when integration of machines with mathematicians, linguists, and codebreakers was still somewhat of an experiment and a learning curve. Some would view codebreaking machines with suspicion in the early days. The designers and constructors of those machines would have to prove themselves to demonstrate they could be used consistently to aid the decoding process, saving time. The many different sections, huts, and parts of Bletchley Park during wartime indicated management's understanding of how complex the subject of codebreaking was. It needed to be properly structured, managed and monitored, as well as being adaptable and flexible to accommodate change over time.

Significance: History in the making. GC&CS started as a small germ of seed back in 1919, with a handful of staff. Bletchley Park gave the opportunity for specialist sections to be developed, exploring a more efficient way of working. The huge number of staff that would occupy the site at the end of the Second World War would be 75 per cent female.

Alan Turing joins Bletchley Park (1939)

Turing joined Bletchley Park in 1939 as a mathematician from Cambridge University. His tutor there was Max Newman, who would also work at Bletchley in a senior capacity. Turing had written a number of papers while at university. Having an inquisitive mind, he would develop his ideas and concepts further, so as to radically change the methodology of approaching codebreaking at Bletchley. The idea of using machines was first used by the Poles, but Turing had in mind a far more sophisticated machine, the Bombe. However, it would need detailed design, engineering, and testing before he could properly prove its benefit to the Bletchley operation.

Significance: A key player in codebreaking at the Park and in developing systems and techniques, based on an inquiring mind and of extraordinary mathematical ability. His influence at Bletchley would help to change the direction of the war against the Axis powers.

Gordon Welchman joins Bletchley Park (1939)

Gordon Welchman, a skilled mathematician, and one with a practical mind that came in useful when the codebreaking machine, the Bombe, was being developed. He would work alongside Alan Turing on probably the most important development at Bletchley Park other than the advanced Colossus machine. Welchman was contacted by Denniston, the head of Bletchley Park, in 1939, to ask him to come and work there if there was another war. He would be one of four key codebreakers, forming a nucleus of innovation and accepting challenges, to break enemy ciphers. The team would expand over time, but Welchman's contribution was considerable. Not only would he become head of Hut 6 at Bletchley, his innovation of 'the diagonal board' circuit would improve the Bombe's efficiency and save the codebreakers valuable time.

Significance: Welchman would prove to be a close partner and colleague to Turing in helping to develop the Bombe, but also in organising people and systems. It would only be the presence of Turing that would take some of the glory away from him while working at the GC&CS headquarters.

HMS *Flowerdown* established as a secret listening base (1939)

HMS *Flowerdown* was near Winchester and acquired fifty ACSWS personnel. They would man fourteen communications links, six of them with high-speed channels, the remainder with hand-speed links. Countries monitored included Germany, Russia, Italy and Spain. Due to personnel shortages, it was decided to have one person manning three high-speed communication pieces of equipment. There were four large steel aerial masts on site.[11]

Significance: Part of a growing network of Y-stations, some more specialist than others, to provide crucial enemy intelligence to Bletchley Park and related organised sites.

Tiltman cracks Japanese codes (1938–39)

John Tiltman, codebreaker, would work on deciphering Japanese codes and ciphers, and with some considerable success. He cracked the Japanese Army's code in late 1938, and followed this up by cracking the Japanese Naval code, known as JN25, in mid-1939. Information would be shared with the United States security services. Tiltman would break the Railway Enigma codes when at GC&CS. A Scotsman, he had a knack for breaking ciphers that no one else at Bletchley seemed to be able to do.

Significance: A skilled operator and cryptographer such as Tiltman would be useful to not only the British, but the Americans, particularly after Pearl Harbor.

EVENTS

Germany invades Poland (1939)

On 1 September 1939 Adolf Hitler gave the instruction to start the invasion of Poland and that triggered the start of the Second World War. Both Britain and France declared war on Germany, to the surprise of Hitler. America would stay neutral until later, when attacked by the Japanese at Pearl Harbor in Hawaii. The state of intelligence for Britain was in its relatively early stages, having already established Bletchley Park and GC&CS as headquarters for codebreaking and cipher analysis. The personnel would increase in quantity over time and specialisms identified to ensure the attack on Enigma would be efficient as far as practically possible. No declaration of war was made by Britain on Russia, who invaded Poland shortly after the Germans. This was considered by the senior politicians, and quickly dismissed as a step too far. It would be quite enough to deal with the Nazis, and their intended domination of Europe. The codebreakers at Bletchley would learn useful facts about Enigma from their contact with the Poles at a meeting in France. The Huts at Bletchley would become a hive of activity as the war progressed, with both successes and failures too. With Italy allied with Germany, intercepts of Italian encoded messages would also be of interest. Many Poles would flee to Britain to fight in the Army or RAF against Nazi Germany, and the RAF squadrons would have a high enemy 'kill' rate. What no one knew at the time of Britain's war declaration against Nazi Germany for the invasion of Poland, was how Poland would end up under Russian communist rule for many years, becoming a satellite of Russia. One dictator would effectively be replaced by another. After all, Stalin had invaded Poland only two or three weeks after Germany. He had held back so the bulk of the blame would be against the Nazis, who started the conflict. Freedom from the Soviets and independence for Poland would take many years to acquire. However, there would be Polish partisan resistance fighting the Russians for many years after the war ended. Freedom for Poland and abandonment of communism would eventually come in late 1991, after much turmoil and complex politics, annexed to substantial loss of life over many decades. Hitler's act of war in September 1939 would have far-reaching consequences for Poland's history.

Significance: The start of the 'recovery' of land in countries other than Germany by Hitler, and by force. This may also have been somewhat of a test to see what reaction other countries and allies of Poland there might be, in spite of threats to intervene earlier. Hitler had reasoned that there would be no or little opposition to his invasion, but he was mistaken.

Churchill agrees location of alternative War Cabinet rooms (1939)

In Dollis Hill, north-west London, a secret underground bunker would house the Paddock, an alternative set of meeting rooms for the Cabinet during wartime. The address was No. 109 Brook Road, Dollis Hill, Willesden, NW2, also code-named 'CWR2'. Churchill, however, disliked the Paddock, which he said was damp and draughty and not suitable for his needs, so it was only used a small number of times. Indeed, reports indicated that it was only used twice by the Cabinet in wartime. This site was adjacent to PORES, or the Post Office Research Engineering Station, which would provide technical support to Bletchley Park. The bulk of War Cabinet meetings were held in the Cabinet War Rooms in Westminster, now called the Churchill Rooms, which houses a museum and exhibition with artefacts and information on Churchill's life. The Paddock was constructed as an emergency War Room underground bunker in 1939, and cost £250,000, which in today's money would be around £10 million. It would also be the emergency base for the commanders of the three principal armed services. By 1944, it was agreed that the bunker had come to the end of its use practically, and after the war was occupied by the Post Office, who had personnel on the site.

Significance: The Paddock was effectively a 'Plan B', in case of the Westminster Cabinet War Rooms being put out of use by the enemy.

Flowers researches valve tubes for use as digital switches

Although tube valves were used extensively for radios and radio receivers in the twentieth century, hardly anyone had considered their use as a switch, or an on-off digital switch. Tommy Flowers, who studied engineering at night school in London, and worked for the Post Office engineering division, had an interest in using valve technology for this purpose. His passion for this technology would become critical in later years, when he would go on to design and build the Colossus decoding machine that used many valves as switches. Not everyone had faith in his concepts and ideas, but he persevered to change history during the Second World War, and arguably shortened the length of the war and potentially saved many lives. His experience in using valves was previously limited to 150 tubes in a previous project, and yet he was convinced he could build a machine with 1,800 valves that would be reliable. A remarkable achievement for someone who had never studied at university. We cannot be sure of the date or time when he became particularly curious about using valves as digital switches, but there were others out there across the world who also had similar ideas, and he may have accessed their technical papers to study them while working at PORES.

Significance: While Flowers would not have known how useful this valve technology and application of it would become in wartime, without his interest and passion for it it is unlikely that Colossus would have been built by the British to challenge the enemy advanced encoding machines and systems. Indeed, history may have turned out rather differently as to the outcome of the war.

Bletchley Park acquires an Enigma (1939)

Codebreaking of a specific piece of equipment or machinery is likely to be slightly less of a challenge if you have that equipment in front of you to study its construction and design. This does not mean that you will break the cipher, but it provides a starting point for your approach. Bletchley Park, the codebreaking HQ in England, eventually acquired an Enigma to study. This was at a meeting held in Paris between the British, French and Polish codebreakers in July 1939, when a replica Enigma was passed to the British by the Poles. However, the Poles had beaten Bletchley to it, as in 1926 the Biuro Szyfrow (Polish Cipher Bureau) had obtained a commercially available Enigma and analysed it. The work done by the Poles would give the Allies a head start in helping to crack Enigma. It is the case that Enigma developed over time, with changes in design and increased security features, but having a physical Enigma machine to study and analyse would be an important step forward for Britain's codebreakers. The military versions were different to the commercial machines, and some would have additional wheel rotors to further increase the permutations of settings. While the original Enigmas were available to the public commercially, this was stopped by the German armed services for reasons of security. There are reports that Britain was offered the Enigma for inclusion in its military communication network, but it was apparently rejected as too cumbersome to operate in the field.

Significance: The acquisition of an Enigma, or of a copy, by the Allies assisted in the understanding of the construction and logic of the machine, but did not automatically allow the decoding of its messages.

Keddleston Hall offered to the War Office for military purposes (1939)

Keddleston Hall in Derbyshire was used by the War Office as an army training camp, but was later utilised by Bletchley Park as a signal's intelligence listening Y-station. Bletchley would carry out any decryption of intercepts necessary.[12] The site contained around forty-five buildings in 1939, and there is evidence of a possible base structure of 7.7m diameter in brickwork for either a revolving large gun or searchlight tower. The majority of the site appeared to be army barracks. Keddleston Hall, as a listed building, is now owned by the National Trust.

Significance: Various country houses and estates would be selected for military support during wartime. Bletchley would be grateful for another listening station, and particularly in the build-up to D-Day in 1944 and beyond.

Enigma finds uses across a wide range of organisations

Enigma as an encoding cipher machine was used by the Luftwaffe, German Army and Kriegsmarine, but also by others. The German Railway network would have several machines. Their allies in wartime, the Italians, would be provided with machines. The Swiss, considered to be neutral in the war, required a quantity of Enigmas and several were supplied. Germany was then able to intercept the

Swiss Enigma machine messages as it wanted to stay informed throughout the war. After all, the Swiss would be the major investment banking hub of Europe, so intelligence on how funds were being used by clients and organisations could be of considerable interest to the Nazis. The *Abwehr* would be monitoring transactions and any potential threats to the Third Reich.

Significance: Given the secrecy surrounding Enigma and the need to restrict access so as to protect the Third Reich and senior officials, allowing organisations such as the railways to use it, and certain other parties, may have compromised security to varying degrees. However, the procedures and protocols developed by the Nazis in the use of Enigma were largely successful. But they had not allowed for the British Bletchley Park and its codebreakers, who would penetrate it over time.

Turing develops concept of the Bombe machine (1939–40)

Whilst Turing was a Cambridge University academic and had written many papers on mathematics and logic previously, his time at Bletchley Park opened new opportunities for him to apply his theoretical knowledge in practice. His work on sketches, calculations, concepts and ideas for a machine to speed up identifying the message settings of Enigma would culminate in the codebreaking Bombe machine. He was aware the Poles had previously built the first codebreaking Bomba machine to tackle Enigma, but Turing's design would be completely different. At least Turing had an Enigma machine to study, unlike William Tutte and his challenge on the Lorenz machine. However, just studying Enigma would only provide a small part of the solution. Turing would sit in the hut at Bletchley Park, develop his ideas, pin the sketches, tables and drawings up on the wall, and work closely with his colleague, Gordon Welchman, on the development of the Bombe. In some ways Welchman was more the engineering type than Turing, and contributed significant solutions to the problems and challenges, although both were mathematicians. The output after considerable testing and failures would help the Allies incorporate a new specialist tool into their arsenal, the British Bombe. All they had to do now was to build it and scale it up for mass production.

Significance: Turing's obsession with advanced machines and logic to help and assist mankind would be converted into a practical codebreaking machine in wartime, to challenge the German Enigma. Although the Bombe was not a computer, it possessed several attributes and features that emulated parts of an electro-mechanical computer, albeit with relatively primitive technology.

Welchman designs the diagonal board (1940)

Keen to make improvements to the Bombe machine design, Welchman designed an electronic accessory called a diagonal board to help reduce the time needed to process the quantity of permutations of message settings. This would be introduced to new Bombes being manufactured, and some added to existing machines as a modification. The change would be a significant improvement in terms of efficiency. The Bombe official registers do indicate some machines had the diagonal board modification added to them, and the relevant dates. The second Bombe machine to be constructed, Agnes or Agnus Dei, had this modification incorporated within it as an improvement.

Significance: The diagonal board would be an improvement that enhanced the efficiency of the Bombe, and came thankfully at a relatively early stage in its development. It would be put to good use and incorporated into most machines built at BTM in Letchworth.

Capture of German trawler and Enigma keys (1940)

A German trawler flying a Dutch flag was captured by HMS *Griffin* on 26 April 1940, where the crew found certain Enigma keys for that month. These were passed back to Bletchley Park for checking.

Significance: Another opportunity for Bletchley Park codebreakers to help crack Enigma, at least for a while.

Mill Hill base established for training Wrens

One of several training bases established across Britain for training WRNS personnel in north London. The usual training period for new recruits was two weeks, but three weeks' training was also provided for some, and many reports indicate that the latter was common. However, no codebreaking activities were taught at the bases, those specialist skills being reserved for selected personnel considered by senior officers as having aptitude for this work. When selected, the Wrens would be appointed and transferred to Special X duties (or PV duties), at either Bletchley Park or one of the five outstations.[13] There would also be training bases in Scotland for the Wrens, and many of those were transferred south after training to work on codebreaking operations.

Significance: A London-based training centre that was part of a network of training bases for Wrens across England and Scotland. Many WRNS personnel would do their basic training here, and some would be selected for codebreaking duties elsewhere.

Bletchley Wrens billeted at Woburn

To cope with the influx of WRNS personnel and others, a billet was required for them not too far from Bletchley Park. Woburn Abbey, a country house estate, was identified as an ideal location as it was possible for Wrens to travel from there to Bletchley and back at night. With a long front driveway, it would take a person almost half an hour to walk to the gate on the road, from the main house; more quickly by bicycle or car, of course. Several hundred Wrens were based at Woburn, and staff were allocated cabins with bunk beds. Outstations would also have a bunk bed sleeping system. The Wrens based there would be mostly 'Special X' duties personnel or designated to work at Pembroke V specialist sites, such as Bletchley or the outstations. Work at both Bletchley and the outstations would be on a shift basis, so there would be much coming and going of Wrens at all hours. In both 1944 and 1945, a number of Wrens would be on shift, operating the Colossus codebreaking machines. The heat output from the valves made the huts very warm, and blackout blinds kept the heat in, making working in the huts extremely uncomfortable, especially in the warmer months. The Wrens were trained to set up the machines and liaise with others on message output via punched tape and optical readers. Cleaning of the Colossus 'magic eye' readers was one of their many tasks to ensure smooth operation. When the message appeared in German, it would be taken to the next hut to be translated. Back at Woburn, there would be some time for authorised leave and passes for the Wrens, with a trip by train to Oxford or to London, to watch a show or go dancing with colleagues. The pressure of working long shifts on the machines did take its toll, with some going off sick through exhaustion due to the intense pressure. Letting their hair down for a few hours would help to refresh their minds for more shift work and perhaps assisting to train newcomers on the machines. Off duty at Woburn, the Wrens would be permitted full use of the estate grounds, which were considerable in size and scale. The presence of deer in the grounds would necessitate some caution at times, when the stags were fighting and establishing a hierarchy. There would be occasional dances at Woburn for relaxation, and they had the space to arrange these. There was an opportunity to meet American personnel from other bases, some not far away in the county. Reciprocal invitations for the Wrens allowed them to travel to those American bases, probably more for the delicious food made available than anything else. Some Wrens would be allowed to be billeted in the main house, others elsewhere in the grounds. The rumour of ghosts and apparitions in the old property made it a challenge to spend a penny at night and most Wrens preferred not to walk along the long spooky corridors. When it was time for D-Day, several Wrens at Bletchley were not permitted to leave for security reasons, and had to monitor incoming messages from German commanders responding to the attack and invasion. Wrens would also operate Robinson machines, which was the predecessor of Colossus but was more complex regarding the need for synchronising two sets of paper tape spools with data. Colossus proved to be more reliable than Robinson, and much larger, with the number of valves running into the low thousands. Access to the Mk2 Colossus would come just prior to D-Day in June 1944, when it was delivered to Bletchley, assembled and set up by the Post Office Engineering Research team. The owner of Woburn, the Duke of Bedford, still lived there while Wrens occupied the estate, but had separate rooms and areas. Some reports indicate he was less than pleased when he discovered Wrens on certain staircases that he considered to be 'out of bounds'. Not all Wrens would remain at Woburn, and many of them moved to be relocated at codebreaking outstations as the war progressed.

Significance: The use of a country house estate in relatively close proximity to Bletchley Park, with ample space for large quantities of Wrens supporting the Park. Additionally, the change of scenery for those billeted there, with walks and wildlife as well as the magnificent house and grounds, would breathe new life into mentally and physically exhausted Wrens, who had worked a long shift on codebreaking machines or in a support role.

Churchill requires a summary of codebreaking intelligence and restricts access to Enigma information (1940)

Churchill had visited Bletchley Park and met some of the codebreakers and support staff there. He had requested sight of all the enemy message intercepts at Downing Street, but it was explained to him this was not possible due to the volume of messages coming through. A compromise would be for him to have a summary of the most interesting intelligence decoded. He would receive this summary in a boxed folder in his office, which kept him up to date with what was going on. He would have to leave it to others to filter out the less useful messages, hoping they had not overlooked something of importance. He would sometimes sit in the garden scrutinising the content and being far enough away from any eyes peering over his shoulder. Early on, Churchill had decided to reduce the number of senior people who were given access to such information and the codebreaking process at Bletchley. He could not afford such information to fall into the wrong hands. On 16 October 1940, he would write to his Head of Defence Office, General Ismay, and make changes to the listing of people for circulation of matters regarding the Enigma machine and codebreaking of it. Few would have access to it, and on 'a need to know' basis. Several weeks later, only thirty-one people of senior capacity either in the armed services or the Government would be on the final list. This was much reduced from the original and gave Churchill some comfort in terms of security. He would raise such security matters again in September 1941, wanting to restrict distribution of Enigma intelligence to commanders in chief of the services, and none below their rank. The establishment at Bletchley Park had taken a good while to develop, with skilled expert mathematicians and cryptographers. It would be all too easy to blow the cover to the enemy, and risk Britain's fate in exposing the secret network behind collecting and analysing military intelligence. There would be situations later, such as in March 1943, when it appeared that Enigma intelligence could have been compromised and that it had been revealed to the Nazis that decoding of it had been achieved. Fortunately, there would be another chance to pull the camouflage over it and maintain the illusion that it was a secure system.

Significance: Churchill wanted to be kept informed of activities and intelligence, so he could be more effective in his decision-making as Prime Minister and head of the War Cabinet. He would be privy to certain confidential information that few others would have access to.

BTM awarded contract to build codebreaking Bombe machines (1940)

BTM in Letchworth, Hertfordshire, won the contract from the War Office to build the Bombe codebreaking machines. They would have to develop the sketches and drawings produced by Bletchley Park to make them into proper and practical engineering drawings, as Turing was but a mathematician and not an engineer. One may ask why BTM was considered for this role, and this was partly due to their involvement with operating equipment and systems for census processing of the population, both at home and abroad, dealing with large volumes of information, together with their having licensing contracts for American-patented Hollerith machines for sorting, filtering, and processing data. They had a large factory in Letchworth with engineering capacity, skilled engineering personnel and physical space for assembly. BTM also had smaller factories around Letchworth for assembly, and these would prove to be invaluable later on. The project was encoded project 'Cantab' by them, probably because the academics behind the concept came from Cambridge University. The project was top secret, and the Official Secrets Act would have to be signed by those involved. Even post-war they would not have been permitted to speak about their wartime work at BTM, or their links with Bletchley Park and Turing. After the war ended, BTM would create advertising plaques stating: 'Machines that think faster than the Mind!' to promote interest in the development of calculating machines and data processing.[14]

Significance: A major contract for the British Government to build codebreaking machines in secret. Few private organisations would have had the engineering expertise, knowledge, and resources to build the Bombes.

Keen in charge of Bombe production at BTM factory (1940)

Chief engineer Harold Keen was tasked at BTM to manage the design and production of the Bombe codebreaking machines for Bletchley Park. Around one quarter to one third of the main factory building would eventually be taken up with the machines. Keen was respected by his workforce and was innovative in providing solutions to the many technical problems encountered. He would provide high-speed versions to process the Enigma settings data faster. Records of these modified machines would be included within the official Bombe registers.

The first Bombe built by Keen and his team at BTM was delivered to Bletchley Park in March 1940. His nickname would be 'Doc' Keen, as he would carry a bag around with him, which gave the impression he was a doctor rushing around to attend to his patients. In one way, he was but his patients were electro-mechanical machines and he and his team were building and modifying them, maintaining the quality control necessary for the output and reliability required at Bletchley, and the outstations.

Significance: The appointment of the chief engineer within the BTM company to lead the Bombe manufacturing programme reflected the level of importance of the project.

BTM coordinates production of Bombes in Letchworth (1940)

Three key sites in Letchworth would bring together mass production of Bombe codebreaking machines during wartime. Firstly, the main factory in Icknield Way, which would construct the final assembly of the machines on a metal frame. The Ascot Government Training Centre in Pixmore Avenue was used for wheel drums and ancillary components, and Spirella, the corset manufacturer, was acquired for war production of Bombe wiring, connectors and components. Everything produced in modular sequence would have to be transported to the main factory for final assembly. Like many factories, they started production on a relatively small scale and then built it up. They used trained personnel, including many women factory workers, brought in materials, allocated space, produced technical drawings and specifications, and opened a quality control department for the testing of components and machines. Keen would be the chief engineer and he would meet periodically with Commander Travis, Turing, and Welchman from Bletchley Park to discuss progress.

Significance: The manufacture of Bombes in a modular form at BTM across a number of different sites in Letchworth required detailed coordination of materials, personnel and equipment, and an understanding of the programme to meet the requirements of Bletchley Park in respect of Bombe output. This was largely achieved in practice.

Cantab project established (1940)

BTM, or the British Tabulation Machine Company in Letchworth was to engineer drawings from the original design and build the Bombe machines from the sketches and details provided by Alan Turing. The project was termed 'Cantab' and the machines coded as 6/6502 by management. It would take engineering knowledge and skills to convert the calculations and sketches into a production machine that worked consistently and reliably. The Bombe codebreaking machines built would occupy more than a quarter of the factory in Letchworth as production increased. BTM had been established in 1909 under that name, and had a track record of becoming involved in Hollerith tabulating machines, which originally were developed in the United States of America. The headquarters office of BTM, in London, would refer to Bletchley Park as 'Bureau B' for security reasons. Post-war, the chief executive of BTM, Phillpotts, would hold a special staff dinner with 'CANTAB' on the menu heading on each table. He would receive a knighthood for his efforts in wartime. Keen would receive an OBE as chief engineer, and his principal assistant, H.J. Morton, would receive an MBE.

Significance: A major project such as building codebreaking machines for the Government would need a project name and reference for project management purposes. Allocation of resources would become critical in the setting up of the factory for production, as well as when the production levels increased significantly.

Bombe transfer system from BTM factory agreed (1940)

One of the decisions that had to be made by BTM in conjunction with Bletchley Park were the security provisions in transporting Bombe machines from the factory in Letchworth to Bletchley or to the outstations. Similarly, in the return of Bombes back to BTM for modification. If a large security convoy was to be provided, that might raise interest by members of the public and any enemy agents or spies. To have minimal security would be a risky strategy but would not raise the profile of the transport used. It was agreed to convey the Bombe machines on a single open truck with a tarpaulin and a single, unarmed driver. The driver would be handed a letter, which he could show others if challenged, that was signed by the Prime Minister. The letter made it plain that anyone obstructing the driver and the vehicle would have Churchill to deal with. This method and process would be used for the transport of Bombes for the duration of the war. No armed guards or outriders would be provided. The tarpaulin would conceal what was underneath. Each of the 211 Bombes designed and built were transported this way. Each Bombe weighed a ton. At least the method would ensure that BTM would not attract any attention and could then continue, building and modifying the machines without interference or needing special armed security on site.

Significance: A decision that involved a relatively low-key approach, avoiding convoys of lorries or armed guards, while maintaining security of the Bombe machines during transportation. A tarpaulin was the only thing between the secret Bombe machine and a member of the public when the lorry passed by. Simplicity is sometimes the most effective method of security, but there would still have been a risk of enemy agents, or perhaps simply curious individuals and members of the public, intercepting the lorries transporting the machines.

Team established at Bletchley to help coordinate Bombes (1940)

A team of three personnel was established at Bletchley Park to help in the commissioning of the first Bombe codebreaking machine, which was based in part of Hut 1. This team was led by Squadron Leader Jones. The personnel grew to some 263 RAF and 1,676 WRNS, or Wrens, the majority being at codebreaking outstations remote from Bletchley Park. RAF personnel were often used in a maintenance capacity on the machines, with the Wrens mainly setting up and operating the Bombes.

Significance: The numbers indicate a substantial operation that required specialist selection and training of staff, robust discipline, technical expertise, levels of high security, and meeting key targets to help the war effort. A team effort.

First codebreaking Bombe machine used at Bletchley Park (1940)

The first Bombe machine was named *Victory* and Bletchley would receive it on 18 March 1940. It would later be sent to Outstation Wavendon, then relocated to Outstation Eastcote on 6 September 1943, partly dismantled, and used for training. Victory would later be renamed *Leo* and returned to Letchworth works for installation of the diagonal boards that improved the Bombe's efficiency. It was installed in Outstation Wavendon, but then found not to work efficiently. In 1942 it was used for training for both RAF engineers and Wrens. On 6 November 1942 it was sent to Outstation Stanmore and renamed London, used solely for instruction until May 1945, when it was dismantled as Leo. This demonstrates the complex nature of the life of a specific Bombe machine over several years. Not all were renamed, but many were.[15]

The first machine initially lacked the 'diagonal board' technical improvement, which was the brainchild of Gordon Welchman. Machines would be delivered on a large truck and be transported via an individual driver with no armed support for protection.

Significance: The culmination of a great deal of work via Turing, Welchman, and by engineers at BTM in Letchworth where the Bombe factory was located.

Philip's valve technology relocated to England from the Netherlands (1940)

At Eindhoven in the Netherlands, on 9 May 1940, the Germans were about to take over the country, and there was a rush of urgency to transfer valves and valve technology from the Philips factory to England before the Germans could get their hands on it. The EF 50 RF Pentode valve was a new type of valve that would change the course of the war, and be the basis for several other designs over time.[16] The stocks of EF50 valves, plus other tooling and components, were driven across to a ferry and transported to England safely. The ferry was attacked by the Luftwaffe, but fortunately it escaped without significant damage. Only a few hours later after the lorries had left the factory, the Nazis had raided it in the early morning of the next day as they occupied the Netherlands, so the timing was crucial.

Such specialist valves were then used extensively in radar equipment and radios. Mullard valves in England were acquired by Philips in 1927, after showing initial interest in the company in 1925, and the company became a source for radio equipment and military communications. This would be relevant to listening Y-stations, and those collecting intercepted data for Bletchley Park. Mullard would have factories in Mitcham and in Blackburn and expand to a total of six overall. Bombing and V1 flying bombs would cause some damage and result in loss of production of half a million valves. By 1944, Mitcham factories had produced 5 million valves, and Mullard, overall, around 6.5 million.[17]

Significance: Prompt action by the Dutch management of Philips in Holland enabled Britain and its allies to retain an advantage in utilising an advanced valve design, which would prove to be invaluable in wartime. Acquisition of Mullard in 1927 would make Philips a significant producer and developer of valves and valve technology.

Second Bombe installed at Bletchley Park (1940)

While the first operational codebreaking Bombe was called *Victory*, the second was named *Agnus* or *Agnes Dei*. This was delivered on 8 August 1940, and it was the first machine to be installed with a special improvement, the Welchman diagonal board. From delivery to operating the machine took around three to four hours. It would be transferred to Outstation Eastcote on 26 June 1944, and used for instructional training purposes.

Significance: The second Bombe had an improved design compared to the first and was far more efficient. Welchman had made a major contribution here. Improvements would naturally form part of the process.

Wrens operate Bombe codebreaking machines (1940)

Initially there would be resistance to using females, Wrens, to operate top-secret Bombe codebreaking machines. Evaluation tests of Wren personnel would be carried out at Bletchley in the early years of the war, and most passed without a problem. Some, however, would not be suited to the role. When appointed to do this work it would be initially termed as 'Station X' duties. Later, as Pembroke V, with bases identified and classified as HMS *Pembroke* V. They would start operating and setting up Bombes at Bletchley Park, later to work at the three country house estates where additional machines had been deployed. Finally, as Outstation Stanmore and Outstation Eastcote came on line, Wrens would be utilised at those sites in the high hundreds of personnel.[18] They would operate Bombes at Bletchley and each of the five codebreaking outstations, their numbers mounting to some 1,673 Wren personnel, with a combination of ratings and officers. They followed the Bletchley instructions on Menus that gave information on setting up the Bombe machines, to selecting and positioning the rotor wheels, to plugging in the cables on the machine, checking the connectors and starting the machines for a run. Then they monitored the 'stops' on the machine, and took readings at the end of the process. The more the Wrens gained experience in this specialist work, the better they understood their role and the more accurate they became.

Furthermore, they would also be tasked with operating the advanced Robinson and Colossus machines, which required a new range of different specialist skills, including aligning punched tape on large reels, using heated glue machines to join the tape, as well as synchronise it over optical tape readers with great precision.

They would make a significant contribution to codebreaking support and data processing, with some Wrens being actual codebreakers on the messages. The equipment operated would not just be Bombes, but extend to checking machines,

Cobra machines, and probably some Typex machines that would be at Bletchley with other staff operators. Some Wrens would also be tasked with training US Signals engineers on the Bombes. While initial training for Wrens would be at one of the training centres such as Mill Hill in north London, detailed training for operating Bombes would not be undertaken until they had been selected for Station X duties, at Bletchley or one of the five outstations. Many women would be in their late teenage years and this was usually their first employment in the workplace. They would use tweezers to align the sharp wire brushes on the rotor drums of the Bombe, and be expected to recognise the symptoms of 'brush bounce', which the RAF engineers would try to rectify during maintenance.[19]

Significance: The resourcing of Bombe codebreaking machine operation could be entrusted to trained Wren personnel, which would release men for other duties. The initial prejudice against using women for this specialist task was soon put to rest, as they proved their worth in efficient operation of the machines. The many hundreds of Wrens who operated Bombes and the later, more advanced machines, demonstrated that they could work efficiently, accurately, and as professionals on what was a highly secret operation.

Capture of Enigma rotors and code books (1940)

HMS *Gleamer* was a British minesweeper operating in the Atlantic in February 1940, when it captured U-boat *U-33*. While German sailors were instructed to dispose of the Enigma rotors overboard to prevent the enemy capturing them, the submariner tasked with this role forgot. As a result, the British managed to recover two of the three rotors, designated VI and VII. In May 1940, the final rotor was recovered from *U-13*. In May 1941 the Royal Navy captured U-boat *U-110*, a type IXB class, with its encryption equipment and its code book material intact. The damaged submarine was approached by HMS *Bulldog*, a 'B'-class destroyer, which sent a boarding party across after threatening to ram the vessel. They were supported by HMS *Broadway*, which had previously dropped depth charges, forcing the submarine to the surface. Once on board, the boarding party from *Bulldog* were surprised to be able to gather up with ease code books, charts, logs, and other important documents. Among the captured material were *Kriegsmarine* cipher code books, instructions, and key lists for different navy and submarine codes. The catch also included an Enigma machine, which was an added prize for Bletchley Park. *Bulldog* radio operator William Stewart Pollock seized the Enigma. The submarine was scuttled and the German crew interned in Iceland. The German high command never realised that the Enigma, code books, and documents had been captured by the British. This bought the Allies a degree of time until new code books were issued and new cipher keys were prepared for issue.

Significance: The need to crack the Enigma codes was paramount, yet the frustration for long periods of failure were compensated to a degree by the capture of enemy documents and rotors.

Radio intelligence passed to Russian HQ by communist partisans

In the battle to suppress Poland both during and after the war, Russian partisans tried to break the Polish resistance and would intercept radio messages on a large scale. These would then be transferred back to HQ for action against the resistance. However, the communists would recruit people from among mobsters, hoodlums and gangs to seek out the Polish underground movement, as younger people would have already been taken into the Polish resistance. The communist enemy were the People's Army and the People's Guard. To make matters more complex, Britain was an ally of Russia during wartime and the Polish Government were in exile in the UK. To fight against Stalin's communist forces would be seen as anti-West, and anti-British. However, they had little choice in the matter. They were fighting for their survival. In 1944 the Red army were joined by NKVD units, which were even more ruthless against the Poles.

Significance: The complexity of war, of loyalty to nations, and deciding in practice who is your enemy. Suppression of Polish resistance was high on the agenda for the Russians.

Swiss Enigma codes broken by Nazis

Switzerland, designated as neutral during the Second World War, had Enigma encoding machines for security. The Swiss military and diplomatic service would use commercially available Enigma machines. Many of the code books were in different languages, which were used by the Swiss, including French, Italian and German. The commercial machines available had less complexity and a much-reduced level of security compared with the developed military machines. It appeared the Swiss used a model of Enigma without a plugboard at the front, a model K. They had acquired more than 250 of these for distribution to their armed services and diplomatic division. The Germans saw the benefit in intercepting encoded messages between the Swiss and a number of other countries that they had dealings with, often for financial purposes, sometimes not. It was established that various messages incorporated a code word at the start, to indicate the content of the message. For example, Merkur would deal with finance, and Wega would deal with shipping. Messages sent from Switzerland to Washington would then have to consider the time difference. Because of this, some messages would be transmitted in duplicate using the same Enigma setting key, making it easy for the Germans to decode. Additionally, sending the message in German and the same message in French would aid the enemy considerably. The German Foreign office codebreakers discovered that the Swiss would put into the Enigma message the encoding machine settings for the next message, and so this was an easy way in to read the content until the system was changed. Wiring of the wheel rotors would be determined, and more detailed probing into the Swiss machines, aided by general sloppiness of their operation of Enigma. The Nazis were particularly interested in possible intelligence exposing Nazi senior generals and others as traitors working with Russian agents in Switzerland. There would even be discoveries of a potential link to people planning the attempted assassination of Adolf Hitler.

Significance: Switzerland would be of interest to all sides during the war for a variety of different reasons. Neutrality of the country would not protect it from subversive activities of spying and intelligence gathering by others. The financial status of Switzerland for commercial business and holding private accounts made it a target for the Nazis to gather essential information.

WAAF expands and provides intelligence support (1940)

The WAAF was established by the RAF in 1939 and by October 1943 had around 180,000 recruits active on a variety of different duties. By spring 1945, approaching the latter part of the war, there would be 1,000 WAAFs at Bletchley Park. Their duties would be a combination of clerical posts, teleprinter operators and Morse slip readers. Additionally, Y-stations such as Chicksands would have WAAFs as listening personnel on Morse code intercepts of broadcasts to the Luftwaffe or other armed services. They would be on shift work through the day and night, filling eight-hour shifts. Many of the WAAFs would already have been trained as competent typists. The speed of Morse interception would increase over time as they became familiar with the sender's 'key'. When taken down in the log sheets, they would be passed on to a dispatch rider, often a Wren motorcycle courier, who would transport the information to Bletchley Park for analysis. The WAAFs would have no idea where the information was sent to, or the significance of the Bletchley Park site. Alongside the WRNS, ATS, and other female organisations, they would play a significant part in wartime activities at different locations in the UK, with some personnel also abroad in places such as Ceylon, now Sri Lanka.

Significance: Recognition that a range of female military personnel organisations would provide important support roles in wartime, whether they were WAAFs, ATS, or WRNS. They would be there to fill resource gaps in the organisations.

U-boats dominate the Atlantic from 1940

From the 1940s the *Kriegsmarine* would dominate the Atlantic and cause havoc with Allied shipping, both merchant vessels and naval. The proliferation of U-boats, many based on the west coast of France, in bomb-proof shelters, were largely free to come and go, aided by mines and nets for protection. The losses as a direct result of the U-boats concerned Churchill more than anything, as the resupply of Britain with fuel, food, armaments and personnel was critical to success in defeating the enemy. Hundreds of thousands of tons of shipping went to the bottom of the sea as the submarines attacked British and American convoys. Bletchley Park was active in trying to focus on the 'Shark' encoded Enigma messages to identify when and where the U-boats would position themselves prior to an attack. Even when the codes were broken at Bletchley, the Allies had to be particularly careful not to give the game away in hinting that Enigma was being cracked by the British. Otherwise, the Nazis would have changed the keys, the sequences, and incorporated other security methods to prevent Enigma being compromised.

A game of 'cat and mouse' ensued, and pressure increased in Hut 8 to make more progress in the intercepts and decodes. One might argue that never more was the responsibility of those codebreakers at Bletchley Park at its peak than the Battle of the Atlantic in the early war years. Britain's survival depended upon it.

Significance: The U-boat threat lasted several years but would peak and then decline due to a variety of different factors. It would be a key objective to disrupt the U-boats by those at Bletchley Park in collecting and deciphering Enigma intelligence, but without giving the game away in terms of how the intelligence was obtained. As much effort went into keeping the Nazis guessing as would be in the actual codebreaking itself.

Hollerith processing commences at Bletchley Park (1940)

The use of machines to assist with processing data on punched cards was seen as potentially useful by management at Bletchley Park. A hut was identified for the processing of messages where they could be filtered and recorded, with even apparent trivia collected as it may become of use when pieced together carefully with other relevant information. Hut 7 at Bletchley was used for the Hollerith tabulating work. A BTM manager was identified, Freeborn, who would run the show, using many women to operate the equipment. BTM, his employer, had connections with the Hollerith company back in the United States and had various contractual licences in respect of the tabulating equipment. Freeborn would have two assistants, and the work was so important that it ran twenty-four hours a day, seven days a week to cope with demand. There would be five shifts of Hollerith operators, three on day shifts and two at night. The process involved punching and then verification of some 3,000 master cards, which when processed might generate some 80,000 detail cards from the master card data. The tasks would be allocated in the morning and procedures established to process in the afternoon. Sorters, reproducers, tabulators, key punch operators, punched card filing clerks, verifier operators, maintenance engineers; all specialist processes, and in many ways the manual precursor of modern computer memory banks and operating systems, where data is stored in the memory, after putting it in folders in a systematic and logical arrangement, on a computer hard drive, for recovering that data in different versions later. Operators could manage two or more Hollerith machines of the same type at once. Women tended to make up the bulk of the Hollerith processing workforce. The quantity of punched cards expanded considerably as the Hollerith processing increased. The volume reached the hundreds of thousands, and even into the millions at their peak. They sat on shelves, in cabinets, on tables, in drawers, on the floor, and the staff were rapidly running out of space to store them, to the consternation of management. A decision was made to relocate the Hollerith tabulating section elsewhere, and Freeborn would be in charge, managing the request for information from Bletchley and supported by his growing team of largely female operators. At its peak, there would be around 300 personnel employed in the Hollerith section. Churchill visited Bletchley and was shown the operation with a planned demonstration for him. Freeborn's assistant would be R. Whelan. The consumption of punched cards would later reach a couple of million per week, and take over the valuable space.

Significance: The application of punched card technology to the codebreaking and data collection operation at Bletchley Park. A dossier on the Hollerith machinery and historical notes on the use of such equipment and under Freeborn in Hut 7 were prepared by BTM covering the period 1935–45.[20] Clearly, the early years from 1935 were unrelated to Bletchley Park, as it was not established until 1939, and it would take time for the Government to award contracts to BTM for codebreaking manufacture and support activities.

Poles establish codebreaking base in southern France in 1940

Three Polish codebreakers who worked for the Polish Cipher Service in Warsaw relocated when the Nazis invaded Poland to Uzès, in Provence, southern France. They occupied an old château, i.e., *Château des Fuzes*, together with other codebreakers in Vichy France to carry out their work and assist Free France and its allies against the enemy. They were located a couple of minutes from the village. The code name was *Cadix*. Around thirty or so specialists were located at the château, comprising Polish, French and Spanish codebreakers. The period of this activity was from September 1940 to 9 November 1942. The Poles worked on cracking Enigma signals from the Axis powers, but also tested Polish codebreaking machines. Eventually, they had to relocate to Spain when the Nazis moved south and occupied the area. They also went to work in Algiers for a period. When the Nazis came to the Provence area, two of the Polish codebreakers, Rejewski and Zygalski, were arrested and imprisoned as they made their way to Spain across the Pyrenees. Eventually they escaped to the United Kingdom. Those codebreakers worked alongside Spanish and French cryptographers, and a plaque now exists outside the château commemorating their specialist work during the war.[21]

Significance: The base at Uzès, Provence, was necessary after Poland was invaded by the Nazis. It was a long way from Poland, but care still had to be taken in not attracting attention to the activities there. The operation at the château bought the codebreakers valuable time before they had to abandon the site when the Nazis closed in.

Knox pulls together his team of codebreakers (1940)

Codebreaker Dilwyn Knox was keen on involving new blood in assisting his team in cracking Enigma keys. He would bring together a group of intelligent women including Mavis Lever, and nurture them to be shown the methods and approach to cracking codes, looking for clues or cribs and establishing a systematic approach. He and his team were very successful in breaking ciphers and codes, although Knox fell seriously ill and died before the end of the war. Knox had been promoted to chief assistant at Bletchley in January 1940, He was allowed to establish a research unit of female assistants, and worked in the stable yard cottages on site. His 'girls' were selected and interviewed by a Miss Moore at the Foreign Office, but he had some control over the qualifications and their suitability. Margaret Rock was chosen as part of the team, and Mavis Lever another. Some could speak fluent German, which would be an asset. Lever and Keith Batey would excel in breaking Enigma keys relating to the eventual Battle of Matapan in the Mediterranean. This battle would be a great victory for the Royal Navy and a feather in the cap of Knox and his team. Knox would unfortunately fall very sick during the war and never lived to see its end. He had made a difference, however, and left a legacy of encouragement and empowerment of females when he was leading his team of codebreakers.

Significance: Knox was both an innovator and risk taker, determined to use the skill of men and women, but particularly of women, to build up his codebreaking team to be effective, and to train those personnel in an environment that was encouraging and would prove successful in terms of output.

The Germans discover part of a Typex machine on a beach in France (1940)

In the early years of the Second World War, a British designed and made Typex machine was left on a beach in France by the Allied armed forces. The Germans pulled it out and studied it. They had seen nothing like it before; it was clearly not a weapon, but a piece of British equipment left abandoned, and they probably came to the conclusion that it was of little significance. The typewriter-type keyboard indicated it was for sending or typing messages, a communication device. In fact, Typex was the British copy of the Nazi Enigma machine, and was the final stage in the use of decoded enemy settings when decoded using either manual methods of codebreaking or using Bombe machines. In some ways it was an improved version of Enigma, but the Germans considered Enigma unbreakable as regards the codes and ciphers.

Significance: If the Nazis had spent longer evaluating Typex, they would have realised this was a version of Enigma created by the British. Why would they do this? To play a part in deciphering Enigma messages and reading them on a version of the machine that was more appropriate to the British way of doing things, and perhaps more understandable in the workings of it. The Allies were most fortunate, as if the Germans had considered Typex a real threat to their encoded communications, Enigma may have been further modified for security, or other advanced machines produced in very large numbers for general use by the army, navy and Luftwaffe.

Nazi Enigma machine version termed 'Shark' by British

The Enigma model M4 Triton had four-wheel rotors instead of the usual three, and this was to increase the quantity of permutations in the message settings considerably. Bletchley Park were arranging for codebreaking machines using three-rotor-based Enigmas, and not four. They named the new challenge 'Shark'. It would be some time before they could break into the Shark encoded settings, and many Atlantic merchant ships would be successfully attacked with torpedoes by German U-boats using the modified Enigma machine as a communication device. Enormous effort and resources were poured into decoding Shark messages, and eventually the effort made a difference to the Allies.

Significance: The understanding by Bletchley Park codebreakers and management that the Germans were using different versions of Enigma for different purposes, and that while the Enigma was universal as a machine in one respect, in others it was not. The four-wheel Enigma would become a headache for the codebreakers.

Discovery of non-Morse messages intercepted in England (1940)

A police station with a listening facility at Denmark Hill in south London would be the first to identify intercepts that did not sound like traditional Morse code. The listening operators then contacted Bletchley Park, who came down to listen to the radio and confirmed this was a new type of system and process, being termed 'non-Morse' messages. The result of this was investigation to establish what exactly was sending this data over the airwaves, and how was it configured? It took the brilliance and perseverance of a mathematician called William Tutte to make the progress needed, after many at Bletchley tried and had failed to make progress. Additionally, new codebreaking machines would need to be designed and built to challenge the advanced enemy machines. The first messages received in this non-Morse format were between 1940 and 1941. A specialist teleprinter attachment was sending them from Germany, and they were intercepted by radio Y-station listeners, as part of the SIGINT network.

Significance: The British understanding that systems other than Enigma were being used by the enemy, but at a time when the source of the equipment was unclear, needing further detailed investigation.

Photo Reconnaissance Unit established (1940)

It would be 18 June 1940 when the Photo Reconnaissance Unit, or 1 PRU, was established, having been evolved from a Photographic Development Unit. Aerial photo intelligence would add to the bigger picture of identifying the enemy resources, equipment and build-up of transported units. This would have assisted traffic analysis when intercepting enemy encoded messages. In later years 1 PRU would be disbanded, and the photo intelligence work distributed across different RAF squadrons.[22] The subject of photo reconnaissance is a subject all by itself, and perhaps beyond the scope of this glossary in detail. It is the case that an aerial photo by itself is useless to the military senior staff without proper, skilled, interpretation of the photos using optical aids, and possibly even stereo-imaging at times. Whole teams of specialists would spend thousands of hours examining photos taken over enemy-occupied territory to evaluate what was of interest on the ground. Peenemünde was one such area of interest, for the Nazi V1 rockets, and later V2 development.

Significance: The relevance of photo-reconnaissance to codebreaking was that it was another important part of the overall picture of establishing the enemy resources and position. Decoded enemy intercepted messages would then consider and analyse what specific evidence of aerial photography had been gained at the time of the fly-over by the piloted aircraft. Of course, photos taken from aircraft of enemy troops, Panzer divisions, and equipment moving across the countryside, could rapidly become out of date. However, there would be times when commanders of operations would look at multiple sources of intelligence, and photos of enemy territory might also support and be relevant to the Traffic Analysis section at Bletchley Park.[23]

Delegation of US Army and Navy SIGINT personnel to Bletchley Park (1940)

An offer was made to the United States to allow a delegation of army and naval officers and personnel to visit Bletchley Park in December 1940.[24] Cooperation was seen as essential where there was a common vested interest.

Significance: Sharing of information in wartime between allies was nothing new, and both Britain and the United States exchanged visits to gain further knowledge on signals intelligence.

Four codebreakers write to Churchill about resources (1941)

Following a visit by Churchill to Bletchley Park in September 1941, four senior codebreakers came together to write and sign a letter to Churchill dated 21 October 1941, making the case for additional resources. Codebreaker Milner Barry delivered the letter to 10 Downing Street. Churchill read the contents and responded with

'Action this day!' stamped in red ink, and giving them whatever they needed in terms of equipment, materials, and manpower. Much of the letter described the need for extra manpower (and WRNS woman power), shortages in key areas, such as in some of the huts at Bletchley, in the Hollerith section, etc. This letter to Churchill was written without knowledge of the management at Bletchley, and they were displeased that their authority had been usurped and bypassed. Denniston commented on the unorthodox approach, and Stuart Menzies was most angry with those involved. However, the outcome was positive and constructive for the codebreakers. The four who signed the letter were Turing, Welchman, Alexander, and Milner-Barry, from Huts 6 and 8. Each one was a senior codebreaker in the huts at Bletchley, and head of various sections. Welchman would draft the letter on behalf of all of them. Without that letter and the response from Churchill there would inevitably have been delays and gaps in codebreaking output, so it achieved its purpose, even if it did inevitably cause some upset. Without Churchill's visit to Bletchley in September 1941, it is likely that such a letter might not have been sent to him, or it would have possibly been later. Either way, that could have had serious consequences in developing codebreaking efficiency at Bletchley and the outstations.

Significance: A bold action in codebreakers writing to Churchill without knowledge of Bletchley Park's management, effectively going over their heads, proved to obtain a positive outcome, with a push for more resources. It was a risk at the time, but worthwhile, and Bletchley's management would also benefit from Churchill's 'Action this day' note and clear instruction on the request for resources.

Y-listening stations expanded to support Bletchley Park from 1941

Although Y-stations had been in existence for a number of years to listen into foreign intelligence via radio and Morse code, expansion of these together with new equipment was necessary to meet the needs of the country. Memoranda and reports held at the National Archives provide strong evidence of this.[25]

Significance: The listening stations were the first stage in intercepting radio traffic from the enemy and via Morse code. While not all would be encoded, a great deal of it was, particularly when Enigma was used in large numbers by the Axis powers.

Bombe Victory is modified (1941)

The first codebreaking Bombe, Victory, was returned to the factory in Letchworth for modification to install a diagonal board circuit, designed by codebreaker Welchman.[26] The National Archive entries in the Bombe registers indicate it was later renamed 'Leo' and sent to Outstation Wavendon in September 1940, relocated from Bletchley Park, but was found to be not working as well as anticipated.

Significance: Machines would be upgraded to improve their efficiency and to save valuable time in the data processing to discover the enemy encoded message settings.

Country House codebreaking outstations established (1941)

In a plan to spread the risk of bombing of the codebreaking facility at Bletchley Park, three outstations were identified, being country house estates. Adstock, Wavendon, and Gayhurst became codebreaking outstations in Buckinghamshire during the war. The machines were in outbuildings, including some in stables. The personnel operating them would be the Wrens, often in cold, draughty and damp buildings, with the risk of electric shock from areas of standing water in the huts and outbuildings in some cases. Dispatch riders would be on motorcycles ferrying information and instructions back and forth to Bletchley Park. Many of the dispatch riders would be Wrens or female personnel in the services.

Automatic typewriters would be installed at some locations to print Bombe 'stops' and to pass this information back to Bletchley Park for instructions.

When some country house outstations closed, their Bombes would be sent to other larger outstations such as Outstation Stanmore in the north-west London suburbs.

OSA Adstock, opened March 1941
OSW Wavendon, opened March 1941. Closed January 1944
OSG Gayhurst, opened September 1942

Woburn, or Woburn Abbey, was only used as a personnel billeting centre, and not as a codebreaking outstation. It housed many hundreds of Wrens who would travel to work at Bletchley Park and elsewhere.

Significance: This was a recognition by senior officials and the military that putting all your eggs in one basket was not a good idea, and that Bletchley Park was potentially vulnerable to a Luftwaffe raid that could cause extensive damage and losses. That would have impacted greatly on Britain's codebreaking effectiveness. The country houses were a compromise at first. Much larger codebreaking bases would come later.

Wren narrowly escapes electrocution at a codebreaking outstation

Country house outstations had a number of Bombe codebreaking machines, and also had Wrens operating them. One Wren on a shift had a narrow escape when attending to her make-up after she positioned her powder compact on the Bombe machine when it was still live electrically. The metal compact shorted the wiring and with a loud noise and flickering of the lights the Bombe stopped working.

The Wren was in shock and fortunately not electrocuted, particularly as there was sometimes standing water on the floor of the huts. A reprimand made sure she would not put her compact anywhere near the machinery again. She would have to obtain a replacement compact as the one that had been positioned on the Bombe had melted to a degree, with the power and heat dissipated. Bombe machines relied on electrical power to operate, otherwise they were mere hunks of metal and components, nothing more. Some Wrens would be issued with Wellington boots and rubber mats in stables that may have been used for the Bombes, as standing water was a problem. Health and safety was not the highest priority in wartime.

Significance: An incident that demonstrated that the conditions in the Bombe enclosures, huts, and stables were usually quite cramped. Operational staff on long shifts took the opportunity to smarten up their appearance, although some clearly forgot they were dealing with live electrical equipment that was potentially hazardous.

Hitler convinced to have a separate and secure encoding system for German high command (1941)

While Enigma was used throughout the German armed services and the secret service in great numbers, Hitler wanted a secure encoded communication system that could only be allocated to him and his German high command officers, i.e., his generals and field marshals. The outcome was the Lorenz teleprinter attachment, which worked on non-Morse encoding and decoding at a very high speed of transmission, in a completely different way to Enigma. It would be far more secure than any of the Enigma models available, although it also worked on multiple rotors on a spindle. Lorenz would have twelve rotors, compared with the much smaller quantity on Enigma.[27] The mathematical permutations of Lorenz and the later 'secret writers' would be astronomically high, and they were made in very limited numbers. There would therefore be two parallel encoding and decoding systems used by the Nazis, and this would become a headache and a challenge for the Allies to deal with.

Significance: Hitler had been told that Enigma was unbreakable, yet he wanted guarantees that his communication with his high command would not be compromised in any way. The teleprinter attachments were the answer, or so they thought. They had not allowed for the determination and brilliance of a young mathematician back in Buckinghamshire, Bill Tutte.

Nazi Lorenz senior military signatories identified (1940–41)

Hitler had been quite specific in wanting to restrict access to the Lorenz advanced teleprinter encoding attachment for sending messages via the German high command. The list of people he approved, mainly generals and field marshals, for access to Lorenz and the various versions, were as follows:

- Adolf Hitler (Führer)
- General von Rundstedt (Later Field Marshal). Western Front
- General Model (Chief of Staff)
- General von Kluge
- Field Marshal von Manstein (Head of German Army)
- Field Marshal Rommel
- Field Marshal Kesselring
- Field Marshal Jodl

These senior commanders would be of particular interest to the Allies when trying to intercept the Fish or Tunny communication links used for the non-Morse teleprinter messages with high command instructions from Berlin and elsewhere.

Significance: Hitler had to restrict access to German high command communications, and apart from the machine operators, the list agreed by him would diminish the chance of leaks and breaches of security. At least, in theory.

Bombes transferred across codebreaking bases (1941)

Evidenced by the official Bombe registers, many Bombe codebreaking machines were transferred across the outstations for reasons of logistics, expansion of codebreaking outstations and closing down others. Some were returned back to BTM at Letchworth for improvements. Others would be improved on site. The renaming of Bombe machines was done in some cases, so that some machines had over their lives more than one name for reference. This can be traced in the Bombe record archives. Several machines went to Outstation Stanmore and a large number to Outstation Eastcote in Middlesex, which would be the last two outstations as well as the largest as regards Bombe quantities. As the larger outstations came into being, some of the smaller ones closed and transferred their machines to them.

Significance: The relocation of codebreaking machines across England was a necessary process for a variety of reasons. Stanmore, in particular, was used as a sort of clearing house of Bombe machines, and a staging post when the larger Eastcote outstation was established, and Bombes moved there. All the movement of such machines had to be done secretly, under tarpaulins, so members of the public had no idea what was under the covers.

First recorded German Lorenz transmissions (1941)

The first recorded intercepts of Lorenz non-Morse wireless transmissions by the Allies were at Denmark Hill, at, or over a police station, which was a listening station at the time. It was June 1941. This would not have been the first actual use of Lorenz, as Nazi tests of advanced machines would have been carried out previously, and possibly even via landline as well. The strange, very fast, staccato-like noises received were quite unlike the traditional Morse code they were used to, and Bletchley Park was contacted by those monitoring transmissions at Denmark Hill for their experts to come and have a closer listen. They agreed this was something quite new and the high speed of transmission indicated a form of automation by the enemy. The problem was, no one knew how this new machine was configured, what it looked like, or anything about it. Bletchley now had to work fast to try and throw some light on it. Ironically, the first experimental transmissions of non-Morse transmissions were probably intercepted in 1932 by the police listening service on behalf of the Foreign Office. The transmissions were on a communication link between Moscow and Berlin. The police would be financed by the Foreign Office to continue monitoring unusual wireless transmissions, at least until wartime.

Significance: The identification of another system used by the enemy other than via Enigma encoding machines for messages. The analysis of non-Morse messages would take some time, and then the infrastructure needed to be established at Bletchley Park, at Knockholt in Kent and elsewhere, to challenge it in a practical way.

Personnel shortages in operating codebreaking machines

In wartime there are always shortages of men, women, food, equipment, materials, and armaments. The Second World War was no different. As production of Bombe codebreaking machines developed and expanded, management reviewed the resources available and realised that manpower would be critical. Men were being conscripted into the armed forces, training for war, fighting abroad, and carrying out a multitude of tasks. The answer was to look at women in the armed forces, and the WRNS or Wrens were one part of the solution. In December 1941, Parliament would make conscription of some groups of unmarried women and childless widows a requirement, with a choice to work in industry or in one of the auxiliary services. More Wrens would be available to be trained as a direct result of this decree.[28] While there would be some initial prejudice in allowing women to operate advanced technical equipment, the tests carried out proved they were more than capable. The Wrens would be selected from the training bases and then given supplementary training to work on the Bombes, the codebreaking machines. Even so, management would raise concerns as time progressed as to the quantities of trained personnel needed to work on a shift rota on the bases and to maintain the quality and consistency needed in setting up and operating the machines. It was like finding enough water supplies to keep topping up the cistern tank in order to keep supplying the population without shortages. While initially the Wrens came on board to the services on a voluntary basis, the conscription of women later would introduce many more staff who could be trained and utilised. Without accessing this female resource there would have been men taken away from other important tasks, depleting the strength of the services. A total of 1,676 Wrens would work on the codebreaking machines, termed

'Special X' duties, and support related to codebreaking. Others would also be in key support roles, in a background capacity along with ATS, WAAFs, and other branches of the services.

Significance: The management of GC&CS and other interested parties had to monitor and to plan ahead for both equipment, skilled personnel, and clerical support. The resources gap in operating personnel of the codebreaking Bombes would become so significant as to cause delays in codebreaking unless dealt with in good time. Memoranda seen by the author of wartime concerns in this respect demonstrates that the training of sufficient numbers of skilled operators of the Bombes needed very high priority to keep up with Bombe production at Letchworth. The training and resources would be monitored frequently by management.

Sinking of SS *Aguila* (1941)

SS *Aguila* was a merchant ship in part of a convoy, OG-71, of twenty-three merchant ships, transferring personnel to Gibraltar from Liverpool. A complement of naval personnel would be en route to Gibraltar including Wren cipher officers, specialist radio operators from Scarborough. A U-boat attack sank many of the ships in the convoy including *Aguila*, with eighty-six naval personnel on board and of these twenty-one would be Wrens. The Wrens had no chance of survival at night in the cold waters. Following this tragic event, the Royal Navy decided to change policy and only allow transport on Navy armed vessels and not merchant ships. A memorial for those who died and a sculpture of a Wren bird on a pedestal is located at the National Arboretum. A lifeboat in Aberystwyth, Wales, was also named after *Aguila* as a commemoration of the loss. Scarborough too has a bench seat marked with the names of those lost in the incident. The chief Wren officer who lost her life, Cecily Monica Bruce Benjamin, came from Pinner in Middlesex, and was only 20 years old.[29] Many of her colleagues were of a similar age.

Significance: The vulnerability of transporting personnel such as cipher officers and others by merchant vessels at sea was demonstrated by the attack of the convoy and sinking of the *Aguila*. The Royal Navy changed their strategy after this event to then transport naval personnel only in military ships.

Cypher No. 3 is compromised (1941)

Enemy codebreakers were reading with ease the British Combined Naval Cypher No. 3 by summer 1941, introduced by the Admiralty in January 1941. This cipher was to be used to communicate on convoy movements in the Atlantic by the British and Americans.

Significance: The leakage of certain ciphers would expose the convoys to U-boat attacks, and the breach needed to be plugged before more ships were sunk.

EVENTS

Turing develops Banburismus (1941)

Turing was keen on finding ways to improve the efficiency of determining the settings of Enigma. This would then save the Allies time and mean more messages could be decoded, giving them an advantage over the Nazis. He developed a system called Banburismus. The process was used in Hut 8 at Bletchley Park to help eliminate some of the rotor wheel permutations by identifying likely matches based on probability. This was then applied by the codebreaking team with a degree of success.

Significance: One of many developments by Turing that would improve the efficiency of codebreaking at Bletchley Park.

Italian codes broken for Battle of Matapan (1941)

Mavis Lever was a codebreaker at Bletchley Park working under mathematician Dilwyn Knox as part of a team. Knox encouraged women who had a mathematical and logical aptitude to develop their skills in codebreaking. It was Lever, with some help from another codebreaker, Keith Batey, who decoded intercepts from the Italians about a planned Naval attack against British warships in the Mediterranean. Using a little of her knowledge of Italian, she worked out certain words and phrases and this was then the basis of further analysis to decode the message. Her intelligence decode would be passed to Admiral A. Cunningham, and he was able to set a trap for the Italian fleet with the information. The result was great success in the Battle of Matapan, in March 1941, with the British assisted by the Australian navy sinking a substantial proportion of the Italian fleet. It was supported with British aircraft dropping torpedoes.

The Italians had originally hoped to entice the British and Australian warships into a potential trap. Merchant ship convoys carrying British troops across the Mediterranean were the target for the Italians, led by Vice-Admiral Angelo Lachino. The Italians had come prepared with thirteen destroyers, a battleship, both light and heavy cruisers. The battle took place at Matapan on the south-west tip of the Greek peninsula between 27 and 29 March. Five Italian ships were sunk and several damaged, with heavy losses of personnel and many sailors captured. British losses were relatively light in comparison and no ships sunk. The interception of intelligence and decoding at Bletchley Park provided key information on the intentions of the Italians, and the British admiral then had a clear advantage. The Italian fleet had notice of the presence of the British aircraft carrier HMS *Formidable* through signals cipher interception, but the Allies would still have the upper hand. Aircraft would spot the flotilla in good time. The defeated Italian vice-admiral recorded that the battle had reduced his operational effectiveness in the area and that there were deficiencies in coordination between their aircraft and naval vessels, as well as poor night attack scenarios.

Admiral Cunningham was so pleased with the outcome that when he visited Bletchley Park later he asked to meet the person or persons who had decoded the message that helped in the victory. He was surprised to be introduced to several females, including Lever, not what he expected at all. Lever went on to eventually marry her codebreaking colleague, Keith Batey, and became Mavis Batey. She would be part of a success story for 'Dilly' Knox and his team at Bletchley. Sadly, her boss died before the war ended. The Director of Naval Intelligence, Admiral Godfrey, acknowledged that success at Matapan was substantially due to the codebreaking work of Knox and his team of girls at Bletchley Park.

Significance: The battle is important due to the effectiveness of intercepted Italian intelligence and prompt codebreaking of messages at Bletchley. It demonstrated that codebreaking could have a direct impact on military naval strategy and save lives. The sharing of intelligence across Allied units and military organisations could help change the balance of power.

Bletchley Park decodes intelligence from Berlin to Tokyo regarding Hitler's military intentions (1941)

On 10 June 1941 Bletchley Park's diplomatic section decoded a message sent from the Japanese ambassador in Berlin, to Tokyo. This advised that Germany was to attack Russia, and this would happen very soon. It was just a week and a half later that Hitler commenced Operation *Barbarossa*.

Significance: Intercepting significant intelligence such as this about an impending invasion of a major European country was like gold dust. There may have been some element of disbelief when Allied commanders read the translation of the message as Hitler and Stalin had non-aggression pacts in place, but Hitler was predictably unpredictable in his military strategy. Stalin had been advised by a few of his senior politicians that Hitler was bound to attack Russia soon, but the Soviet leader dismissed this and then the opportunity of surprise and possible advanced military preparation. It is not clear if the intelligence feeding Tokyo was passed to the Russians before the invasion of Russia by Hitler. Even if it was, Stalin would not have believed it. Stalin trusted Hitler to a degree, and would have been dumbfounded if Russia was attacked by its ally.

Operation Barbarossa commences (1941)

Hitler had previously agreed a non-aggression pact with Russia to ensure that Germany would not be attacked, at least not without warning. However, it was already in his mind for him to attack Russia and take control of the country to obtain its useful mineral resources and eliminate a potential threat. He despised the Bolsheviks almost as much as he despised the Jewish people. It was just deciding the right time to act. Operation Barbarossa, in June, 1941, would surprise the Russians, who were largely unprepared for an invasion and Stalin looked for scapegoats among his team of advisers when it occurred. The plan was to capture the capital, Moscow, and also Stalingrad in the summer months. However, it went badly wrong for the Nazis, who were bogged down with their men and equipment in seas of autumn mud, followed by an extreme winter. Losses would be huge on both sides. Many saw this operation as Hitler's biggest mistake in the war. It overstretched his forces, and diverted supplies away from France, Italy and other occupied areas. Hitler was left fighting a war on several fronts.

The intelligence from the east was as important as from elsewhere. Bletchley Park decoded intercepted messages from both the Nazis and the Russians, even though Russia then became Britain's ally. However, Britain would also feed back to the Russians key intelligence about enemy preparations and their build up for attacks and counter-attacks without giving away the source of the information. Churchill and Roosevelt were suspicious of the Russians, but Stalin's feeling was mutual. For a time, Bletchley would stop spying on the Russians and concentrate on the Germans, Italians and later the Japanese. Russia became the west's ally, at least for a few years until the Cold War changed things again. Russia lost some 27 million military personnel and civilians helping to defeat Hitler, more than any other country in the war. Hitler had seriously underestimated Russia, its resources and people. The Russian winter was more effective at slowing down the Nazis than a thousand tanks but Hitler had not planned for the campaign to last that long.

Significance: Hitler had always intended to attack Russia; it was just a matter of getting the timing right. It would be a major mistake strategically for the Nazis, as the resources of the Russians were huge, in manpower, in comparison to the Germans. However, Hitler had banked upon a swift penetration into Russian territory, destroying its airfields, and capturing major cities quickly. He had not bargained for the resolve of the Russian people. As winter approached, the whole campaign started to go badly wrong. Despite numerous counter-attacks against the advancing Soviets, the Nazi forces would never recover and it was the beginning of the end for them.

A burglary in Rome at the embassy (1941)

The American embassy in Rome, Italy, was burgled by an Italian military intelligence officer. The intelligence obtained was the diplomatic code book used by the US military attaché when communicating with Washington. How could this have been permitted to occur? Security was poor in September 1941.

Significance: The lack of security would help the Italians, and probably the Nazis too. The Allied response would be to improve security systems to avoid a repeat.

German Lorenz operators make errors in transmission (1941)

One of the aims of a codebreaker is to look out for clues or cribs in encoded messages from the enemy. These can be a small crack in the armour of the coded message, and open up potential for identifying other letters or numbers. These all save time, and time is precious in codebreaking during wartime. On 31 August 1941, one German teleprinter operator re-sent the same encoded Lorenz message a second time to his recipient, but without changing the key, a fatal mistake. Some of the second messages even had abbreviations within such as 'Nr' for number. Lorenz was a teleprinter attachment that could send non-Morse encoded messages for the German high command. When discovered by Bletchley Park codebreakers, and William Tutte, this opened up an opportunity to crack the message settings and read enemy messages in some detail. It was not straightforward, however. Tutte managed to identify a pattern in the message text, and deduced the number of teeth on the rotor wheels of Lorenz, and the quantity of wheels, which was twelve in total. This was without Tutte ever having seen the Lorenz machine, which was an extraordinary achievement.

Arthur Scherbius, the inventor and designer of Enigma, had always been aware that the protocols for security must be adhered to by the Enigma operators at all times, to prevent mistakes. However, people are human, become tired, bored, and look for short-cuts in systems to save time. This is exactly what the Allies needed. Creating a small crack in an open door, as with the same message transmitted with the same set key, one could detect patterns in the sequencing, and make progress in decoding the message settings. Also, the fact that the design of Enigma prevented the keyed letter being illuminated as the same letter was a weakness in the design. If the message setting tried out at Bletchley gave an identical letter on paper, then the codebreakers knew it was incorrect, and an 'L 'could not show up as an 'L' when the key was pressed down on the machine. Only one of twenty-five remaining letters could appear on the illuminated lamp board.

Finding out the weaknesses of Enigma was a two-pronged attack. Firstly, knowing and understanding the design weaknesses and limitations of the machine, and secondly, looking for operator errors in setting up the machine and in use. Enigma may have appeared to provide random letters for the encoding process, but the truth was that it was not random, only pseudo-random. The objective was to understand the operation of the machine so well and so thoroughly that one could look for patterns in certain sequences, and to test those patterns either by hand or with the aid of machines. The permutations of 158.9 million, million, million settings, made this task a real challenge for the codebreakers. The Lorenz and secret writers, by comparison, had much higher mathematical permutations, such as 10^{170}. A very large number; in fact astronomically large.

Significance: The errors made by Lorenz operators would be seen as a way in to crack the codes by the British. They would be sloppy mistakes and errors, but very useful to the Allies.

Japan communicates a coded message in fourteen parts (1941)

American codebreakers were kept busy trying to keep up with intercepting and decoding Japanese intelligence between embassies, and the build-up to an act of aggression against the USA, which was suspected. The problem was that the Americans had no idea of the timing or the location. A fourteen-part coded message was sent to the Japanese embassy in the US via diplomatic communication using a machine that the Americans called Purple, which was a version of Enigma but looked quite different. The last message part sent by the Japanese told the recipients to destroy and burn all the paperwork as attack was now imminent. The key information was never communicated in time to the US military in Oahu, Hawaii, where the surprise attack would occur early one Sunday morning. Commanders had thought Japanese action would perhaps most likely occur in the Philippines, and that the Naval base at Hawaii was too well defended with aircraft and of high risk to the Japanese, but they were wrong.

Significance: The failure of the Americans to intercept the Japanese intelligence in time to make a difference at Pearl Harbor and be prepared for a surprise attack by the Japanese. There were examples of inefficiency and poor communication, and of disbelief that the Japanese could carry out such an attack.

Pearl Harbor (1941)

The surprise attack by the Japanese on Pearl Harbor on 7 December, 1941 on the island of Oahu in Hawaii brought the Americans into the war. President Roosevelt was enraged. The Americans were deciphering a string of coded messages sent to the Japanese embassy in America about a build-up to some important event or action, but the last part was not decoded in sufficient time, or at least the output was not communicated in good time to the commanders on the island. Many ships were sunk in the harbour, but fortunately the principal American aircraft carriers were out at sea.[30]

Japanese spies were on the island before the attack, monitoring naval ship movements and conveying the intelligence back to Japan. After the attack on Pearl Harbor, many Japanese-Americans were interned in Hawaii and on the mainland without almost any warning. Although Pearl Harbor was a tragedy for the Americans, Churchill saw it as a turning point to obtain an alliance and military support from the USA to strengthen a weakened Britain. The Neutrality Acts would be overturned due to the surprise attack and the need for America to defend itself.

Significance: The surprise attack on the United States naval base had the consequence of bringing the United States into the war, and not just against Japan. Hitler's declaration of war on America sealed that fate. Churchill was pleased, however, to have another active ally in wartime, and one with substantial resources.

US Senate allows Lend-Lease facility for European allies (1941)

The Lend-Lease Act, enacted on 11 March 1941, was a key tool in providing funding and resources to allied powers by the USA during the war. It was subtitled 'An Act to promote the defense of the United States'. Churchill had even suggested the concept of Lend-Lease to Roosevelt at the end of 1940. After Pearl Harbor, it would be easier to pass the Bill through Congress. Extraordinary large sums of money and equipment was provided to Britain, Russia, and many other countries to help with the war effort. This included a considerable amount of radio equipment for transmission and for radio receivers. Much was used in various Y-stations or wireless listening stations in the UK and abroad, being robust and with ample spares for maintenance. The agreement stipulated that items not used at the end of the war should be returned to the US or were to be paid for. The Lend-Lease facility was a saviour for the UK inasmuch it enabled a bankrupt nation to rearm and prepare for further conflict, and as part of a much greater allied force together with the United States. Britain was one of the first countries to benefit from the Lend-Lease Act, and others would soon follow.

The process involved the Office of Lend-Lease administration allocating resources to Britain and others in huge quantities. The US would receive around $10 billion of so called 'reverse lend-lease' as compensation, and a number of financial settlements post-war, although a fraction of what the US had supplied. The money would generally not have to be paid back, although other loans made to Britain did have to be reimbursed. In October 1941 the US Senate passed a $5.98 billion Supplemental Lend-Lease Bill, bringing the total commitment to around $13 billion at the time. This would later increase substantially as more and more countries were added to the list or recipients of wartime aid. By early 1945 the US had spent around 15 per cent of its entire war budget on Lend-Lease to other countries. The investment into the Y-stations as regards equipment would ensure Bletchley Park and the outstations were kept operational in decoding the enemy intelligence, to the benefit of the Allies. A complication under the Lend-Lease agreement involved the convertibility into Sterling, which had to be later adjusted and then dispensed with as it disadvantaged the UK post-war in terms of trade with the US, affecting British monetary reserves. The US treasury was repaid in full by Britain in December 2006, when the last payment was made. The amount borrowed under Lend-Lease was some $50.1 billion across some thirty-eight countries. For comparison, this was the equivalent value of $690 billion at 2020 rates. Considerable levels of funding and military equipment would also be provided to Russia by America when it was an ally fighting Nazi Germany with the West. It was a logistical challenge during wartime, and there were concerns by President Roosevelt that urgently needed machine tools for US factories were being sent abroad. A balance had to be struck as regards the priorities in food, fuel, armaments, materials and other resources that left the shores of America.

Significance: Lend-Lease would be seen as a major economic help for Britain and many of its allies. Without this facility, Britain would not have been able to continue fighting the war against Germany and the other Axis powers. Britain was running low on materials, armaments, fuel and food. Russia also benefitted considerably from the Act, with substantial supplies delivered. The modern equivalent of this degree of financial support is the American 2022 Ukraine Democracy Defense Lend Lease Act, signed by President Biden.[31]

American Signals Services Stations established and expanded (1941)

The Second Signal Service company of the United States had seven listening stations by December 1941, which would later be expanded further. The stations were as follows:

> Fort Hancock, New Jersey
> Fort Scott, Presidio of San Francisco
> Fort Sam Houston, Texas
> Post of Corozal, Panama Canal Dept
> Fort Shafter, T.H.
> Fort McKinley, P.I.
> Fort Hunt, Virginia

In addition, they were also supported by the US Navy in intelligence gathering, with Bainbridge Island, Washington, and with Bar Harbor in Maine.

Eleven stations existed as the war progressed, including the following locations:

> Vint Hill Farms, Warrenton, Virginia
> Two Rockranch, Pet Aluma, California
> Indian Creek Station, Miami Beach, Florida
> Fort Shafter, Territory of Hawaii
> Amchitka, Aleutian Islands
> Fairbanks, Alaska
> Bellmore, Long Island
> Tarzana, California
> Guam
> Plus two others, unnamed here

Significance: A diverse range of listening stations across America and the Pacific would be needed to keep up to speed on intelligence gathering.

Stowe School considered for an outstation (1942–43)

Following the use of three country house estates for codebreaking Bombes there was a need for much bigger sites and premises to support Bletchley Park. One option was to provide Bombes for codebreaking at Stowe School in Buckinghamshire. This was fairly remote in the countryside and had much land available. It was a public school for those with the appropriate funds. However, it was decided not to use Stowe, probably much to the relief of the headteacher, assuming he was consulted at the time. Stowe School's grounds are now part of the National Trust. If Stowe had been used as an outstation it is probably unlikely that Eastcote or Stanmore would have been used. The exact reasons for Stowe not being accepted for an outstation are unclear. Manchester was also considered as a possible place for an outstation at one time, but probably not proceeded with due to the likelihood of general bombing by the Luftwaffe.

Significance: Exploration of a range of different sites and locations was all part of the management process to identify a strategic approach to reduce the risk of Luftwaffe attacks damaging Britain's codebreaking facilities. It just so happened that Stowe was dismissed and Stanmore selected as a new outstation location, followed by Eastcote in Middlesex.

Turing visits America (1942)

In 1942, Alan Turing went to the USA to discuss matters of Bombes and intelligence with his opposite number and colleagues but was surprised to find the Americans refused the offer of one of his designed Bombe machines. This was due to them designing and building their own improved version of the Bombe. He visited the National Cash Register Company in Dayton, Ohio, where he discussed the design of the new four-rotor-based American Bombe machines. He also gave some advice at Bell laboratories in the USA in the design of the advanced voice-encoding SIGSALY machine, eventually used by Churchill for international calls with the American President in Washington. Turing was most interested in speech encoding and speech scrambling technology, and how it could benefit the security of private Allied conversations. At one point there was resistance to allowing Turing to enter the American research facilities, but this problem was soon overcome.

Significance: The US visit was part exploratory and part educational for Turing. He would meet a range of people to discuss equipment, systems, ideas, and this may have helped shape his thoughts in machines, machine intelligence and design.

Tests in London arranged for potential new codebreakers (1942)

Advertisements were placed in a newspaper on 13 January 1942 in connection with a challenging crossword puzzle for readers. Those who could complete the crossword within a given time should contact a number, where they were later invited to attend a test in a room with others. Very few of the candidates who took the test were selected from this test to be interviewed at Bletchley Park to be trained to work on codebreaking. It does not always follow that if one is good at completing crossword puzzles that one would make a good codebreaker. However, those who are consistently good at them may possess a mind that thinks logically, and applies their memory and reasoning ability in a practical way to arrive at a solution. The test they had to carry out would explore other aspects of logical thinking, puzzle solving and approaches to finding clues in a mathematical or other task. With an appropriate range of individual test questions, those at Bletchley could filter down those who were good at crossword puzzles to those who had other skills and could adapt more easily to attacking a complex enemy cipher. Of course, those who carried out the test in that room had no idea what the organisers were looking for, nor what work they might ultimately be engaged in, and the relevant significance and importance of that specialist work. If you were selected to go forward from the test, following interview you would have to sign the Official Secrets Act like others at Bletchley Park and the outstations.

Significance: Advertising for crossword puzzle-solvers was one way of finding individuals who were good at logic and problem solving. However, being good at such puzzles far from guaranteed they would be a competent and robust codebreaker. It was simply a process of filtering out those who had certain attributes that Bletchley Park understood were essential for analysis. Few would remain to be selected from the many contacted to do the test. Those in charge could not afford to waste the time of existing codebreaking staff if new people were not up to the job, and they had to be ruthless in the selection process.

Capture of Enigma code books by HMS *Petard* (1942)

The crew of Royal Navy destroyer HMS *Petard* managed to capture the Enigma code books from U-boat *U-559* after sinking it off Egypt. These were passed over to Bletchley Park, which gained a considerable advantage in using the intelligence. The books contained the Triton cipher keys, which the U-boats relied upon in the Atlantic war against Allied merchant ships and warships. Using the information to analyse enemy Shark (Triton) intelligence between 13 December 1942 and 10 March 1943, Bletchley would solve almost all the messages based on the decoded settings (i.e., for a period of ninety out of ninety-nine days of activity in intelligence intercepts). Between 10 March 1943 and the end of June, the codebreakers at Bletchley Park broke all the Shark messages over eighty-seven days out of a total of 110, a success rate of over 77 per cent in terms of time alone. This was made largely possible by the capture of the Short Signal code book by the crew of *Petard*.

The capture of the code books on 30 October 1942 was a stroke of luck. Despite the German captain trying to sink his vessel before the enemy could obtain any valuable equipment on board, the code books were recovered intact.

First Lieutenant Antony Fasson and Able Seaman Colin Grazier swam across to *U-559* in darkness. The men went across naked as they realised they would have limited time to capture important documents and equipment from the U-boat, which had been brought to the surface by their depth charges. Sailor Tommy Brown, who worked in the canteen and was aged 16, had also jumped from the ship on to the U-boat as it came alongside. A boarding party of sailors from *Petard* had also gone across in a boat. Brown took documents and papers as they were passed up to him from the conning tower. Unfortunately, the two sailors who had swum across from *Petard* drowned in the U-boat as it filled suddenly with water and sank. Brown managed to escape with his life, as did the rest of his colleagues. He had made three trips back to his ship with the items they had captured. Brown received the George Medal for his action, and the lost sailors also received posthumous military decorations for bravery. The code books and enemy documents recovered and passed to Bletchley Park would be so significant that the crew of *Petard* were never told what they had actually acquired. It was too secret, and anyway, they would know nothing of codebreaking, or of Bombe machines, or of Triton. It might have been a different language to them. The tables had turned, at least for a bit, for Bletchley's codebreakers with this new intelligence handed to them. It was like a gift from the gods.

Significance: If the brave sailors who had drowned at the time of the incident had not acted as they did, then certain key Enigma documents would not have found their way to Bletchley Park, and many more could have lost their lives to the action of enemy U-boats. Any capture of enemy code books and documents would be crucial to the Allies. The key issue here was to save valuable time and find a way into the enemy's cipher system.

Britain is exposed in the Atlantic via BAMS (1942)

BAMS was the British and Allied Merchant Ships Code, and was critical to the communication and strategy when moving convoys across the Atlantic. By April 1942, the enemy was reading BAMS communications, assisted by capture of code books elsewhere. U-boat commanders could identify how the convoys were configured when they were planning to make a crossing to either the USA or Britain. The weakness has not been plugged, resulting in heavy losses for the Allies.

Significance: Weaknesses in intelligence occurred on both sides, but the penetration of BAMS communications was a relatively easy task for the Nazis.

Photo reconnaissance of Peenemünde by Allies (1942)

On 15 May 1942 a photo-reconnaissance Spitfire photographed the research centre at Peenemünde in northern Germany on the Baltic island of Usedom. The unusual embankments on the photographic images were initially dismissed by staff as being relatively unimportant. It would be the following year that the evidence for a rocket base was confirmed. In April 1943, a De Havilland Mosquito was over the north coast of Germany after an operation where its cameras recorded a huge cloud of steam, and that apparently turned out to be a V2 rocket missile on a test. Valuable intelligence was also collected by the Polish Home Army and the Luxembourg Resistance, at great personal risk. The Americans were keen to photograph the island, and there would be several sorties over time, particularly in 1943.[32] The SS Enigma key, Quince was intercepted, and information obtained about the rocket fuel quality at the time.[33]

Significance: If the Allies had acted more quickly then perhaps fewer Nazi missiles would have hit the UK, and British lives perhaps could have been saved. It is not known what degree of enemy intelligence traffic was intercepted via Enigma of activities in the area. It is likely that Enigma would have been used to call up supplies, resources, rocket fuel and equipment.

TRE relocates to Malvern, Worcestershire (1942)

The Telecommunications Research Establishment, TRE, was originally based in Dorset on the south coast. However, due to a daring raid by British Commandos in France, a German *Würzburg* radar was captured and brought back to TRE for investigation. There was great concern that the Luftwaffe might then attack TRE and the decision was taken to relocate it much further north in Malvern, Worcestershire. This switch would take place in May 1942. This would be a significant move and TRE would be enlarged with both personnel, space, and equipment over time. Several thousand personnel would eventually occupy the site. It would occupy a boys' boarding school and college, and remain there until the end of the war. The King and Queen would visit TRE during wartime, demonstrating its significance in the war effort. However, the base was secret and not advertised to the public.

Significance: A risk reduction and relocation for TRE, to avoid bombing of the facilities where it had previously been on or near the Dorset coast. The space available gave TRE the room to expand over time.

Ultra code word adopted

Previously, SIGINT or Signals Intelligence was referred to as 'Special'. However, instructions were given that all SIGINT material was to be referred to as 'Ultra'.[34]

Significance: The new code name for SIGINT would be referred to in confidential and secret reports, which would be seen by high-level officials including the Prime Minister.

Introduction of four-wheel Enigma (1942)

The four-wheel Enigma was used extensively by the German Navy, and increased the permutations significantly on the Enigma message settings with an additional rotor wheel. The version was known as M4 Enigma. The Allied codebreaking machines had been based on three-rotor Enigmas, and different solutions were tried to cope with the added complexity of a fourth wheel. One such device was termed 'Cobra', an attachment of some size and enormous connecting cable to a standard Bombe. The US Navy built their own version of the British Bombe, but it was a design targeting the four-wheel Enigma, and this can clearly be seen in photographs of the machines. The US version was largely successful in intercepting U-boat intelligence. The Americans had the advantage of seeing the British Bombe before designing their version.

Significance: The moving of the goalposts by the Nazis with the introduction of the four-wheel Enigma caused the Allies a lot of frustration for lengthy periods. It bought the U-boat commanders a lot of time and success in the Atlantic in sinking large quantities of merchant shipping bringing resources to Britain.

Midway in the Pacific (1942)

The battles in the Pacific with the Japanese came to a head in early June 1942 when deception tactics were used against the enemy.[35] Over five days, 3–7 June, the US Navy, with considerable air support from their carriers and island airbases, dealt a hammer blow to the Japanese, sinking numerous ships and carriers. This action occurred around six months after the attack on the American naval fleet at Pearl Harbor.

Significance: Use of military intelligence and various tricks played on the enemy identified a breach in Japanese naval codes, which were then used to the advantage of the US Navy at Midway. The enemy was ultimately caught by surprise as to the location of the American fleet and suffered great losses, losing most of their aircraft carriers.

ETOUSA established in London (1942)

ETOUSA was Headquarters European Theatre of Operations US Army. It was established in London, on 8 June 1942. US Signals Engineers would come to England in later years to assist Bletchley Park and some of the codebreaking outstations such as at Eastcote. Until the establishment of the Supreme Headquarters Allied Expeditionary Force (SHAEF) on 13 February 1944, ETOUSA participated in operational planning for the Allied invasion of Western Europe. It performed administrative and service functions for US Army troops, equipment, and facilities in the following areas:

> United Kingdom and Iceland 1942–45
> North Africa November 1942–February 1943
> Western Europe, 6 June 1944–1 July 1945

The headquarters moved from London to France on 1 September 1944 and to Paris on 14 September 1944.

It was redesignated HQ USFET on 1 July 1945, with its main headquarters at Frankfurt, Germany, and rear headquarters at Paris, by General Order 130, HQ ETOUSA, 20 June 1945.[36]

OSG, Outstation Gayhurst established (1942)

Outstation Gayhurst was established in 1942 near Bletchley Park to house operational Bombe machines on a country estate. This was one of the satellite outstations to help spread the risk in case Bletchley Park as headquarters was bombed by the enemy. Initially it had five machines, operated by Wrens. It would be the sole surviving country house outstation out of the three stations established to support Bletchley. Adstock and Wavendon would later close, although they had their part to play in accommodating a quantity of Bombe machines in outlying buildings on the estates.

Significance: One of three country house codebreaking outstations, intended to spread the risk of bombing Bletchley Park by the Luftwaffe yet geographically close enough to the headquarters to be useful.

US naval intelligence visits Bletchley Park (1942)

It would be July 1942 when US naval intelligence officers from section OP-20-G visited Bletchley Park in England and signed the visitors' book. These were Robert B. Ely and Joseph J. Eachus, anxious to learn and develop codebreaking machines themselves back in the United States. American Solomon Kullback had also visited on 20 June 1942.

Significance: An example of the British sharing information on intelligence and codebreaking with their American allies, at a time when the war was largely in favour of the Axis powers.

WAVES established by US (1942)

WAVES stood for *Women Accepted for Volunteer Emergency Service* and were women conscripted to work on a variety of specialist tasks including assembling and building codebreaking machines in America. They would play an important part in helping to build and operate the newer US Naval Bombe codebreaking machine, being a development of the British Turing/Welchman Bombe. On 30 July 1942 President Roosevelt signed the *Navy Women's Reserve Act* to make women available to help release American men for other naval duties in wartime. The establishment of WAVES came out of this process, and it was formed in July 1942. The recruitment was women between the ages of 18 and 36, and female officers between 20 and 50. Most of the WAVES would serve in naval aviation units, and only a proportion would be involved in codebreaking or building codebreaking machines.

Significance: The recognition of the US Government that they had a resources problem, and that women of a certain age group would fill that gap across a variety of tasks in wartime. The equivalent in Britain might be the WRNS or Wrens, although these were part of the Royal Navy, with some being voluntary and many later conscripted into the service. Both are examples of the need for women in wartime, many of whom gained useful skills to assist the war effort.

Traffic analysis at Beaumanor transferred to Bletchley Park (1942)

Traffic analysis of enemy communications was an essential tool for the Allies during wartime. The use of direction-finding equipment could identify the location of enemy radio and signals stations. Call signs could be recorded and mapped. Teams of specialists called 'log readers' would sort the messages while noting who was communicating at either end of the transmission, logging the radio frequencies, and noting this down manually on printed paper log sheets. At Beaumanor, 6IS or No. 6 Intelligence School would be a key player in this work, but in May 1942 it would be transferred to Bletchley Park, largely due to recommendations earlier by codebreaker and mathematician Gordon Welchman. The new section at Bletchley would later be termed 'SIXTA' in 1944. It would have almost 400 personnel in that section approaching D-Day.[37]

Significance: A realisation that traffic analysis of enemy signals was a key tool in the eventual defeat of Nazi Germany and may assist codebreaking by discovering certain words, phrases, cribs and patterns in enemy communication. The relocation to Bletchley Park from Beaumanor was part of a rationalisation of the traffic analysis and the streamlining of it. The methods, systems and training of personnel would be improved and pay dividends as D-Day approached that summer in 1944.

Bletchley fails to crack U-boat codes for a specific period (1942)

The progress at Bletchley Park in cracking Enigma was limited when four-wheel rotor machines were introduced. The *Kriegsmarine* were quick to utilise them for communication with the U-boat fleet. The date of 1 February 1942 would be a game-changer for the enemy as from then on the 'Shark' communications to and from U-boats would be based on four-wheel Enigmas. This improved security at a stroke, with many more possible permutations of the cipher settings. Several months of intense work in the Bletchley huts and particularly Hut 8 left them still unable to penetrate the Enigma cipher, allowing U-boats to sink thousands of tons of merchant ships supplying valuable and essential resources for Britain and its allies. Three keys of the Shark cipher were broken between February and the middle of December 1942, a tiny fraction of what was required. What they needed were the current Nazi Enigma code books, and cribs or clues to apply to the messages. A spot of luck would eventually help the codebreakers after almost nine months of frustration, when certain specific enemy code books were captured at sea from a sinking U-boat, aided by brave men on board the destroyer HMS *Petard*. The frustration and failures in 1942 in codebreaking were only part of the overall picture, however. The codebreakers knew that they were breaking other enemy 'keys', including those in the Mediterranean. Also, there were more advanced codebreaking Bombe machines being developed with the help of the Americans that could be based on four-wheel Enigmas. It was just a matter of time.

EVENTS

Significance: The consequence of the failure to crack Enigma for a long duration of months would be hundreds of thousands of tons of shipping from Allied convoys going to the bottom of the Atlantic ocean due to the U-boat threat.

Bill Tutte cracks the Lorenz encoding machine (1942)

A young mathematician employed as a codebreaker at Bletchley Park was handed the Tunny-based message data that had been intercepted on non-Morse messages to see if he could establish the basis of the system. Others who had tried had no success. Over a period of weeks and months, Tutte worked systematically on the problem and using a variety of methods was able to identify the structure of the machine from a mathematical viewpoint, and a way of breaking the cipher. A cryptographer colleague who would later work on Lorenz and would write a book on the subject, Captain Jerry Roberts, commented, '*I saw him staring into the middle distance twiddling his pencil and making counts on reams of paper for three months, and I used to wonder whether he was getting anything done. My goodness he was!*'[38] He broke the Lorenz cipher in spring 1942. The Lorenz encoding machine would only be declassified in 2002. It would be far more sophisticated than Enigma, and have astronomically high mathematical permutations for the settings of the message due to its design. The Bombe codebreaking machine used to tackle Enigma could not be used against Tunny non-Morse messages, so a new machine, or machines, would have to be developed.

Significance: A huge leap forward by Bletchley Park codebreakers due to one young mathematician in understanding the configuration of the German Lorenz teleprinter attachment without ever having seen it. This was a key stage in developing systems and machines to help decode both the message settings and the messages.

Vernam-Baudot encoding becomes significant in wartime

This would be a system used on punched tape that incorporated instructions and would prove to be invaluable for business, but also the Nazi advanced encoding machines linked to teleprinters for communication. The Baudot system comprised thirty-two characters or spaces, with twenty-six reserved for the alphabet. It used XOR operation logic to encode the characters within the Baudot code. Gilbert Vernam patented his system in 1917 and would later work at AT&T in the USA. Bletchley Park would have to become familiar with the system when the Nazi Lorenz SZ40 and other advanced encoding machines were used as a teleprinter attachment. Decoding machines would have to read the characters on punched tape using 'photo-electric eyes'.

Significance: The adaptation of a relatively well-known encoding system on punched paper tape in conjunction with new machines would give the enemy, the

Germans, a degree of flexibility in the design of advanced machines for encoding and decoding.

Royal Navy and WRNS abandon term 'Station X' (1942)

Following a directive from the top, the Wrens would no longer refer to Station 'X' for duties in relation to codebreaking from 15 November 1942. The replacement term would be designated as 'Pembroke V', and bases for codebreaking would be designated HMS *Pembroke* V, being onshore naval bases.[39]

Significance: The change of a name with formal approval from the top. The confusion would arise whereby everyone from (part of) Bletchley Park to Outstation Eastcote would become 'Pembroke V' or 'PV'.

Polish codebreaker Rozycki dies (1942)

The trio of polish cryptographers including Jerzy Rozycki fled the Nazis, from Warsaw to Spain, then France and as the Germans occupied more of France, across to Algiers. In January 1942, when Rozycki was transferring back from Algiers to France by sea, he died. He was on his way back to Uzès, at the Cadix codebreaking centre, at the time a château in Provence. His two colleagues had to continue their specialist work without him. Rozycki had been one of twenty mathematics students in 1929 who were accepted to attend a secret cryptographic cipher course for the Polish military. As a civilian, he worked in the General Staff Polish Cipher Bureau and work with colleagues Marian Rejewski and another to make codebreaking history against the Enigma encoding machine. His two colleagues would later escape to England, to work on Russian codes and ciphers for the Allies.

Significance: The loss of Rozycki was a blow to the Polish codebreakers and to the Allies. But work had to continue in order to challenge the Nazi encoding machines.

Codebreakers in America form new research team (1942)

Following some non-productive work on Enigma earlier, a new section was established called OP-20-M, with the task of finding the most productive way of designing and building an American codebreaking machine to tackle the Naval Enigma, which was based on four-wheel rotors. Commander Wenger appointed Commander Howard T. Engstrom to this important task, linked to OP-20-G. Two naval officers were permitted access to Bletchley Park to learn as much about the British Bombe as practically possible. Their feedback was that the machine needed redesign and improvement, with photo-electric cells for faster and more reliable operation. In November 1942 the NCR Company in Dayton, Ohio, started building the new American naval codebreaking machine for the Codebreaking Division of OP-20-G. Joseph Desch at NCR, head of electrical engineering, led the project. Commander

EVENTS

Denniston had been replaced at Bletchley Park by this time. The new machines would be operated by WAVES, or Women Accepted for Voluntary Emergency Service. By this time, Bletchley had some success with cracking the four-wheel Enigmas with three-wheel rotor British Bombes. However, America and NCR proceeded to build the Naval Bombe, a different design to the British Bombe but using some of the original elements and ideas, and improved as regards operational efficiency. The two allied nations worked together, albeit independently and competitively, to arrive at a codebreaking solution to help win the war against the Nazis. The real driving force behind this were the terrible losses in the Atlantic to U-boats, which were sinking both military and merchant shipping, with considerably more of the latter affecting the resourcing of the war against the enemy.

Significance: OP-20-M and OP-20-G would be the key to designing and building the new Naval Bombe to tackle the U-boat threat using four-wheel Enigma machines.

Production policy of Bombe machines affected by differences of opinion

While BTM in Letchworth would be manufacturing and assembling the Bombe machines for Bletchley Park and the outstations, several people had an input in the production policy. This was partly due to the need to identify types and modifications to certain machines, as well as tracking the quantities of Bombe machines required to meet the demand of the codebreakers. Those principally involved would be Harold Keen at BTM, Wynn-Williamson of TRE, and Welchman, based at Bletchley Park. However, it transpired that the Post Office Engineering Research Station would also want somewhat of an input, and Thomas Flowers, a senior engineer, would then make certain suggestions and recommendations as to the Bombe production policy. Gordon Welchman objected strongly to this and would write memos at Bletchley Park stating that '*the influence of Dr Radley and Mr Flowers must be removed ...*'. Radley was Flowers' boss. Welchman later criticised Flowers for his idea of using large quantities of tube valves for an advanced decoding machine as irresponsible and wasteful of resources in wartime.

Significance: There may have been an element of class snobbery here as Welchman was university trained as an academic, whereas Flowers was not and had studied engineering at night school to gain his qualifications. Welchman required control of the Bombe production policy in conjunction with BTM, who built the machines. He could accept Dr Wynn-Williams' input, to a degree, as he was making design modifications that improved efficiency. Radley and Flowers were seen as interfering busybodies, but it was the case that the input of Flowers and PORES would go on to make a significant difference to the ability to decipher enemy Nazi messages from the German high command, which were transmitted via advanced machines such as non-Morse data and specialised teleprinter equipment.

Fletcher writes a report on Bombe status and personnel (1942)

Bletchley Park tasked H.D. Fletcher from Hut 6 to write a critical progress report that would outline the quantity of Bombe machines available, the type and location of them. This would be on 2 June 1942, relatively early in the war and in the development of Bombe codebreaking machines. Fletcher suggested that management should be keeping their eyes peeled for 'a really large site' so the Bombes could be further expanded in terms of scale and quantity. It was then that Stowe School was mentioned as an option. The status of Bombes at the time, i.e., mid-1942, across various locations were as follows:

Hut 11A Bletchley – 8
Outstation Wavendon – 16
Outstation Adstock – 5
Outstation Gayhurst – 16

It transpired that Stowe would not be selected as an outstation, even though there was plenty of land there. Fletcher was also looking at the resources of operational Wrens, how many needed training to cope with Bombe expansion and an increase in the outstations. Wavendon had 100 Wrens and Gayhurst 150, but when planning for new sites one had also to take into account that the work was carried out in shift patterns, that there would be people on leave and away training, and sickness had to be allowed for too. An intake planned at around twenty Wrens per week was considered, but there could well be delays when new Wrens came into an outstation from basic training. It would take a while to get the Wrens fully up to speed operationally. This delay might be around a fortnight from arrival at the outstation, so it had to be allowed for logistically.

Looking ahead at BTM's production planning for the Bombes, there was an estimate of another 400 to 500 Wrens in addition to the ones already on site. It was acknowledged in the report that number may also increase further over time. The analysis of exact numbers of WRNS personnel was complex, as BTM would also be producing high-speed Bombes and modified versions of them. The management would need to reappraise and monitor the situation on a regular basis. To run out of Bombes would be a poor show, but to have the new Bombes but no one to operate them consistently would be a travesty, and could not be permitted to occur. In the end, Outstation Stanmore came to the rescue, and was later followed by Outstation Eastcote around a year later. These two outstations would become the largest codebreaking outstations in terms of Bombe quantity and in terms of operational personnel.

Significance: The monitoring of logistics in respect of codebreaking operations was an essential management task. This was taken seriously, as to run out of space, locations, and skilled, trained personnel when Bletchley Park needed them more than ever would have been catastrophic and limit British intelligence gathering.

OSS, Outstation Stanmore established (1942)

Due to the need for continued expansion and growth to find space for more Bombe codebreaking machines, a site in Stanmore was identified. It was not far from Stanmore station and at the junction of a major crossroads leading to Elstree in the north and Edgware in the south. Outstation Stanmore would be established in 1942. The plans were to provide dormitories for 250 Wrens, who were to work up to sixty-five Bombe machines.[40] Wren personnel would rise to around 571 over time. The task of finding a supply of sufficient quantities of skilled personnel to operate the increasing quantity of machines was a real problem for management. The base would have some seventy-six Bombes at the end of the war.[41] Some machines would be transferred here from the country house outstations like Wavendon. Stanmore was a very important codebreaking site as many Bombe machines would be transferred there from other sites as well as it receiving newly built Bombes from BTM in Letchworth. By February 1943 there would be approximately 440 Wrens on site.[42] The paperwork alone would have been a challenge with machines coming and going, modifications, and later liaison with the last and largest outstation, Outstation Eastcote, not far away. The site was also not far distance from the RAF fighter control station of Bentley Priory. The Stanmore outstation site does not exist any longer, having been redeveloped for housing.

Significance: The establishment of Outstation Stanmore was a major site expansion for the suite of codebreaking outstations in wartime. It gave BTM the opportunity to transport many more Bombe machines to a large site, where space and resources were available to support Bletchley Park.

Knockholt established (1942)

At Ivy Farm in Knockholt, Kent, a site was identified as being slightly elevated for the geographical terrain and not far from the coast, to obtain relatively good radio intercepts from Europe. It was first approved in August 1942. The land, around 30 acres initially and a farmhouse, would be formally requisitioned in September of that year.[43] The site of Ivy Farm was acquired from a local farmer, and formal permissions obtained for war work. This was some time after the first non-Morse radio intercepts were discovered in south London and subsequently confirmed by Bletchley Park specialists to be non-standard encoded messages, i.e., non-Morse. The site was also known as Knockholt Pound, which was the name seen on maps of the time. It would eventually have large aerials, as well as a farmhouse and Nissen huts built to house ATS, WRNS, and FORDE staff, plus civilian operators, among others. The race would be on to identify the machine and system that encoded the messages. Knockholt would become an important and specialist listening station to feed intelligence data back to Bletchley. However, the volume of messages intercepted would not be as large as those via the Enigma machines, as the teleprinter attachments such as Lorenz used to encode the message were manufactured in much smaller numbers. However, the encoded messages often contained valuable German high command intelligence. The base was managed by a Mr Kenworthy, who had experience in signals intelligence intercepts. He was the pre-war head of the Denmark Hill SIGINT station.

Training courses for personnel at Knockholt ensured that there were ample staff both for home and abroad in processing the enemy intercepts. It is the case that the deciphering of the message settings would be undertaken at Bletchley Park some distance away, and that teleprinter links installed between the sites assisted with this process. Dispatch motorcycle riders would also be used for transferring information between the sites, with many of these Wrens.

Significance: The recognition of the need for a base suitably positioned geographically in south-east England, with an elevated position to aid radio reception, to intercept non-Morse messages and pass these on to Bletchley Park for analysis. Knockholt would become one of the most important listening bases in the war for intercepting messages from advanced enemy encoding machines.[44]

Newmanry and Testery established (1942)

Once the discovery of Tunny intercepts and Fish intelligence was identified by Bletchley Park, efforts would be made to establish which machine was being used and how was it configured to send non-Morse high-speed messages. Bill Tutte, a young mathematician at Bletchley Park worked this out using a combination of trial and error and pure brilliance in intellect. He had succeeded where others had failed. Manual methods could be use to crack Tunny, but a better solution would be to build a machine, or machines, to take out a large part of the donkey work and reduce the large volume of settings for messages. In order to make this work efficiently two new sections would be established. Firstly, the *Newmanry*, headed by Max Newman and concentrating on the machine side of codebreaking. Then, the *Testery*, headed by Frank Tester, to lead a team of cryptologists and mathematicians to take the part-decoded settings and finish the job manually. It was still a complex process. The *Newmanry* and *Testery* would be contained with Block F at Bletchley Park.[45]

The communication between the two sections was virtually non-existent initially, until Bletchley Park management knocked heads together and encouraged both formal and informal communication. There would be no place or time for inter-departmental rivalry, or holding back information. The management changes made a significant difference. It would be a two-tier solution, part machine and part manual codebreaking. The machine processing of the enemy message would save time. Deciphering the message settings would become the real prize to progress further. Even the *Newmanry* machine section had to have instructions and logic systems managed to communicate effectively with the machines. It became a sort of sophisticated production line to reach the end objective of breaking the ciphers and codes of the advanced enemy encoding machines. Later, it would become even more efficient with the introduction of the Colossus decoding machine, with an increase in staff.

Significance: The realisation at Bletchley Park of the need to have separate specialist sections with experts to analyse the advanced enemy message intelligence, and to utilise specialist machines to break the codes.

British worried about Russian cipher vulnerability to enemy (1942)

The relationship between the western Allies and the Russians was always going to be a challenge. There was a fear that the Russians' ciphers were exposed to the enemy and vulnerable. This was discussed in detail with suggestions how to approach the Russians on this sensitive issue.[46] The Allies did not wish to allow the Nazis to intercept key intelligence that could affect their plans in Europe. There was evidence from five Bletchley Park reports that the Germans were already exploiting Russian communications, and this needed to be addressed urgently.

Significance: Any breach of cipher security among the Allies could open military tactical or strategic opportunities for the enemy. The approach to the Russians about how to overcome this would be difficult but necessary. The Russians would not be aware of the source or sources of the information that let the allies know there was a problem that had to be overcome.

Ultra intelligence used for Torch landings in North Africa (1942)

A combination of cracking Enigma keys and deception tactics assisted the Allies in the Operation Torch landings in North Africa. The operation took place between 8 and 16 November 1942. Ultra intelligence decrypts kept GC&CS and Bletchley Park busy for months prior to the landings. The trick was to gather sufficient intelligence and to deceive the enemy so that large convoys of Allied shipping approaching North Africa would escape mass destruction by the Axis powers in the Mediterranean, particularly the Luftwaffe, U-boats, and Italian Navy. The amphibious landings that resulted were a success, and an example of how effective joint signals communications between the Americans and the British could help defeat the enemy. This was strategic deception on a large scale. The principles were to form a model of approach by the Allies later in Operation Husky at Sicily and Overlord for the Normandy invasion in France. The AFHQ or Armed Forces HQ was established in 1942 and made use of Ultra intelligence and also of local listening Y-stations. They would crack Vichy France meteorological ciphers and Luftwaffe ciphers, among others. Coordinating all the intelligence and obtaining feedback on deception tactics would take a massive, coordinated Anglo-American effort. The breaking of Italian ciphers such as those based upon the C38M machines would add to the overall intelligence gathered. The complexity of the build-up to Operation Torch was such that it is perhaps outside the scope of this book, but much detailed information can be obtained by reference to US Navy (Retired) Commander John Patch's report of 2008: 'Fortuitous Endeavour – Intelligence and Deception in Operation TORCH', in *Naval War College Review* Vol. 61, No. 4,

Article 9. This account, involving Ultra intelligence, is superbly written and comes highly recommended.

Significance: Arguably the first use of Ultra and special intelligence for the planning and execution of a large-scale military campaign using strategic deception.

Double agent 'Garbo' works at a safe house in London (1942)

Double agent 'Garbo', real name Juan Pujol Garcia, and code-named 'Arabel' by the Nazis, worked for the British to help deceive the Germans during the war. Although he had been working in Lisbon, Portugal, he was eventually accepted by MI5 as being of use as a potential double agent. He was taken to 35 Crespigny Gardens in Hendon, north London, considered to be a 'safe house', and managed by a handler to send and receive transmitted messages to and from the house and to the Nazis. He moved around the corner later in 1942 to 55 Elliot Road, but would return frequently to Crespigny Gardens to weave his web of deceit against the Nazis via his contacts in Europe.

Significance: The site would become important as the base where much of the double agent's work would be done, and particularly the lead-up to D-Day and *Operation Fortitude South*. A blue plaque now adorns the front external wall of the house, and records that Garcia lived his extraordinary life from 1912–88, and spent time at the house helping the British and the Allies to defeat Nazi Germany. He was awarded an MBE by the British in December 1944, in secret.

Bombe No. 1 renamed and relocated for training (1942)

The first codebreaking Bombe, *Victory*, having been moved to Outstation Wavendon in late 1940, was relocated again to OSS, Stanmore, on 11 September 1942. It would become an early machine installed at the new and expanding outstation, and renamed Leo. This machine would be used to train and instruct Wrens and RAF personnel in the operation of such codebreaking machines. It would relocate again in 1943.[47]

Significance: Several bombes would be moved to other sites over their operational lives, be modified and renamed. Victory would end up as a training tool across several bases, and with different names.

Eastcote site considered for a military hospital

The site at Eastcote, in Middlesex, consisting of a small number of large open fields linked together near the main road was identified for a possible military hospital base, in case there was a major invasion back into France against the enemy, effectively D-Day. The site had been appropriated from the owners, the Telling Brothers, by the British Government. After carrying out feasibilities and erecting several buildings and huts, the project was abandoned, possibly as being too far distant from the coast. It would soon be tasked with a completely different use, that of a codebreaking outstation. The site was converted into barracks together with the space for codebreaking machines and would form a shore-based naval operation, HMS *Pembroke V*.

Significance: A site with a use that was considered and then abandoned for various reasons. If it had been used as a military hospital, then another site would have had to be found as large as Eastcote, to house more than one hundred Bombe machines. The post-war use for Eastcote would also be significant as GCHQ, taking over the reins from Bletchley Park.

Britain regains confidence in its naval code books (1943)

In June 1943 the Royal Navy changed its codes for the fourth time after serious failures and sinkings. Prior to this, the Germans were able to easily read the codes but from then on they were prevented from doing so. The Battle of the Atlantic was about to see the tide turned in favour of the Allies. Add this to improved air superiority over time, plus other factors including the spotting of enemy submarines on the surface by centimetric radar for aircraft, and the U-boats soon became a liability for Hitler and Dönitz. Their effectiveness reduced over time.

Significance: The improved security for Allied intelligence would make a difference in the Atlantic and help reduce the losses of convoys and shipping.

Rejewski and Zygalski relocate to England (1943)

Following a period in a Spanish prison, after escaping from Vichy France in the early years of the war and working at Uzès in Provence, Polish pioneering codebreakers Marian Rejewski and Henryk Zygalski came to England. They worked as part of a team near Hemel Hempstead, in Hertfordshire, mainly on deciphering Russian codes. This carried on until the end of the war.

Significance: The Polish codebreakers had worked in Poland, France, Algeria, and fled across Spain only to be imprisoned. They were released and managed to extract themselves to Britain, where they were relatively safe during the remainder of the war. It is interesting that they would be working on Russian codes and ciphers for the Allies, leaving others to tackle the Nazi message codes.

BTM approaches Spirella for production and manufacturing support

The need for expansion in terms of space and workers to build components and modular sections for the Bombe machines increased as time went on. The

BTM engineers and management approached those at Spirella, down the road in Letchworth. It was agreed that Spirella would transfer its corset production to London to make space for making and assembling components to support BTM in their programme of production. The workers would not be aware what the end finished product would be or what it was intended for. The vast majority of workers would be female, and some would work on Bombe component assembly as a change from corset production, while others would be brought in and recruited for the task. There would be a camaraderie between the women workers, even more so than previously, as they realised they would be helping the war effort. Parts of the factory would make parachutes, so were used to adapting their workforce.

Significance: BTM considered Spirella as an opportunity to expand production of key Bombe machine components. It was geographically relatively near to the main BTM factory for final assembly on to the Bombe frames. It also had skilled female workers, some of whom would remain after corset production moved to London during wartime.

Concept of high-speed Bombes developed

H. Keen at BTM in Letchworth would help develop high-speed versions of the Bombes for faster processing of the settings. There are many references in the official Bombe registers with 'HSK' written against the names and numbers of the machines and this stands for 'High-Speed-Keen' version. It is thought that Wynn-Williams from TRE may have contributed to the design of these specially modified versions. Faster rotation of Bombe rotors would have to be considered and managed very carefully to ensure that the wire brushes would still make physical contact with the brass contacts at the rear, and that no malfunction could occur. A symptom of high-speed operation might be Bombe rotor bounce, and concern that the relays may not operate quickly enough. These problems would need to be addressed to ensure the high-speed machines were sufficiently robust and reliable.

Significance: Faster processing of message settings saved valuable time, but a robust system was required and then developed by Keen, the BTM chief engineer.[48]

Siemens relays copied by the British

Siemens was a respected German manufacturing and engineering company and made a variety of equipment and components before and during the war. Their relays were of particular interest to the British, and were copied to be used on the Bombe machines, which improved their reliability and efficiency. German engineering, therefore, arguably, helped to a small degree the Allies in winning the war against them. Some of the Bombe registers record the mention of Siemens relays against specific Bombe entries, where installed. Not all Bombes would have them. Siemens went on post-war to establish itself as a major company in engineering and electronics. Outstations Stanmore and Eastcote would both be supplied with Bombe machines that had the Siemens copy relays for greater efficiency.

Significance: The British recognised that German engineering was exceptionally good, and could be adapted to benefit the Allies, without making this apparent to the enemy. The evidence that German engineering was, on the whole, excellent, can be seen in the design of their armaments, optical systems, radio equipment, teleprinter attachments and other equipment. However, even a significant weapon such as the Mk II Tiger tank had encountered reliability problems with its engines.

Siemens uses forced labour in its factories during wartime

Siemens was much in demand during wartime for electrical and electronic components and equipment for the Nazi war machine. The principal problem was the lack of staff and personnel to assemble the components and equipment and to work on the materials necessary. Women played a big part in the factories, but the high command relentlessly put the pressure on factories such as Siemens to increase output. The company would send vans around the locality broadcasting to recruit for the factory. But as so many German men were in the military, training and fighting the Allies, they turned to acquiring forced labour to close the resources gap. They were not the only factory or firm to have done this. Starting in 1940, forced labour was introduced and included Jews, Roma, and others, and later, concentration camp inmates. The numbers increased dramatically over the entire wartime period to around 80,000 people in order to meet their expected manufacturing targets. All these people had to be transported, trained, managed, clothed and fed. It is difficult to know what the working conditions were like at the time. The equipment produced was mainly electrical equipment for the armed forces, but with only a very small amount of armament in comparison to other factories. Additionally, around 400 Siemens' manufacturing, design and production facilities were relocated during wartime, often into Nazi occupied countries or areas. These also used forced labour to meet production targets. Siemens produced several Siemens and Halske 'Secret writer' teleprinter attachments during the war. The British had recognised that the Siemens relays were exceptionally well designed and manufactured, so much so they copied the design and used it in Turing's Bombe machines and in other equipment. Siemens factories and assets were taken over by the Russians and Allies after the war and were all dismantled. Financial reparations were made as compensation in part. The Siemens company formally acknowledges its part in the National Socialist Wartime period and regrets the activities, but has since rebuilt the company into a major worldwide modern organisation.

Significance: The sad realities of wartime meant that almost any measures would be taken to keep production at a high level in Germany and the German-occupied states, and this meant slave labour was used in large quantities.

Outstation Stanmore receives high-speed machines (1943)

It would be 1943 when Outstation Stanmore would receive high-speed (HSK) Bombe machines, with HSK short for High-Speed-Keen, a reference to BTM's chief engineer in the factory at Letchworth, Hertfordshire, where the Bombes were manufactured in quantity. They would have four sets of rotor wheels and the ultra-fast wheels would turn twenty-six times to every single revolution of normal fast position, and a three-wheel run could be completed in one and a half minutes. It was reported that the first of these machines, No 101, remained at Letchworth for testing, and the first operational machine was No. 102, also called 'Darwin'. Wynn-Williams of TRE also worked on high-speed Bombe machines in August 1942.

Significance: High-speed machines would increase the chances of eliminating the permutations of the settings of the enemy Enigma machine much more quickly and efficiently.

Knockholt is expanded (1943)

With the threat of advanced German encoding machines and new systems, there was a need to build Knockholt listening station into a formidable site, with the appropriate skilled personnel and equipment to intercept encoded messages. Large aerial arrays would be erected across the land and cabled back to the buildings, complete with substantial electrical power supplies and transformers, so as to assist in the interception of non-Morse enemy messages. Facsimile transmissions could also be intercepted, which would be a first for Britain. The site, like Bletchley Park, was top secret, although the aerials could be seen from a distance. The elevation of the site made it more suitable for its use. According to certain memoranda seen by the author at the National Archives, aerial masts had to be procured for a wide variety of listening stations and Knockholt was given a high degree of priority due to its importance. The expansion and acquisition of additional land from the initial 30 acres increased the site to more than four times the size of the original. Personnel increased substantially to several hundred skilled staff at its peak. By 30 December 1944, 717 people worked at Knockholt. By 15 July 1945, 585 personnel were working there, excluding the guards to the perimeter and security staff. One third of staff worked on shifts. Around 400 staff worked on daytime shifts, the remainder at night. Aerial masts were listed in various sizes and heights, with some 48ft high and others 70ft. At times there would be shortages of the taller masts for receiving sites, based on memoranda seen by the author at the National Archives, but these difficulties were eventually overcome.

Significance: The increase in non-Morse transmissions and intercepts required more listening stations, more aerials, and additional personnel. Expansion of Knockholt was essential as the war progressed.

EVENTS

Facsimile intercepts by the British (1943)

The first intercepts of facsimile transmissions were made at Knockholt listening station. It is believed this occurred in 1943. It was a fax transmission from a Japanese civilian to Tokyo, giving details of US bomber squadrons and certain strategic information. The intercept was passed to the Americans for action. This base was for specialist purposes and principally for intercepts of advanced enemy encoding messages. The large aerial arrays installed across the base proved to be very effective in conjunction with the staff in the huts and farmhouse with technical equipment.

Significance: The use of new technology to intercept both images and text based upon data transmission. Knockholt would expand over time in terms of personnel, equipment, and expertise, to support Bletchley Park.

Teleprinter use increases at outstations (1943)

Teleprinters were being introduced on a large scale and improved efficiency at outstations and at Bletchley Park for communication. By the end of 1943 there would be some ninety-nine codebreaking machines in operation, and many teleprinters sending information back and forth in respect of the Bombe 'stops'. Staff were trained to operate the teleprinters, which would be extremely noisy if several were working together in the same room or space.

Significance: Improved communication via teleprinters saved time and probably lives too.

Hut 4 redesignated Pembroke V (1943)

The naval influence across the codebreaking activities extended to Bletchley Park when on 27 April 1943 Hut 4 Naval Section was designated part of Pembroke V. Previously this was under 'Special Duties X', until the designation changed. Naval Wrens would be directed to various sites across the country including codebreaking outstations, to Pembroke V, or HMS *Pembroke* V.

Significance: A change of name, but more in line with WRNS and naval protocol, with shore-based naval stations operated by Wrens using HMS *Pembroke* V instead of Station X. Station X was really Bletchley Park, so the name PV fitted better according to some.

BRUSA cooperation established between Britain and America (1943)

BRUSA stood for British–United States Agreement, and was established in May 1943 to enable and encourage sharing of cryptological message intercepts and technical codebreaking methods between the allied nations. Bletchley Park and the US War Department would become the signatories of this agreement. It would be principally about information exchange, and sharing knowledge and experience on codebreaking, aiming to defeat the Axis powers with Britain's partners in war. Of course, this only occurred after the USA was brought into the war via the attack on its Pearl Harbor naval base. Prior to that the US had been considered as neutral. The sharing of information and intelligence would make the Allies more effective against the enemy. Machines, systems and knowledge would be exchanged, with specialist equipment such as 'Purple' brought over, and there would be new opportunities for both parties. None would be so pleased with such measures as Churchill and the American President, Roosevelt. Later, as a result of such cooperation and agreement, the Americans would develop their own version of the British Bombe in their factories, using some of the concepts of Turing's machines, but with improvements to the design and with four-wheel rotor versions to challenge the U-boat attacks in the Atlantic, which caused so much destruction to the convoys.

Significance: Recognition that allied nations are more effective in dealing with challenges in the specific area of gathering intelligence, codes and ciphers than by going it alone. The same approach is adopted with anti-crime agencies and the sharing of intelligence.

American cryptanalyst visits Bletchley Park (1943)

The cryptanalyst F. Friedman visited Bletchley Park on 7 May 1943, at the same time as the Anglo-American cooperation agreement was being arranged. He was shown various information and equipment, aware that some of his American colleagues had visited in earlier years. Friedman was part of the Signal Security Agency (SSA).

Significance: It made sense to use the BRUSA agreement in May 1943 as an opportunity to meet with Allied signals intelligence personnel to share and exchange information on traffic analysis and codebreaking matters.

Hollerith data processing relocates to Drayton Parslow (1943)

Originally based at Bletchley Park, the Hollerith tabulating section had to relocate some miles down the road to *Prospect Farm*, Drayton Parslow, a small village. This was set up by BTM manager Fred Freeborn, who would build the unit into a considerable workforce with mainly women to carry out data processing using punched cards. These cards would have been coded to collect certain items of intelligence once messages had been decoded from Enigma enemy machines, obtained via Y-stations. So much information was intercepted and this would include much trivia, and by itself appear of little interest. However, when filtered and sorted and put together with other information, the intelligence may reveal useful information. Bletchley needed the space for other uses, and could not cope with the ever-expanding volume of punched cards on its tables, shelves, and cupboards. There would be constant communication between the two sites with requests for data and information from Bletchley. There are reports of some bad feeling between those managers at Bletchley Park and with Freeborn, as the headquarters wished to dictate the sequence of data and prioritisation. However, Freeborn resisted this, and would be in control of priorities as far as practically possible, managing the huge amounts of data and punched cards that would pass through the site. A compromise was reached, however, and this enabled the objectives to be met at a practical level.

Drayton Parslow would rise in capacity to have several hundred personnel, mainly women, operating equipment, maintaining logs and supporting Bletchley Park. There would be five shifts of operators on a twenty-four-hour shift basis, and the most urgent work would be for Hut 8 at Bletchley. That processed Naval Enigma or 'Shark' traffic. There would be women punching and verifying the high-level or master cards, and if there were 3,000 of these they could generate a further 80,000 cards with detailed data and information. There would be sorters, reproducers and machine tabulators involved. The sequence of processing and management of it would be critical in providing Bletchley with useful output when requested. The quantities of staff were substantial as the need for data processing via punched cards developed. One report stated that at least 500 people were involved, and the 'consumption' of punched cards was around two million per week.

Freeborn, his wife and a few senior BTM personnel involved in the operation initially lived in a rented country house, The Horseshoes, in the nearby village of Nash. When that was vacated, they moved to The Lodge in Drayton Parslow. BTM would fund the accommodation for the duration needed by senior personnel. Freeborn was always looking for opportunities to make his section more efficient. The courtyard area and stables at The Lodge were developed to form space for the Hollerith operational process, and an extension to the machine room, together with additional offices. A large barn was demolished to make way for the alterations, with further additional residential hostel accommodation for staff also constructed there. One assumes that all the necessary permissions and consents were acquired prior to the development. Commander Travis from Bletchley would monitor the situation, and have meetings and discussions with Freeborn from time to time. The system seemed to work well on the whole. Prior to the move to Prospect Farm at Drayton Parslow, the Hollerith section had moved to Block C, at Bletchley Park. The lack of space and growth of the section necessitated the move outside Bletchley. Teleprinter lines would be connected to Bletchley Park for communication. Post-war the Farm and Hollerith machine site would become a training centre for the GPO.

Significance: Relocation of the Hollerith tabulating operation to Drayton Parslow, some miles away from Bletchley, gave new opportunities for additional space, expansion, and scaling up the operation to support the experts at Bletchley Park.

Battleship *Scharnhorst* sunk with intelligence aided by Bletchley Park (1943)

The German battleship *Scharnhorst* was a real threat to the Allies, being extremely well armoured and of enormous proportions. It was a potential target waiting to be attacked, but it used a number of tricks and deception to avoid being located.

Eventually, intelligence was decoded at Bletchley Park, and this helped contribute to the sinking of the famous battleship. Richard Pendered was one of the Bletchley codebreakers working on 'Shark' who may have contributed to the deciphering of the messages leading to the location of *Scharnhorst*, concealed in the Norwegian fjords.

Significance: Perseverance in using listening stations for radio and Enigma transmissions together with coordination with Bletchley Park codebreakers, would pay dividends and put back Hitler's naval force significantly.

Outstation Gayhurst remains after two country house stations closed (1943–1944)

Three country house codebreaking outstations were established, Adstock, Gayhurst and Wavendon, but as Stanmore and Eastcote were later developed and expanded as outstations, Bombe machines would be transferred across. Only Outstation Gayhurst would remain operational. It was a fraction of the size of Stanmore and Eastcote, but still had an important role to play.

Significance: As the Bombe machines increased in quantity, there would be a need for more and larger outstations. It was inevitable that some of the smaller ones would close and transfer their machines elsewhere. Gayhurst, geographically not far from Bletchley Park, had a reprieve to remain open.

Denniston visits codebreakers in America to dissuade them from building their version of the British Bombe

Commander Denniston, the head of Bletchley Park back in England, travelled to the United States during wartime. He was made aware that the Americans would be designing and building their own 'Bombe' codebreaking machine, based on a four-wheel rotor Enigma. Denniston tried to persuade Commander Laurence Safford, the Head of OP-20-G, not to build their own version and to use the British Bombe. However, the Americans knew that the British had problems in maintaining consistency of codebreaking with the Nazi *Kriegsmarine* Shark codes, and there were long gaps when progress was not made at Bletchley Park. Safford went ahead with the production of a naval codebreaking machine, an improved version of the British Bombe and based on four-wheel Enigmas.

Significance: Denniston's pleadings with the Americans probably had the effect of making them even more determined to proceed with the design of a four-wheel Naval Bombe. It would be as much about pride as anything else. If Britain could build a codebreaking machine, American engineers could do one better, and improve on it. They had the advantage of not being as limited in obtaining materials, equipment, and resources.

EVENTS

Cobra developed to tackle four-wheel Enigma machines

Cobra was a high-speed auxiliary piece of motorised equipment with thick multiple cables to support the Bombe codebreaking machines. It was principally to assist the three-wheel-based Bombes have a fourth wheel, and emulate the four-wheel Enigma machines. These machines were installed at both Outstation Stanmore and Outstation Eastcote, the two largest outstations. The auxiliary equipment was extremely noisy, created a lot of dust and vibrated when in use. It was a compromise compared to the US naval four-wheel, purpose-made Bombe codebreaking machines built later. The equipment would be positioned within a raised bund wall to keep the dust and oil contained. It was developed jointly by TRE's Wynn-Williams and the GPO's Thomas Flowers at the Post Office Research Engineering Station, but was found to be unreliable.

Significance: An auxiliary piece of technical equipment to improve the Bombe machine. It would not be the answer to the four-wheel Enigma, but more of a stopgap measure and a compromise.

Swiss warning on Enigma goes unnoticed (1943)

Warnings were passed in October 1943 to Swiss intelligence from America that Enigma had been compromised by the allies. The Abwehr were notified, but the warning went unheeded and no action was taken. This was fortunate for the Allies.

Significance: Missed opportunities by the Nazis may have helped change the course of the war for the Allies.

Robinson codebreaking machine is built (1943)

An advanced decoding machine was built for Bletchley Park by a combination of suppliers and engineers including the Post Office Research Engineering Station, TRE, and BTM in Letchworth. The first machine was delivered to Bletchley in 1943. This was named the *Robinson*, from Heath Robinson, a name coined by the Wrens who used it due to the rather haphazard appearance of the machine with several pulleys, cables, a large frame and electronic equipment, tape readers and motors. It contained a handful of tube valves, but only a fraction compared with the far more advanced Colossus decoding machine built later. It was operated by Wrens, who cursed the synchronising of the dual paper tapes to make the thing work, and the need to connect them together with hot glue. It would be temperamental, and break down from time to time, but it was a start in the challenge to Lorenz, the German advanced encoding machine, and Fish intelligence from Europe.

Significance: The need for greater efficiency in utilising an advanced codebreaking machine to attack the Lorenz teleprinter attachment used by the Germans, where messages were sent between Hitler and the German high command.

Robinson delivered to Bletchley Park (1943)

The Robinson decoding machine was an attempt to break the Tunny/Fish communications of non-Morse messages sent by the enemy, using advanced technology. Robinson would be a rather clumsy design and difficult to set up as witnessed by the Wrens, who had to synchronise large reels of punched paper tape so they could be read by optical readers or 'magic eyes'. It was assembled and brought together by various contributors and engineers, including the Post Office Research Engineering Station, who built a large part of it. Frank Morrell and Tommy Flowers would work on it for many hours, weeks and months. Tommy Flowers, a PORES engineer, was eventually dismissive of the design and was convinced he could design and build something much better. Later he would have his opportunity to prove that he could make substantial advances and improvements, but it would be a completely new machine, using valve technology on a large scale.[49]

Significance: The first advanced codebreaking machine to deal with non-Morse messages. It would be a stopgap measure until something more efficient could be designed and built, i.e., Colossus. Tunny machines would provide the final conversion of the decoded message.

Wrens trained in operation of Robinson and later the Colossus machines (1943)

With extensive experience in operating codebreaking Bombes and setting them up, when new decoding machines were introduced, such as the Robinson, the Wrens were trained to set up and operate those too. The quantity of these advanced decoding machines would be a fraction of those with Bombes, so far fewer personnel had to be trained in their operation. The Wrens would work together in pairs checking each other's work and helping to load drums of punched paper tape on to motorised spindles. They would glue together long lengths of the tape using heat clamps and have to synchronise two separate reels of tape exactly.

Things would improve slightly when the Colossus machine came along, as there would be no longer the need to synchronise the reels. The setting of switches and controls in conjunction with their written instructions and operation manuals would become critical in getting the machine to operate correctly. The intense heat from many hundreds, even thousands, of valves on the Colossus decoding machine would be extremely uncomfortable, particularly in the warmer summer months. The Wrens operating these machines would not be aware they were operating the world's first semi-programmable digital computer, and making history.

Significance: The resourcing problem of the British and the Allies would introduce WRNS personnel to help operate and set up the advanced codebreaking machines. There would be a mirror image in the United States, where the Naval Bombes could be operated by WAVES personnel.

SIGSALY used by Churchill for transatlantic communication (1943)

Churchill was in urgent need of a robust secret transatlantic communication link to have dialogue with the American President. Previous systems were insecure, until the Americans built SIGSALY, a complex, enormous speech-synthesis communication system, using Pulse Code Modulation techniques. The second machine built by the manufacturers would be installed in 1943 in the basement of an annexe to the department store Selfridges. This would be top secret at the time. It worked using 'one-time pads' to add noise to speech and used record discs on large players that had to be synchronised across the Atlantic to work. So large and bulky was the system, it needed its own air-conditioning and ventilation system due to the electrical power it used, and the enormous heat output. SIGSALY utilised advanced methods of technology for the time, but was dismantled after the war and sent back to the United States, having served its purpose during wartime. Part of the equipment can be viewed in the National Cryptologic Museum in Maryland, USA.

Significance: The SIGSALY system closed the gap in terms of plugging leaks of confidential transatlantic telephone calls between the US President and the British Prime Minister.

America builds its Naval Bombe machine (1943)

In 1943 the first US Naval Bombe machine was put to use operationally, to decode and tackle the U-boat enemy messages. These were four-wheel based machines and built by WAVES, a special group of mainly women, together with some male naval enlisted men and civilians who worked night and day to assemble them in large numbers. They built them at the NCR factory in Dayton, Ohio. Around 121 machines were constructed and moved to Washington near the east coast for the OP-20-G group. Detailed production drawings were produced before the machines could be manufactured. The advantage for the Americans was that they had access to the British Bombe design, and had opportunity to improve it, to obtain materials more easily and in greater quantity, with more speed. Alan Turing was aware this machine was being built and had visited the site in 1942 when he travelled to America.

Significance: The decision of the United States to proceed with building a four-wheel Bombe progressed the codebreaking of four-wheel Enigma machines, helping considerably in the Battle of the Atlantic. It would be a more efficient version of the British Bombe.

Newman approaches Flowers of PORES for assistance (1943)

Alan Turing would introduce Max Newman of Bletchley Park to Flowers of the Post Office Research Engineering Station. Turing was aware that Newman had the idea of creating a machine to assist with the decode of the Nazi advanced non-Morse Fish intercepts or Tunny. Newman was Turing's tutor at university. The discussion that followed with Flowers culminated in a new machine, designed and developed over many months, and utilising valve technology as digital switches. Not everyone at Bletchley was convinced this was such a good idea, and many thought the project wasteful of valuable resources. However, Flowers and Newman proved them wrong. Newman understood that if an advanced codebreaking machine could be designed and built to counter the non-Morse messages, this would save valuable time for the Allies. It is likely that Newman saw the proposed new machine as being part of the decoding process and still requiring manual intervention by mathematicians, but increased speed could be gained with such a machine. Turing's Bombe would be of little use against non-Morse messages as it was not designed for that purpose.

Significance: Newman recognised this was both an engineering task as well as a mathematical one, and he needed an engineer on board who could help him design and build a codebreaking machine to crack the German Lorenz and associated equipment. A high-speed codebreaking machine with inherent reliability would be required, and he could work alongside Flowers and his team.

Tommy Flowers commences building Colossus (1943)

Max Newman of Bletchley Park was keen to have a processing machine to tackle at least part of the Lorenz messages. Flowers, a research engineer at Dollis Hill, north London, agreed to design and build such a machine using valves as digital switches, with input from Newman. Over many months Flowers, with a team of Post Office engineers and support from his boss, Radley, put together the Colossus semi-programmable computer for decoding the 'Chi' part of the Lorenz messages, known as 'de-Chi'. Nine months would take its toll in terms of resources, cost and time. Flowers even contributed £1,000 of his own money to fund the completion of the project. Although Newman could see there would be a great advantage in having such a machine built, if possible, many at Bletchley would be highly sceptical of a valve-based machine as it would require around 1,500 valves to work. Valves were very expensive at the time, and in short supply due to the multitude of equipment needing valves to operate. Flowers' belief in himself, tenacity and perseverance in the project resulted in the world's first semi-programmable digital computer, Colossus (Mk 1).

When assembled at Bletchley Park after being transported from Dollis Hill and tested, it worked. The process of decoding would still require human intervention, but having Colossus would reduce the number of permutations of settings considerably, for skilled humans at Bletchley in the 'Testery' section to complete the job manually. The Colossus would save the codebreakers much time and increase the ability to decipher many more enemy messages than if they relied purely on manual techniques alone. Flowers had achieved an extraordinary objective together with his Post Office engineering team. It was a gamble for him, which had paid off. Ironically, Bletchley Park had been reluctant to consider the project as viable at the start, but could appreciate the advantage in having it in their arsenal of codebreaking tools, if it worked reliably. Newman, however, was convinced from the start that Flowers was the correct person for the job, and he had faith in him. It would be Newman who knew what he wanted the machine to achieve, and Flowers would create the design to meet Newman's brief as best he could with his engineering team.

Colossus was nothing like the codebreaking Bombe machine. It was a much more advanced design and the basis of an early computer, although only semi-programmable. Whereas the Bombe could only be utilised for one specific task, it was possible with the correct and appropriate knowledge and skill to programme Colossus to carry out calculations other than to break advanced encoding machine ciphers and codes. It was a far more flexible machine than the Bombe, although the Bombe was essential at the time, and therefore two separate and parallel decoding systems would be necessary until the end of the war. This is often overlooked by the media and others. Media presenters have previously assumed there was but one codebreaking machine and confuse the names of Enigma and Colossus. It is a complex subject, however, and guidance needs to be given to interviewers in advance of interviews of specialists or of Ex-Wrens, who operated machines in wartime. There was a place for each of the systems to help defeat the Nazi enemy and their supporters.

Flowers was asked to build a machine by mathematician Max Newman from Bletchley Park, at a time when many others at Bletchley dismissed the idea as unworkable, extravagant use of wartime resources, and a waste of time. Welchman was particularly vocal in condemning Flowers' idea for designing and building the Colossus. However, it would prove to be a game-changer in the fight against the enemy, and highly successful, although it would only eliminate part of the cipher settings, and manual methods would need to supplement the machine-codebreaking for a combined team effort in the Testery section at Bletchley Park.

Ten Colossus machines were built, with an eleventh partly constructed as the war came to an end. The process of designing and building Colossus was a real challenge, as there were no manuals or drawings of the machine initially as it had to be developed. Flowers would obtain considerable support and resources from Radley, his boss at PORES, who arranged access to skilled engineers and materials. Flowers was pleased that he had been proved correct about the usefulness of the machine and its reliability, but was saddened that he did not receive the true recognition for his efforts over many months of work. He would not be permitted to work on a further advanced machine after the war ended. Flowers would, after the war, apply for a bank loan to build an advanced computer with his knowledge, but was turned down, so became frustrated and despondent.

Significance: The development of Colossus would be a mammoth undertaking, both from a technical engineering aspect as well as one of obtaining all the resources and skilled personnel to do so. The meeting of minds with Max Newman and Flowers, the engineer, resulted in a project that was like no other, and yet it had to succeed. It has to be stated that without support from Flowers' boss, Radley, the project would not have even started, and Colossus would most likely not have been built in Britain, or perhaps not at all.

Kursk (1943)

Allied intelligence would assist the Russians when engaging with the Nazi enemy at Kursk. The source of the intelligence was not divulged, but Kursk was seen as a possible turning point for the Russians, who were able to make real progress, albeit with heavy losses. The Battle of Kursk, when the Soviets resisted a significant Nazi counter-attack, was between 5 July and 23 August 1943. Hitler's troops had already lost the Battle of Stalingrad, and to lose at Kursk was of great concern to Hitler and his generals. The German attack was named Operation Citadel. Reports have indicated that it was not just Allied intelligence via Enigma intercepts that provided clues as to the intentions and plans of the enemy. Defectors, and local intelligence used by the Russians also played a significant part too. The key point here was that the Nazi counter-attack failed, and was a devastating blow to Hitler's plans. By 13 July, Hitler had cancelled Citadel, and was concentrating on the threat in Sicily from the Allied advance.

German equipment was specially picked for the battle, including many new Tiger tanks direct from the factory. The troops also, were battle-hardened and elite sections and divisions, but they could not make headway against the Russians in sufficient strength. Although the Germans did make progress at times, they were overwhelmed by the Russians, to Hitler's immense disappointment. Some of the German tracked armoured equipment could not cope at short range, and losses were high. The T-34 Russian tanks were vulnerable and no match for the Tiger, but volume and quantity of equipment won in the end. The element of surprise was a tool used particularly by the Russians to conceal tanks in the forests, and based on the Doctrine of Maskirovka, or masking. This approach had been developed back in the 1920s. The losses at Kursk on both sides were huge, with the countryside and landscape littered with tanks, equipment abandoned lorries and trucks. Kursk was a true turning point in the war against fascism and the Nazis.

Significance: There are many factors in the success of Kursk as a location for a major offensive and counter-offensive. While intelligence was one aspect in the equation, the resolve and determination of the Russian soldiers was also critical.

Outstation Eastcote established (1943)

Originally planned as a military hospital, but rejected for that use, Eastcote was adapted and established in September 1943 as Outstation Eastcote and part of HMS

Pembroke V, operated by the WRNS. It was run as a shore-based naval station and built up the supply of codebreaking Bombe machines until there were 103 at the end of the war. These were situated in long huts and finger blocks across the footpath in Block 'B', with the administrative, sleeping quarters and galley kitchen and dining in Block 'A', on the south part of the site. Wrens had to sign the Official Secrets Act to work at any of the outstations or at Bletchley Park.

It is relevant to explain the link between Outstation Stanmore and Outstation Eastcote here. Stanmore came prior to Eastcote and took not only new Bombes from the Letchworth factory, but existing examples from some of the country house outstations. It would almost become a type of clearing house for processing Bombes. Some machines would go onto Eastcote after that site was established in late 1943. The author has studied the movement, allocation, and distribution of Bombe machines across Bletchley and the codebreaking outstations in some detail. Each machine has a history recorded in the Bombe registers.

Eastcote would be the largest codebreaking outstation in the Second World War, having almost 50 per cent of the total codebreaking machines. Blocks 2 and the northern parts of Block 3 would be used to house codebreaking machines during wartime. Both Stanmore and Eastcote would be sent 'Cobra' machines, which speeded up the Bombes' operation as an auxiliary attachment. Eight hundred Wrens supported by others would work shift patterns during both day and night, on a continuous basis, to meet the needs of HQ, Bletchley Park.

An unusual aspect of the codebreaking base was the public footpath that ran through the site, dividing it into two parts, and this was potentially a security issue.[50] It is surprising there were no measures taken to close the footpath during wartime, although that might have indicated there were sensitive matters on the site, which might have otherwise alerted enemy agents or suspicious interested parties. Armed guards, Royal Marines, would protect the entrances and exits to the site. Several of the WRNS operators of the codebreaking outstations are now on the Bletchley Park Roll of Honour.

Significance: The final and largest codebreaking outstation, Eastcote would grow over time to house in excess of 100 codebreaking Bombe machines, and with a personnel strength of more than 800 Wrens. Together with Outstation Stanmore they would house around 85 per cent of the Bombes, making a valuable contribution to the processing of Enigma message settings. The spreading of the risk of bombing codebreaking machines and personnel being destroyed by the enemy was a good strategy at the time. However, it complicated the logistics of the codebreaking operation considerably, and systems would have to be in place to ensure the correct instructions were sent to the appropriate outstation, as well as maintaining a high level of security.

Bombe Number 1 relocates to OSE (1943)

The first Bombe, Victory, had a chequered history. It was moved from Bletchley Park to Outstation Wavendon (OSW), to Outstation Stanmore (OSS), and finally to Outstation Eastcote (OSE), on 6 September 1943, when the final codebreaking outstation base was only just being established and opened. The machine would be redesignated there as 'London' and partially dismantled. A sad end to a pioneering codebreaking machine.[51]

Significance: A journey of a significant codebreaking machine that helped to change the war, courtesy of Turing, Bletchley Park, the codebreaking outstations, Wrens, and RAF personnel, not to dismiss the listening Y-stations who provided the crucial source material. It was a great pity that the machine could not have been saved and shown to the public at Bletchley Park.

Increased Security at Codebreaking Outstations (1943)

With codebreaking machines such as the Bombes being hidden away on sites such as Stanmore and Eastcote, increased security demanded Royal Marines personnel with guns to guard the bases from intruders or inquisitive members of the public. At Eastcote, the site was split into two parts, with a public footpath down the middle. This did not occur at Stanmore, however. When shift workers, Wrens, walked across from Block 'A' to Block 'B', the huts where the codebreaking Bombes were held, the women would be asked to show their identity passes even though the guards recognised them and were familiar with their faces and names. High walls and barbed wire helped to make access difficult for intruders. Warning signage would be in existence. Even post-war, armed guard security was maintained for GCHQ Eastcote, later RAF Eastcote.

Significance: The sensitivity of these codebreaking sites was such that members of the public had to be prevented from knowing what was being done there, or what activities. Even personnel in Block 'A' who asked a Wren what they did over at the other part of the Eastcote site would get short shrift, as the Official Secrets Act was in force. If you did not have official written authorised access to Block 'B' huts, you did not need to know what went on there. There are also some reports that indicated local public houses should not be used by codebreaking personnel, and were out of bounds as a precaution against a loose tongue giving away information.

6813th US Signals operates at Bletchley Park

As part of the BRUSA agreement between America and Britain, various detachments of American US Signals Engineers came to Britain to help in a support role on cryptographic matters. Some would operate Bombe machines. The units would be the 6811th, 6812th, and 6813th detachments. The 6813th US Signals went to Bletchley Park and contributed to codebreaking in Hut 6, after certain training initiatives. The American contingent was relatively small as a proportion of the personnel in Hut 6, probably around 10 per cent, if that. The designated sub sections that involved American signals engineers included 'Watch', Machine

EVENTS

Room, Army Research, Air Research, Control, Identification Section, and a section at Beaumanor. Some changes were also made to personnel on the approach to D-Day.[52]

Significance: The involvement of US signals engineers across Bletchley Park, in Kent and at Eastcote in Middlesex, would prove beneficial in the fight against the Axis powers.

Colossus codebreaking machine delivered to Bletchley Park (1943)

The mammoth task of designing and building a new innovative codebreaking machine fell to the Post Office Research Engineering Station and Tommy Flowers, aided by codebreaker Max Newman. The machine, with 1,500 tube valves as digital switches, was far more advanced than the Robinson machine used at Bletchley, and more reliable. It would be delivered and demonstrated at Bletchley on 8 December 1943. This was not an easy task, as it was so large it had to be dismantled into modules or parts at Dollis Hill, where it was being built, then transported, assembled, connected up and tested. It worked. There would be a faster, more efficient version, the Mark 2, in 1944, and this would require 2,400 valves but would be considerably faster to read the paper tape data optically through its magic eye sensor. But as a first machine, the Mark One Colossus was very welcome indeed.

Significance: This was a significant turning point in the war, with a reliable codebreaking machine able to analyse, determine and eliminate a significant number of permutations of the Lorenz and secret writer message settings from the advanced enemy encoding machines. It was much more reliable and simpler in many ways to use than the punched paper tape in the complex Robinson machine. Manual input by mathematicians would still be required to arrive at the message settings, but this machine saved much time thanks to engineer Flowers, and also Max Newman, who worked well together. The next challenge would be to design and build an improved version in time for the forthcoming invasion of northern France in the summer of 1944.

First Bombe machines delivered to Outstation Eastcote (1943)

Between September 1943 and December 1943, the first ten Bombe codebreaking machines were delivered to Outstation Eastcote, being the last of five outstations. The establishment of the largest codebreaking outstation provided a degree of flexibility for the management team, who had to organise the resources in terms of equipment and personnel. The site would increase the quantities of Bombe machines significantly in the next eighteen months, and the complement of WRNS operators would grow to 800. One of these early machines had started its life at Bletchley Park in 1940 as the first codebreaking bombe machine, Victory.

Significance: It would take time to build up the quantity of Bombe codebreaking machines on a new site. Many of the machines would come from other smaller, codebreaking outstations, and the rest from new machines built by BTM in Letchworth.

SIXTA established at Bletchley Park (1944)

The combination of various traffic analysis departments and sections spread around London and England would form the backbone of traffic analysis, with Bletchley Park playing a key role in organisation. However, in February 1944, the section would be established formally as SIXTA. This would assist the decrypting of messages via data analysis of the intercepted radio or Morse code traffic, to find out as much as possible about the source and recipients. This would include call signs, enemy unit names, and numbers, frequencies, and other information. The support service of traffic analysis was based at Bletchley from 1942, but was relatively fragmented in organisation, spread across various huts. The benefits of effective traffic analysis were huge to the whole process of intelligence gathering and cryptography of encoded messages, and should not be underestimated. Log readers would play their part in helping to filter down the information so it could be kept on card indexes, or be processed via a Hollerith machine either at Bletchley Park or at Drayton Parslow. Unusually, a number of the log readers were informed about the breaking of Enigma, so they had more incentive to do the specialist work in long shifts.

Significance: Traffic analysis was not an optional extra in wartime. The management at Bletchley realised that there could be enormous gains in decoding messages and identifying key intelligence if one spent the time and resources in the analysis of the source of messages, as well in the message content itself. Traffic analysis therefore, over time, became as important as the decoding process of message settings of Enigma machines. The biggest issue was perhaps in managing the volume of data that was recovered in an age well before computers and digital hard drives for storage.

Bletchley Park intercepts intelligence on V2 rockets (1944)

V2 missiles had been tested for months beforehand but became operational in 1944 and caused havoc and loss of life in London. They were much larger and more destructive than the earlier V1 rockets. However, Bletchley Park had managed to decode certain Enigma transmissions relevant to the weapon. The Peenemünde/Blizna Enigma network termed 'Corncrake' had been broken by Bletchley codebreakers. The parallel threat of V1s and V2s, albeit launched from different sites, and the mobility of the latter missiles' launching pads, caused the Allies havoc after D-Day, when Hitler wanted retaliation for the Normandy invasion. On 15 June 1944, even though the Allies had thought that the Germans could no longer make significant attacks on London, 30 per cent of the 244 V1s launched that day got through.[53] This was alarming considering the effort that had been put into the D-Day invasion. It had to be stopped.

Significance: The tracking and identification of the location of the V1 and V2 rocket launch sites and support facilities was crucial after D-Day in avoiding mass civilian casualties. All intelligence, whether by Enigma decodes, reports by resistance forces, or photo-reconnaissance, would be needed to find and destroy the infrastructure of Hitler's weapons of mass destruction.

Double agent Garbo commences his build-up of false information reports leading up to D-Day (1944)

Double agent Garbo was located in a safe house in Crespigny Road, Hendon, north London, and sending false reports to his Nazi contacts in Europe.[54] Garbo was really Pujol Garcia, a Catalan who was working for the British. He played a key role in providing false information in the build-up to the eventual D-Day invasion under *Operation Fortitude South*. At this time the Allies did not know the date or even the month when D-Day would occur, but the stage was being set to report on the fictitious First US Army Group in southern England in an attempt to try to convince the enemy the invasion would come at the Pas-de-Calais and nowhere else. Garbo's British MI5 handler, Tomás Harris, oversaw the messages and responses as a check. The wireless operator at Crespigny Road was Charles Haines. A network of twenty-seven fictitious spies or agents were created over time by Garbo, convincing the Nazis that intelligence was being fed back from them to him on a regular basis. It was all lies, a brilliant deception, which would prove invaluable as D-Day approached.

Significance: Garbo would play a dangerous game on behalf of the Allies, which could easily have backfired and either delay the start of D-Day or postpone it by another year, giving Hitler valuable time to develop his weapons of mass destruction.

Incendiary bomb hits Outstation Eastcote during an air raid (1944)

A general air raid covering north-west London resulted in an enemy incendiary device being dropped by the Luftwaffe and hitting huts at Outstation Eastcote during the night. The damage was to a hut, some plumbing and building services, but fortunately the bomb did not fully ignite. The fire was put out by Wrens and other personnel on the base. No damage occurred to the huts containing the Bombe machines. Churchill was informed the next morning and was most likely relieved that the damage was considered as minimal. The Wrens helped residents in a bombed residential property over the road after their fire had been put out. A fire practice by Wrens at Eastcote with a hose and trailer had been abandoned some weeks, or months previously, due to the tender not being able to fit through the gate. It is not known if this same fire tender was used in the dampening of the fire that night.

Significance: The reality that the outstations were not immune to general bombing, but thankfully escaped lightly. No codebreaking machines were affected, and therefore progress in decoding could proceed at a steady pace to support Bletchley Park.

American signals engineers arrive in Britain to operate codebreaking machines (1944)

As part of the BRUSA agreement between Britain and the United States, signals engineers came to England, to Bletchley, to Kent and to Eastcote in Middlesex. The 6812th Signals Engineers were trained by Wrens at Outstation Eastcote to operate a quantity of Bombe machines. Eventually, ten bombes in total were allocated to them. The Americans were based in Ruislip Woods as an encampment, and travelled in daily and at night to operate the Bombes. There were five US officers and around 120 enlisted men to work in shifts on the machines. The commander was Major M.H. Stewart.[55] They named each of the ten Bombes after an American city, and they successfully processed message settings to a high standard, both in terms of speed and consistency of output. Efficiency would be approximately 38 per cent better than British operators at its peak. There was later a large American contingent of military and support personnel at Eastcote after the war ended. The 6812th Signals personnel broke some 425 Enigma keys in their use of the Bombes allocated to them. A detailed report of the operation of the Bombes was written by senior staff in 1945 towards the end of the war. The period of activity at Outstation Eastcote with American input on Bombes allocated to them was 1 February 1944 to 7 May 1945, a total of around fourteen months.

Significance: Recognition of the value of sharing information and resources across the Allies, by allowing American signals engineers via ETOUSA to locate to various sites in England, including at Outstation Eastcote. Trust was essential here, and to be comfortable with giving access to the Americans to some of Britain's most secret equipment at the time.[56] It is interesting to note that while Americans operated a limited number of British Bombe machines, when they designed and built their Naval US Bombe, no British codebreaking personnel were given the opportunity of operating them in Washington. At least, not officially.

American signals engineers – details of ETOUSA orders (1944)

Under the BRUSA agreement & ETOUSA organisation, personnel from the American military would come to Britain during wartime to learn techniques and systems, such as codebreaking and operating British Bombe codebreaking machines. These would include detachments from the US Army Signals 6812th and 6813th detachments among others. Those who went to Outstation Eastcote would be trained by the Wrens to operate up to ten Bombe machines. Once operational, the 6812th US Signals would prove to be very successful in breaking message settings, and in setting up the Bombes. They would have a good understanding of the machines. The

US Naval four-wheel Bombe would be built in America during wartime, to counter the Nazi U-boat threat, and would prove to be very successful. The orders for US Signals redeployment to the United Kingdom in 1944 were listed as follows:

> Headquarters European Theater of Operations, US Army.
> Organization of Field Detachments for Signal Intelligence Division.
> To Commanding General CBS, SOS, ETOUSA, APO 887
> Commanding Officer EBS, SOS, ETOUSA, APO 517

The following units were provisionally organised, effective 1 February 1944 at stations indicated:

> **6811th** Signal Security Detachment – Hall Place, Bexley Kent, APO 887
> **6812th** Signal Security Detachment – Eastcote, Middlesex, APO 517
> **6813th** Signal Security Detachment – Bletchley Park, Bucks, APO 128

The 6811th US Signals Engineers were transferred to Hall Place in Bexley, Kent via the ETOUSA organisation. They were established here within a specialist listening station with large aerials positioned across the roof of the main house. Intercepts concentrated on Morse-generated, Luftwaffe-based Enigma messages.

These were Specialist American engineers relevant to intelligence gathering and processing during WW2. Particularly of importance were the 6811th, 6812th, and 6813th US Signals Engineers who visited England in 1944, some allocated to GC&CS at Bletchley Park, others to Outstation Eastcote, (a Bombe machine codebreaking outstation), with some allocated to Kent. *See ETOUSA.*

Significance: The incorporation of Americans within a secret codebreaking outstation would be good for morale, and ensure specialist skills could be taught and shared across the pond. A detailed technical report was produced by US signals engineers on the operation and design of the Bombe machine after the war, based upon their experiences at Eastcote.[57]

The allied cooperation via the BRUSA agreement and ETOUSA orders in the USA, enabled the cooperation of technical engineering Signals personnel to learn codebreaking techniques from the British, and apply their expertise to help the war effort in a variety of ways. This included using Bombe codebreaking machines, listening to Luftwaffe Enigma Morse messages, and assisting with codebreaking and traffic analysis.

Selected OSE Bombes given American names (1944)

At Outstation Eastcote, the largest outstation for codebreaking, the Bombes were operated by Wrens. However, when the 6812th US Signals, Americans, joined the outstation to operate machines, ten Bombes were allocated names of American cities. These may have helped the US signals personnel become less homesick in a strange country. These names included *Houston, Atlanta, New York* and *San Francisco. Houston* would suffer from ongoing technical problems on 29 November 1944, but these were rectified by early December. Bombes would be numbered as well as named. For example, *Rochester*, the tenth Bombe, was numbered 313 even though there were only 211 Bombes manufactured in total.[58]

Significance: The naming of Bombe machines with American cities would give recognition to the Americans as Britain's allies in wartime and possibly increase morale when the US signals were setting up and operating the codebreaking machines at Eastcote.

BTM builds the 'super-Bombe' (1944)

Innovation and experimentation would form a significant and substantial part of the process between BTM, Bletchley Park, and other supporting organisations. It was decided to build a Bombe codebreaking machine called 'Giant' based upon four individual Bombes linked together physically and electrically. This project was carried out in 1944 and by June it was ready for use. This was not considered to be a success operationally, however. Evolution of the codebreaking sections identified that it was effectively obsolete by the time it had been built. Speed of operation was now the key, and faster machines were built and some were modified accordingly. It was also so large and heavy it could not be moved in one piece, and therefore never went to Bletchley. It was used for a time at BTM in the factory, under conditions of secrecy, but eventually was dismantled into four separate machines and distributed across the outstations, several of the units going to Bletchley Park, and one unit being sent to Outstation Eastcote. Wrens did not operate Giant, at least not when it was configured as one connected machine at the BTM factory in Letchworth. Once at Bletchley Park and at Outstation Eastcote, Wrens would just see those Bombes as just another codebreaking machine, to be set up and operated conventionally. There would be no clue as to its origin, or of abandonment of the Giant project. BTM and Bletchley would, however, have learned something from the exercise.[59]

Significance: An attempt to make a more efficient codebreaking Bombe machine, but the outcome was not successful. Risks were taken, and would not always be worthwhile. At least the machine could be recycled and still used as individual units, spread across Bletchley and the outstations.

V1 Bomb hits Stanmore at OSS (1944)

Outstation Stanmore was fortunate not to have sustained major damage when a V1 flying bomb exploded on 18 December 1944 at the perimeter wall of the site. No codebreaking huts were damaged, and the breached wall was promptly repaired. There were also reports of a V2 bomb detonating not far from RAF Bentley Priory, near Outstation Stanmore. Fortunately, it failed to hit the base and avoided disrupting the RAF Fighter Command operations. While an incendiary bomb did hit Outstation Eastcote, it did not detonate completely, and the damage caused was minimal.

Significance: A random attack not aimed specifically at the codebreaking outstation, but still of concern. Damage to the perimeter wall was limited and the base operated as normal afterwards.[60]

Last Bombe machine allocated to Americans at Outstation Eastcote (1944)

Bombe number 313 was named Rochester, under the operational authority of the 6812th US Signals engineers. This was the last of the ten machines allocated to them, all others being operated by the Wrens. A direct teleprinter link from Eastcote connected to Bletchley Park for the Menus of instructions needed.

Significance: The allocation of ten codebreaking machines to the Americans at Eastcote was a measure of their being entrusted with top-secret codebreaking equipment, helping the Allies to defeat Germany and the Axis powers.

Enigma adapted to improve security (1944)

While there would be many versions of the Enigma encoding machine, in 1944 a special version was developed and introduced. This was the Enigma *Uhr*. It was connected to a supplementary and auxiliary wooden box by a series of cables and a manually operated dial. The outer part of the dial was numbered up to thirty-six. The cables were connected from the front plugboard to the separate box. By turning the dial, it was possible to select up to thirty-six, possibly more, plugging arrangements without physically changing the plugs on Enigma. This was designed to increase the permutations of settings further than before. The National Archives at Kew has photographs of this model. It was introduced during wartime without any warning, so was a surprise for both sides. However, it was deciphered by Bletchley Park shortly after its introduction and used to send and receive messages. Uhr means 'clock'.

Significance: The designers of the Enigma were always considering further improvements to the machine in order to increase the level of security. This one was unusual in that it incorporated a separate auxiliary box with equipment linked by cable to the machine. It was more difficult to use 'in the field', as compared with the one-box Enigma.

Mark 2 Robinson is built (1944)

Certain improvements resulted in a Mark 2 Robinson codebreaking machine being built for Bletchley Park, but it was still very much a compromise design until the more successful Colossus was developed. It was designed by Flowers and could run four tapes instead of the original pair of punched tapes. This version was nicknamed 'Super-Robinson'. It still relied largely on electro-mechanical switches. It is reported by TNMOC that one of the Mark 2 Robinsons went to Eastcote after the war ended, and it may have been operational until the 1950s. Curiously, the Colossus and Colossus Mark 2 were being used very successfully in mid-1944 and were much more reliable than Robinson. They were also much simpler to set up.

Significance: The development of a more efficient version of the Robinson advanced codebreaking machine to improve speed and robustness in operation.

Michie and Turing discuss advanced machines while playing chess

Both Donald Michie and Turing were mathematicians and codebreakers at Bletchley Park. They shared a love of chess and like many other codebreakers would sometimes play the game in their lunch breaks together. But this was also an opportunity to talk about a shared interest, that of advanced machines that could take away the work from man, to perform calculations and logistical problems. They also discussed artificial intelligence, which was to become significant in both Turing and Michie's future work, post-war. But Michie lived longer than Turing and became an expert in that subject, chairing various committees and leading the way towards the modern world, with computers as the basis of the next industrial revolution. Michie was interested in the application of logic and algorithms to computers, as part of a process to be humanised, as he saw early computers as a tool. It was not the actual computer that was clever, it would be how one used them effectively and efficiently for the benefit of mankind that mattered. The lunchtime chess games may have formed a framework for this, with discussions, ideas and concepts shared between two highly intellectual people, who were surely ahead of their time. Michie's study of human anatomy in later years and associated specialist work indicated his breadth of knowledge and expertise beyond machines.

Significance: The event indicates there was effective communication between Michie and Turing, both very different personalities. A game like chess could be a sounding board for ideas between these advanced and intelligent minds.

Bletchley Park spy feeds Russians intelligence

John Cairncross was a translator at Bletchley Park. He decoded to feed the Russians information on Enigma and intelligence while working in Hut 6 at the Park. Hut 6 had, arguably, one of the most important collections of codebreaking individuals working on cracking Enigma. At university, Cairncross had made links with the KGB. But he found out that the Russians were not told about the British cracking Enigma for fear that a leak could compromise the Allies' position. Some reports indicated that the British knew he was a suspect and were monitoring him while at Bletchley Park. Cairncross claimed that he had assisted the Russians with crucial intelligence to enable them to defeat the Nazis at the Battle of Kursk. He was known as one of the Cambridge Five, spies who passed British secrets to the Russians. He defected to the East after the war.

Significance: The fact that there were leaks in intelligence and spies in both wartime and post-war demonstrates that no matter how many security systems one has in place, there is always the opportunity for a determined agent to steal secrets.

Speech encipherment project progressed by Turing (1944)

A speech encipherment project was developed over time at Hanslope Park, a large eighteenth-century country house in Buckinghamshire. The property was used as a major listening and receiving station. It was known as the *Delilah* project. Turing drove the project forward, but others played their part too. The completed unit with a terminal could fit on a table. The Americans had their own speech encipherment system, SIGSALY, used by Churchill and extremely complex with vast amounts of machinery and power consumption. The basement of Selfridges in Oxford Street in London had the second production machine on loan. Delilah was tiny by comparison. Delilah was needed because of the vast amounts of information that had to be sent back and forth to America as part of wartime communications. Turing had gone to Hanslope House, around 10 miles from Bletchley, in 1943. Delilah would eventually be designed for local shortwave, or VHF transmissions, but would not work efficiently over very long distances. Its use would be limited, but the project proceeded. Turing arranged for Delilah to be taken for evaluation at the Post Office Engineering Research Station in Dollis Hill. By the time the war ended, its use was no longer required. It was a case of problem solving, designing test equipment to test circuits and ideas, building parts, doing the mathematics, and making improvements. The development was all too slow and not seen as a high priority at the time. The final version of Delilah in 1945 did work, but it was just too late for make any significant difference to the war effort. This fact must have been extremely frustrating for Turing.

Significance: The development of a speech enciphering system by Turing was not used practically during wartime, due to the timing. However, the research and development may have proved beneficial to others.

Use of teleprinters at codebreaking outstations increases

Dispatch riders, usually on motorcycles, were largely WRNS personnel and sometimes from the GPO and elsewhere. They would ride between outstations and Bletchley Park in all weather and conditions, during day and night, to deliver instructions, Y-station logged data, and Menus of instructions. However, as teleprinters became more reliable and widely used, there would be such facilities at many of the codebreaking outstations and including Knockholt, where non-Morse messages were being intercepted. The use of the teleprinter gave feedback between sites much more quickly than using motorcycle couriers or dispatch riders. The cables had to be run between the various sites by the GPO and tested prior to operation. Of course, the Germans also used teleprinters, and connected an attachment to encode messages for the German high command – Lorenz and the secret writers – which were to cause Bletchley Park a headache until advanced codebreaking machines were later developed to tackle Lorenz. While the enemy did use some landlines to connect the Lorenz and secret writers, the majority were used via encoded non-Morse radio transmissions, which were the only practical systems to be intercepted by specialist listening stations.

Significance: Speed was essential in codebreaking and intelligence gathering in wartime. The advantage of using an advanced teleprinter and Lorenz encoding attachment for communication could benefit those commanders and admirals making key military decisions. However, there was a false sense of security when those at Bletchley cracked the Lorenz keys.

A lack of trust in the Nazi codebreaking sections (1944)

Codebreakers within the German OKW-Chi or Pers-Z were not always trusted by senior officers in the Third Reich. This was even more so after the attempted assassination of Hitler. The SS and Goering had established their own codebreaking operation separately. In 1943, one Abwehr report obtained by an agent in the US told of 'an outstanding aid in the Naval Intelligence Office in England against the U-boat threat'. Because the message did not include the word 'Enigma' within the text, and for other reasons, Admiral Dönitz did not take this information seriously and maintained that Enigma would remain secure. Here was an opportunity to investigate further the possibility that Enigma was already compromised, but the Nazis failed to do so. It is the case that from time to time reviews would be carried out on the security of Enigma, the improvements needed and so forth. But to receive from an agent in an allied country to the United Kingdom information that could be crucial in terms of it having major security implications and to dismiss it is poor judgement. The opportunities to act quickly diminished further as the war progressed, and particularly after the second front in France had been established. The Nazi codebreakers such as within OKW-Chi were not able to get the intelligence gained to be used effectively or speedily against the Allied forces. Strategically, the Third Reich's planning was beginning to crumble. While there may have been isolated pockets of intercepted Allied intelligence used to the advantage of the German army in battle, it was a case of too little and too late. The key issues for the Germans would be resupply to the front line of troops, ammunition, tanks, food, medical supplies, and most importantly, the need for increasing volumes of fuel to supply the military armour and equipment. And all this while the Allies were constantly bombing troop trains, fuel dumps, airfields and bridges to slow the Nazis. The advantage to the Allies would be the vast planning for years in advance of D-Day in terms of how these supplies could be managed logistically. Hitler had to spread his resources far and wide in France,

Belgium, Norway, Italy, Russia, Poland and Germany, and stay in command when his generals were telling him facts he did not wish to believe.

Significance: Inter-section rivalry and jealousy in Germany and the occupied countries may have impeded the sharing of key intelligence and information. Logistics would be affected by Allied bombing and severing lines of communication as the war progressed. All this made efficient use of intelligence more of a challenge, whereas the Allies appeared to have their systems much better managed in comparison to the Axis countries.

British spying on captured German generals and senior officers while in captivity in England

The Allies introduced secret microphones and listening equipment to listen to conversations between captured German generals and other senior officers who were imprisoned in Britain during the war. None of them would realise their private conversations were being 'bugged', monitored and recorded by British staff who spoke German in adjoining rooms and areas in the large houses where the Nazis were kept under guard. Some of the secret listeners were foreign Allied soldiers of Jewish origin who wanted to gather evidence of war crimes against the Nazis. Thousands of hours of recordings and transcripts would be typed up, studied and filed, with more than 100,000 transcripts accumulated. There were three principal locations: at Latimer House and Wilton Park in Buckinghamshire, and one at Trent Park near Cockfosters, north-west London. These were stately homes. Trent Park concentrated on German generals, the others on *Kriegsmarine* and Luftwaffe officers. At the peak, around fifty-nine Nazi generals had been monitored at Trent Park.

The detailed conversations gave an insight into how the captured prisoners considered their position and that of Germany as the war progressed. A few Nazi officers were anti-Hitler and shocked the majority of the others, almost seen as traitors of the Third Reich for their radical views. However, several others could see how badly the war was going for Germany, and that nothing but a miracle could turn the war against the Allies. They were permitted to listen to the BBC radio news broadcasts, which also shocked them when the Allies made real progress in Europe and closed in on Germany, with the Russians also attacking from the east. Many realised that the invasion of Russia by Hitler was a serious strategic mistake. Some of the evidence indicated that several staff were aware of the Holocaust and mass destruction of Jews and others, even actively participating themselves and boasting of their involvement as though they saw it as a sport. This shocked the secret listeners and those who were permitted access to the transcripts and recordings. One Luftwaffe officer described in detail his activity in shooting and killing innocent civilians, Jews, and thought nothing of it. The SS were clearly complicit in the Holocaust from the conversations recorded. But, for various reasons, no action was taken against the officers and generals, and the secret recordings were kept on file and are now held at the National Archives.

The listening was carried out in what was known as the 'M' room at the properties, and extreme care had to be taken by the Allies not to give the game away. Microphones and wiring had to be concealed. Some important information was gathered from the conversations as to the location of the V2 rocket base at Peenemünde, which would attack London and south-east England. Bombing of the site was then implemented by the Allies. Information could be pieced together with other data collected from Y-stations or deciphered from other sources, including Bletchley Park. This was something of an intelligence operation, and utilised various detective methods to identify and prioritise action arising from the bugging and monitoring process.

At Latimer House, near Amersham in Buckinghamshire, the operation, as elsewhere, came under CSDIC, or the *Combined Service Detailed Interrogation Unit*. This was run jointly between MI5 and MI6 and was so secret that Parliament had no idea it existed. It would become operational from 1942 to 1945. The cover story was that Latimer House was a supply depot, so it did not attract attention from the public. Some prisoners would be moved on elsewhere, after several weeks' monitoring. Some clandestine listening techniques were also carried out at the Tower of London during the war, when it was used as a prisoner of war site.

The operation under CSDIC listened in, monitoring around 10,000 Nazi prisoners of senior officer rank. It gave the Allies an insight into how German enemy minds worked, their backgrounds, activities, and crucial information which almost certainly helped to reduce the length of the war. That the whole operation was kept secret and fooled the German prisoners is astonishing over such a sustained and prolonged period during wartime. Overall, in CSDIC there would be 1,000 staff and almost 100 secret listeners hidden away, monitoring conversations. CSDIC was run by Colonel Thomas Kendrick of MI6, with around 200 intelligence officers across the three sites.

Significance: A clandestine operation to eavesdrop on enemy prisoners at different locations to learn useful intelligence. This process would have occurred on both sides to varying degrees, but probably on a much larger scale in Britain.

Luftwaffe intelligence withdraws (1944)

In October 1944 German Luftwaffe signals intelligence withdrew from the eastern Mediterranean and other areas, moving closer to Austria and Germany. These units would have been monitoring radio traffic in the area.

Significance: The failure of intelligence infrastructure would make the Luftwaffe less powerful and much less efficient as the war progressed.

End of the U-boat successes (1944)

A combination of factors resulted in the end of the *Kriegsmarine*'s U-boat strategy in the Atlantic and the loss of Allied shipping. These included better Allied spotter aircraft, use of centimetric radar, and fewer support personnel and vessels available to support the U-boats. Fuel supplies were also running low. By July 1944, Admiral Dönitz was devastated that his elite force had not won the Battle of the Atlantic, with many of his prize U-boats sunk or captured. However, there was still monitoring of Allied naval movements by Germany in the Baltic headquarters. The impact of U-boats on shipping at D-Day was relatively minimal due to the Allied strategy for naval and air cover.

Significance: Dönitz would have been disappointed to have to withdraw his U-boat forces and control his increasing losses in the Atlantic. He would eventually take on a new role to support Hitler in defending the last few weeks and days of the Third Reich.

Germans listened to military police radio prior to D-Day (1944)

With the mass build-up of troops, equipment, and supplies prior to D-Day in England, there was considerable radio traffic from military police directing traffic and helping to organise the situation. However, there is evidence that such radio transmissions were sometimes intercepted by the enemy in France, Holland and Germany. This gave the enemy a clue that something big was about to happen, but they would not know where or when. Hitler's assumptions were based on the premise that the Allies would come across the Channel to the Pas-de-Calais, and the Germans would be waiting for them in considerable strength. Large sections of the Atlantic wall had also been strengthened should a landing be attempted elsewhere. The irony of the radio intercepts by the enemy was that with the fictitious army of FUSAG having been created by the Allies, a certain amount of radio traffic was intended to be intercepted to give a false illusion that major forces were coming across the Channel to the Calais area. It is not fully understood how well the Germans could piece together the military police intelligence, which was not intended for them, and how well coordinated they would be to usefully apply the collected information to their best advantage. It is also the case that while British television transmissions were no longer available to the general public in wartime, some military TV monochrome transmissions were most likely intercepted by the enemy. The content of those television transmissions, however, may have been classified.

Significance: With such a large-scale operation and build-up to D-Day, troop movements in England would become known to varying degrees to the enemy, with a combination of both accurate and purposefully misleading accounts, which would confuse the enemy. Nevertheless, it was unintentional that unencoded military police radio transmissions could be intercepted by the Germans. In the bigger picture of things, this was not that significant, but if the enemy had been better prepared and shared information more constructively that intelligence may have given them useful data to add to their resources and strategic planning.

'Morrison Wall' intelligence at Bletchley prior to D-Day (1944)

Bletchley Park had gathered a great deal of information and intelligence across a wide range of sources, including Bombe, Robinson and Colossus deciphers of enemy intercepts. Y-stations would pick up useful trivial information too of transmissions, and even enemy tests of their communications. This information included the hierarchy and structure of the map of enemy communications in Europe. They were pinned on to a large wall, and the information collected via SIXTA and Hut 6 at the Park was positioned in their respective locations relative to other German communications stations. The chief organiser of this group was Major Morrison. Direction-finding equipment further amplified the schematic diagram of enemy communications stations, and it would be an ongoing task to provide as much detail as practically possible. Understanding how the enemy communicated across their personnel and divisions would be extremely valuable for the Allies. Traffic analysis log readers would draw simple diagrams of enemy communications networks and these would be passed to the organisers of the Morrison wall to build a more complete picture of the networks, including call signs and associated information.

Significance: This demonstrates the need to fully understand the communications arrangements of the enemy in wartime, and doing so may reveal key information as to movement of Panzer divisions, the renaming of divisions, and the merging of divisions for redeployment elsewhere. From the field marshal and generals giving instructions based upon Berlin's objectives, to the lone radio operator in the battlefield trenches sending numbers of casualties or an urgent need for fuel, supplies, and ammunition back to Command, the Allies needed to map out the communication links to give the forthcoming D-Day a high chance of success.

Colossus Mark 2 delivered to Bletchley Park (1944)

The Mark 2 Colossus machine would be to tackle the Lorenz and secret writer encoded messages intercepted from Germany. It would take many months to build by Flowers and his engineering team at Dollis Hill in London. It was delivered to Bletchley Park in June 1944, just a few days before D-Day, on 6 June.[61] This new machine would contain almost double the number of valves, at 2,400 in total. It would operate five times faster than the original and save the codebreakers much time. There would be a single tape for an optical reader 'eye' to read the punched holes, and no need for the synchronisation of two separate reels of punched tape, a huge improvement over the Robinson codebreaking machine. There was considerable pressure on the Post Office engineering team to deliver the Mark 2 machine to Bletchley Park before the start of D-Day, and this was only just achieved, with many hundreds of hours of testing and assembly. The increased speed of processing data would save time in the 'de-Chi' stage in the Newmanry at Bletchley, leaving manual methods to strip away the remaining settings, allowing the messages to be read.

Significance: The intense pressure on the Post Office Research Engineering Team at a critical time in the war made the completion of the Mark 2 Colossus a challenge, due to limited time and resources. That it was delivered a few days prior to the start of D-Day was extraordinary.

EVENTS

Mark 2 Colossus modified by Michie (1944)

Donald Michie was a close colleague of Turing and a codebreaker, a classicist, and mathematician, later to become an expert in artificial intelligence. As the Mark 2 Colossus codebreaking machine came to Bletchley Park a few days prior to D-Day in June 1944, Michie made a few modifications to it to improve its efficiency. He would later go on to study bio-medical techniques with his wife, and to develop and write papers on AI. Michie worked closely with codebreaker Jack Good to make small improvements to Colossus on technical issues. It is not clear if Flowers, the Colossus designer, was aware of these modifications made by others.

Significance: The modification of advanced codebreaking machines could only be done if the modifier understood the workings and logic of the machine, and the consequences of their modification to the output. Michie knew what he was doing.

D-Day assault at Normandy (1944)

The D-Day invasion at Normandy on 6 June 1944 was the largest sea-borne invasion in history. Bletchley Park and agents operating for MI5 in England would be constantly monitoring enemy radio traffic as well as non-Morse messages intercepted at Knockholt in Kent and elsewhere. It was important to identify the Order of Battle adopted by the German generals and field marshals, to stay one step ahead of the enemy. Intelligence signals units would also be on the Normandy beaches listening out for enemy transmissions and feeding back information to HQ. They would move inland cautiously, as the troops made progress. The decision for D-Day assault and implementation would largely be weather dependent, there was also the need to establish via the double agents' feedback to the Nazis the triggering of useful German high command messages. It was essential to build up a picture for the enemy, of an illusion, to tie their key Panzer divisions up away from Normandy. It would be inherently risky to move thousands of ships and troops across from England to the Normandy beaches, but it had the element of surprise. The Met Office became critical in advising the allied Supreme Commander, Eisenhower, of a possible gap in the poor weather to start the assault. Bletchley would erect radio receiving aerials at the Park to intercept intelligence, taking a further risk of being seen by enemy aircraft, but seen as worth it at the time as the Allies dominated the airspace over the Channel in June 1944. Wrens at Bletchley Park caught up in D-Day would not be allowed to leave or go to the canteen for security reasons, and then worked on coordinating the incoming messages from German commanders reacting to the Normandy invasion. Flowers and others would meet Eisenhower before D-Day to report on how Colossus was proving invaluable to the Allies in terms of decodes of enemy intercepts and deception of the Nazis. Eisenhower would have an enormous weight on his shoulders and had written two speeches, one telling the public about the success of the Normandy landings, the other disappointment in the failure of them. The latter, fortunately, never needed to be used.

Significance: D-Day was the culmination of years of planning by the Allies for a second front, with all the risks associated with it. Success or failure, these were the two possible outcomes. Failure would put the Allies back by years and give Hitler's weapons of mass destruction an opportunity to destroy Britain and America. Thankfully, this did not occur.

Enigma intercepted after D-Day referencing Army Group 'B' (1944)

On 9 June 1944, a few days after the Normandy landings, a German signals operator sent a message via Enigma to request supply data for XLVII Panzer Corps be made available to both the chief ordnance officer and the chief quartermaster. This Panzer division was positioned just north of the River Seine. The operator was using a three-wheel Enigma, the most common type. There were two personnel involved in setting up the machine and taking down the encoded letters in groups of five. This encoded message was then sent by Morse code. The Y-stations in Britain were listening in, intercepted the coded message and passed it to Bletchley Park. Hut 6 would be busy at Bletchley. A 'Menu' was devised to be passed to Hut 11, where a small handful of Bombe codebreaking machines existed, the majority being at the outstations. The wheel settings had been found for the daily key, which was changed by the enemy every twenty-four hours. The Bombes had done their job. The settings code was broken. A Typex machine, or Type 'X', was operated by female personnel and the settings incorporated within the machine, to spell out the plain text in German. All one needed now was a translator, to convert the message into English. Hut 3 would become involved in the next stage. An 'adviser' would study his database index and assess the relevance and importance of the message. He would make comments and pass a signal to operational command. On 11 June 1944, Hut 3 would release the full decoded message after checking. The content was of great interest, as it showed the enemy requesting data appertaining to XLVII Panzer Corps and the Seventh Army. The implication was that the Panzer corps was mobilising to the area of battle nearby. This was further complicated by reports that Seine crossings, 20km north of Paris, were destroyed. This could only mean that the Panzer corps would have to use road and rail links north of Paris to mobilise. This information was passed to commanders and Allied bomber command was then able to target key rail centres and crossings in the area. This did not happen overnight, of course, but time was certainly of importance in order to have the maximum disruptive effect on the enemy, and slow them down before they could attack the Allied armies. One should appreciate that the logistics of the pre-battle period, i.e., the build-up, was as important as the battle itself, as one relied on fuel, armaments, ammunition, medical supplies and food in great quantities, and on both sides. For the Allies, these supplies had to come via the sea, from England, via the Mulberry harbours, on a continuous basis. Once ashore, they had to be transported up to the front line, and to reserve positions. Not so easy when you are under fire from the enemy transporting those supplies. Air superiority of the Allies, however, also played a significant part in the outcome.

Significance: An example of how breaking Enigma messages was just as important and critical after D-Day as before it. As a concession, Bletchley Park had a Y-station on site for the D-Day operation, even though the aerials were probably conspicuous from the air. This may have saved some valuable time in reception of enemy encoded messages. Furthermore, the Lorenz encoding teleprinter was being used simultaneously by Hitler and his generals for German high command messages, and Bletchley would utilise both Robinson and Colossus machines to tackle those. Two very different but parallel encoding/decoding systems.

Garbo misleads the enemy via a message on D-Day (1944)

Double agent 'Garbo' (real name Pujol Garcia) was based in north-west London in a residential house and monitored by his MI5 handler. He was given special permission to contact the Nazis early on the morning of D-Day with the authority of the Supreme Allied Commander, General Eisenhower. It would be risky, and with extremely high stakes if things backfired, but Garbo sent a message to his contact in Madrid, which was encoded by Enigma and subsequently forwarded to Berlin. Garbo had to convince the enemy that from activity seen by him and his agents, it was clear that a major operation was commencing with many ships and craft leaving England. He was also indicating that a substantial force, FUSAG,[62] headed by General Patton, remained in England awaiting to cross the Channel. The ploy was to convince the enemy to keep much of its Panzer divisions in northern France near Calais, awaiting an invasion across the Pas-de-Calais, which would never come. Agent Garbo had gained the trust of his opposite number, and had fed the Germans intelligence that had elements of fact attached in small amounts, but the bulk of his information was fictitious. Even his network of agents under him was an illusion, and did not exist. His message was not initially responded to by the Germans due to the radio receiver not being manned until early the next morning, and he complained vigorously, stating that he was risking his life to provide this information and intelligence. Garbo would then receive a profuse apology and they thanked him for his efforts. It was some time before a reply would be forthcoming. Both Bletchley Park and Knockholt were waiting to see if the Tunny advanced message for German Field Marshal von Rundstedt would be forthcoming over the airwaves. If so, what would those instructions be from Berlin? The Allies needed to know if the Germans had fallen for the trap, and for Garbo's story. Garbo was but a pawn in this situation, albeit an important one and trusted by the enemy.

Significance: Deception as a strategy is not always practically possible in wartime, but when it works it can have profound consequences for both sides. What surprised the Allies was just how successful this one was, and how much time it bought them after the D-Day landings.[63]

Operational Bombe machines at end of 1944

According to Bletchley Park text, there were 192 Bombe machines operational by December 1944.[64] Of course, there would also be the more advanced codebreaking machines to supplement these, notably Robinson and Colossus. The Bombes would concentrate on the much more widely used Enigma encoding Nazi machines.

Significance: The majority of Bombes would be available operationally to the Allies several months after D-Day. Enigma was being used on a daily basis by the enemy as a principal method of military communication. Dual systems with non-Morse traffic would have to be resourced and managed by the Allies.

Meeting of trio of world leaders in Yalta (1945)

In February 1945, the three Allied powers represented by their leaders, Churchill, Roosevelt and Stalin, met in Yalta, in the Crimea. This meeting looked at the occupation of Germany post-war, the split or apportionment of Germany, Austria, Poland, and other countries to obtain agreements in the 'slicing of the cake' of Europe.[65] The conference was monitored by Turkish spies, who were intercepting the Russian signals. These were also being intercepted by Hungarian intelligence, and then reached Berlin. Some German generals refused to accept or believe the decrypted information.

Significance: Carving up the spoils of war was one of the points of discussion at this conference. Poland was not represented, and would have been disturbed at what was being suggested in respect of Polish land being transferred and made available to the Russians.

President Roosevelt dies (1945)

The death of President Franklin D. Roosevelt of a cerebral haemorrhage on 12 April 1945 was a shock to the American nation. This was still wartime and a new leader had to be found, who would be Harry Truman. Truman would become America's thirty-third president. Churchill dealt with both men during the war and maintained the important alliance between Britain and the United States. Truman continued to liaise with Churchill on both political and strategic issues. They communicated across the Atlantic using new technology with a special machine encoding and decoding their speech conversation in the basement of Selfridges department store in London.

Significance: Although Roosevelt had been ill for some time, his death was still sudden and a shock for the nation. Churchill would have to deal with a new President in his strategic and political discussions on the war, and in post-war plans.

TICOM informed of Russian Fish intelligence (1945)

TICOM, the British, and later joint-British–American, committee, had received a stroke of luck in May 1945 when they obtained information that Russian Fish communication equipment, signals intelligence and secret documentation had been discovered, based upon reports by a captured German prisoner of war. Several tons of such Nazi specialist wide-band receiving equipment were located and removed for analysis and study. Machines were then reassembled and operated successfully.

EVENTS

Significance: This indicated that the Germans were intercepting and deciphering Russian intelligence, and clearly had some insight as to their military planning. This was at the latter stage of the war, but it showed that the Germans could intercept and decipher teleprinter-based advanced encoded messages with their equipment. This surprised the Allies and TICOM.

Efficiency of codebreaking Bombes operationally reaches a peak

The efficiency of utilising the codebreaking Bombes during the war may have varied from year to year, but overall, and based on 'Jobs up', or data runs on Bombes that were confirmed to be successful by Bletchley Park, of the total jobs tackled, the efficiency amounted to some 97.6 per cent. This must be seen as an extraordinary high record in wartime. Of course, the efficiency measured as a whole was dependent upon various factors, and not just the input of Bletchley Park:

(a) The quality control at BTM in building the machines and coordinating production via chief engineer, H. Keen.
(b) The RAF engineers maintaining the machines on site.
(c) The Wrens setting them up, plugging the cables in and running the jobs on shifts, 24/7 and 365 days a year.
(d) The 6812th US Signals engineers working at Outstation Eastcote on a total of ten Bombe machines.
(e) The codebreakers at Bletchley Park establishing the Menus for the operators at the outstations and at Bletchley Park.
(f) Those maintaining the power supplies to the machines in wartime irrespective of the air attacks and bombing raids across the country.
(g) The personnel in subsidiary factories making and assembling Bombe components for BTM, such as at Spirella in Letchworth.
(h) The Typex operators at Bletchley Park, being mostly female personnel, who took the output settings from the Bombe rotor wheel runs, and fed them into the Typex machine, and entered the encoded messages to be decoded.

One can see from the above that it truly was a team effort.

Significance: A high efficiency rate indicates that training of tasks related to this work was also efficient, conveyed with the minimum of fuss, correctly applied, and consistent across the Wrens, the RAF engineers, the 6812th US Signals engineers, the Bletchley codebreakers, and other associated personnel. Everyone knew their job, the limits of their role, and while they may not have been permitted to know what others were up to in the chain of the operation, to a large degree that did not seem to matter. It was, in effect, a production line, similar to working on a factory floor, but with varied and different skills to be applied at different stages. Initially, the rules were made up as the process was developed, but soon became formalised with instruction manuals and so forth.

Jewish personnel involved in codebreaking and intelligence

Over a period during the war, a good number of Jewish people would support Bletchley Park and other organisations against Nazi oppression. They would take on a variety of different tasks and roles. This included Jack Good, a famous codebreaker at Bletchley, with the real name *Isidore Jacob Gudak*. Within the 'Newmanry' at Bletchley, Max Newman would be in charge of this specialist division, utilising machines to help crack the advanced German Lorenz and other teleprinter attachments. There are too many to list here, but sufficient to say a substantial quantity of personnel had a Jewish heritage and background. Codebreaking and support of this area was just one way of getting back at the Nazis, who were carrying out outrageous activities back in Europe, with genocide being their objective. While the religious background of people may seem to be almost irrelevant to some readers on the topic of codebreaking and intelligence, the active involvement of this group of people who were being targeted specifically back in Germany and elsewhere, with various levels of skills, ability and innovation, would help the Allies crush the enemy, and would save lives. The Jewish Virtual library has much more detail on this subject, worth studying. Those with families and links back to these brave Jewish people who were active during wartime should be very proud of their heritage. The author of this glossary considers it wholly appropriate to insert reference to the Jewish contribution in codebreaking, particularly given the horrific nature of the Holocaust and attempted destruction of the Jewish race by Hitler. The Jewish people contributed significantly to the eventual defeat of Hitler and Germany, along with the Allies.

Significance: A wide range of Jewish people would contribute greatly to the Allied war effort in helping to defeat Hitler. Hitler would have been enraged that Jews were in a position to disrupt and help dismantle the Third Reich using their many skills, both men and women.

Fish communication links after D-Day (1944)

There would be continued attacks on the Fish communication links by Bletchley Park after D-Day as intelligence for the commanders in France would be essential to understand the build-up and organisation of enemy Panzer divisions, etc. But the success rate was quite variable and we set out below (courtesy of Dr David Kenyon of Bletchley Park) the statistics in achieving the Fish communication decodes of daily cipher keys:

Post 17 June 1944 'Jellyfish' link – One key broken in June
July 1944 'Jellyfish' link – Three keys broken in July
August 1944 'Jellyfish' link – Five keys broken in August
July 1944 'Bream' link (Italian) – Six keys broken in July
August 1944 'Bream' link (Italian) – Five keys broken in August

Success rate:

> 3.1 per cent of Fish intercepted messages in June 1944
> 1.9 per cent of Fish intercepted messages in July 1944
> 1.8 per cent of Fish intercepted messages in August 1944
> Decrypted characters increased to 2.1 million in July and August 1944.[66]

Of course, breaking a daily key meant that intercepted messages for that day could largely be decoded, and the number of actual enemy messages would vary. Even single broken message on a Fish link gave the Allies a snapshot of communication between the German high command, or the Italian equivalent.

Significance: Although the Allies had the Colossus Mark 2 machine at Bletchley Park just before D-Day, the team still had to work hard to break the Lorenz and the 'secret writer' daily keys. It was a two-pronged attack, partly by codebreaking machine and partly with mathematicians in the Testery section at Bletchley. As time went on, with the Allies punching through France and other countries, more sources of intelligence would add to the overall picture, including interrogating German prisoners of war and local tactical wireless interception. These all were useful sources for the commanders as to what the enemies' resources were at any given time, and their military strength.

VE day (1945)

The coming of Victory in Europe Day, with the German surrender, could not come quickly enough. The date was 8 May 1945, and there would be considerable celebration across the British nation. There was also the realisation that a war was still in full swing in the east, with British, American and Commonwealth forces still fighting the Japanese. A transfer of Wrens and military personnel to listening stations and codebreaking bases in the east helped to tighten the noose on Japan and its allies. The men and women transferred had to cope with high ambient temperatures and humidity, also tropical storms, which played havoc with some of the radio equipment and wiring cables. Many had never left Britain before, so they needed to adapt to their new surroundings quickly. Some were also transferred from Africa and parts of the Mediterranean area. The codebreaking needed to intercept Japanese radio messages and decode 'Purple', which was the enemy encoding machine that the Americans and British eventually cracked with their skilled personnel and methods. The Americans had a nickname for the intelligence that came from 'Purple', referring to it as 'Magic'.

Significance: VE day was a time for celebration in Europe, but the start of a lengthy process to find missing persons, record the dead and wounded, provide infrastructure to allow food, fuel, medical supplies and materials to be transported and distributed, and to record the horrors of the Holocaust, with a view to finding those responsible and bringing them to justice.

VJ day and end of the Second World War (1945)

Victory over Japan day was recorded as 15 August 1945, being the day after the official Japanese surrender. By then, the Japanese encoding system had been broken and intelligence was routinely being obtained through radio intercepts on troop movements, supplies, and much other valuable information. Those at listening stations in Ceylon and elsewhere could start to demobilise and come home after years of war and turmoil. This included many Wrens who had been in the east for some years, and others transferred from Britain after VE day. Some would use their new skills to go into commercial industry, such as the manufacture of radio, electronic and test equipment. Others might teach Morse code in the military or set up post-war listening posts, preparing for the Cold War that would soon exist with Russia as the enemy. Valves would soon be replaced by modern transistors, and a whole team of electronics engineers would be required to understand them and apply them to the modern world. A small handful of Japanese soldiers deep in the jungle and forests would not be aware of the surrender to the Allies. Some would remain hidden for years before being made aware of their defeat.

Significance: This was the official end of the Second World War, with all hostilities ceasing, aided by the use of nuclear bombs in Japan at Nagasaki and Hiroshima. This would change the world and start the race for nuclear arms across nations.

Final Bombe count at Eastcote at end of the war (1945)

Calculation of the final quantities of codebreaking Bombes at Outstation Eastcote, the largest outstation, is tricky. This is because there was considerable movement of several Bombe machines back and forth between Outstation Stanmore and the Letchworth factory at BTM. However, from studying the official Bombe registers on loan at the National Archives, the author has established that at the end of the war there were 103 Bombes at Eastcote, by far the largest number of all the outstations, and considerably more than at Bletchley Park. From inspection of the registers, some Bombes did get transferred to Stanmore from Eastcote and it is possible that more than 103 Bombes may have existed for a very short time, but the final number is 103. Stanmore had seventy-six Bombes, although some reports have stated previously that forty-nine were operational. That is not the view of the author, or at least there may have been forty-nine Bombes operational at one time, but many more came online soon after. Adding the total Bombes at Stanmore and Eastcote at war end, there was a total of 179 Bombes at the two largest outstations, representing some 84.8 per cent of the 211 built at BTM. While these were mainly used for data processing, they did contribute greatly in assisting Bletchley experts to arrive at the solutions of decrypting thousands of enemy messages.

The number of WRNS personnel was roughly proportionate to the quantities of Bombes at the outstations, allowing for round-the-clock shift work and miscellaneous other duties. At Eastcote, the ratio for staffing the Bombe machines operationally worked out approximately at between seven or eight Wrens per Bombe machine overall. At Stanmore, it was around eight Wrens for each Bombe overall. Three separate shifts would make up the twenty-four-hour outstation Bombe rota. American US signals engineers at Eastcote who arrived later in the war also helped to operate up to ten of the machines for a fixed period. However, the Wrens would have been involved in training these men. The Wrens would all be part of the Royal Navy, working at shore-based naval bases. The 'Special X' duties would come under HMS *Pembroke* V for the Wrens. The coordination and liaison between the outstations and Bletchley Park as HQ appeared to work, on the whole, extraordinarily well. This is even more remarkable considering that the vast majority of Wrens would have no idea of the role of Bletchley Park, or even of the existence of Enigma. That was allowed only to a privileged few.

Significance: The statistics given are merely the distribution of the Bombe machines and the personnel needed to operate them. However, they are important as they give an indication of the scale of the operation of codebreaking, linking into the codebreaking function of Bletchley Park and also the Y-stations, which collected the Morse code intercepts as part of the first stage of the process. It could not have been easy to manage the logistics of building the Bombe machines, maintaining quality control, distributing, maintaining, and staffing them with skilled and semi-skilled personnel.

Total codebreaking Bombe quantities by end of the war (mid-1945)

We provide a table of the Bombe machine quantities, and the US Bombes are included in the last row as a comparison, being based on four-wheel Enigmas:

Early three-wheel Enigma Bombes	73
Four-wheel Bombes (BTM/H.S. Keen)	57
Four-wheel Bombes (GPO/BTM) Cobra	12
Later three-wheel Bombes with high-speed, Siemens-type relays incorporated	69
Sub-total British Bombes	211
United States four-wheel Bombes	121*
Grand total Bombes (British and US)	**332**

* NB Some reports indicate this number was higher at 145 US machines, but this cannot be substantiated by the author.

In terms of allocation of operational staff to set up, monitor and operate the Bombe codebreaking machines, as an example at Outstation Eastcote, there would be between eight and ten Wrens per machine allowing for the shift work around the clock and that Wrens tended to work in pairs, checking each other's work. Based on eight Wrens per machine, and three shifts per day, plus personnel off on leave and allowing for sickness, and operational cover, we have 103 machines × eight persons average per machine, which gives 824 operational personnel total. This is very close to the 800 Wrens reported to have been at Outstation Eastcote, plus administrative staff.[67]

Significance: The statistics are of general interest to illustrate that different types of Bombe machines were used in codebreaking. Some of these were evolving from experimentation at BTM and PORES, as well as other sites, aided by Wynn-Williams of TRE and H. Keen of BTM. The Bombes with Siemens-type relays were utilising copies of the excellent German Siemens relays, and much more efficient than those produced by Britain during the war.[68]

Milner-Barry writes to thank US Signals detachments (1945)

On 10 May 1945 codebreaker Milner-Barry at Bletchley Park wrote to the US signals detachment commanders and thanked them for their contribution and that of their skilled personnel during the war in cryptographic and support roles in England.

Significance: Despite some trepidation initially upon their arrival in England, Bletchley Park and other locations found the US signals (6811th, 6812th, and 6813th) detachments to be extremely valuable to the British war effort. The apprenticeship and training was taken on board without question, and they applied themselves to the tasks efficiently. Bletchley Park codebreakers and management were pleasantly surprised, as were those at Outstation Eastcote where Bombe machines were allocated to the 6812th US Signals, trained by WRNS personnel.

Churchill orders destruction of codebreaking machines post-war (1945)

Churchill was fearful of the Russians accessing the British codebreaking machines after the war ended in Europe. Consequently, he gave instructions before he lost power in that summer's General Election for all codebreaking machines to be dismantled and destroyed. The Wrens and some of the others who had been involved with the machines were tasked with the dismantling process. One Wren commented that she and others would playfully roll the Bombe rotor drums across the floor as if they were playing skittles, and was sad to have these machines dismantled. Wrens and RAF technicians had previously spent thousands of hours attending to the Bombe machines to ensure they operated correctly to give a useful output, but now times were very different post-war.

Not all the machines, however, were dismantled, and around fifty Bombes were retained at Outstation Eastcote. Of these, sixteen were retained for operational use. It is thought they were used to monitor intelligence from central Europe in case there was a Nazi resurgence from diehards. Used in an experimental capacity at Eastcote in secrecy, they would eventually be transferred to GCHQ at Cheltenham by the mid-1950s and were dismantled and destroyed by the 1960s. The remaining

Bombes were also be dismantled after a time. All machines were dismantled post-war in stages, and none remain today, only replicas at the National Museum of Computing at Bletchley (TNMOC).

Two Colossus machines were sent from Bletchley Park to Eastcote, coded Red and Blue. Eventually the Colossus machines were sent to GCHQ at Cheltenham before being destroyed later, by the 1960s. Even drawings and blueprints had to be destroyed, and codebreakers and engineers at Bletchley and elsewhere remembered putting machine blueprints into furnaces and boilers to watch many years of hard work burn to a cinder. Perhaps it was premature of Churchill to order the destruction of important codebreaking equipment? New machines and techniques would be required for the modern world with the introduction of solid-state components and computers. Would the Russians have accessed the codebreaking technology from the British if it was available? Probably. However, in hindsight, Churchill's instructions to dismantle codebreaking machines were probably ill-advised. Russia would be acquiring Nazi Lorenz machines and advanced secret writers as they swept into Germany as it was defeated. Being able to decode their messages would be of great interest to the Allies. There would be limited clues as to the design and construction of complex machines such as Colossus to build a working replica many years later, but incredibly this was achieved in the mid-2000s, headed by a team of volunteers and Tony Sale at Bletchley.

Significance: Churchill's fear of the Russians gaining access to the British codebreaking machines and systems was perhaps based on paranoia. It would possibly be argued later that the machines could have been retained and secured, with little risk to the Allies of Russian intervention. Others may have concluded that destruction of the codebreaking machines set Britain back in terms of competition with the USA and others. The Official Secrets Act became a burden as much as a benefit to the nation.

Bombes retained at Eastcote (1945/46)

In spite of Churchill's instructions after the war to dismantle and destroy all the codebreaking machines and burn all the drawings, some would escape destruction, at least for a time. Around fifty Bombes were retained at Eastcote after the war, and of these sixteen were kept running and operational for a time. The rest were mothballed. Eventually these were all dismantled and destroyed.[69]

Significance: There was some disagreement that all codebreaking machines should be dismantled and destroyed after the war. Churchill would not have been informed that some machines escaped destruction at Eastcote. He would lose the next general election and be out of power, this being a complete surprise to him.

Cantab dinner at BTM (1945)

Philpotts, the BTM Chief Executive, decided to hold a special celebratory dinner for staff who worked on the Bombe machines after the war ended. The menus had

'CANTAB' as a heading, the code name for the Bombe design and production. It was arguable whether such a display of information breached the Official Secrets Act, as it still applied after the war. It was Philpott's way of thanking his engineers and staff for their efforts in making the Bombe machines such a success. The assembly of parts in different locations across Letchworth in Hertfordshire and surrounding villages, bringing them together as sub-assemblies and installing them on to large, manufactured, bronze-coloured frames was no easy task, with more than 200 machines made and delivered to Bletchley Park and the five codebreaking outstations. BTM would go on to bigger things in a post-war world, with a historical wartime track record to be proud of.

Significance: A celebratory dinner at BTM, for staff and management, celebrating the achievements in building the Bombe codebreaking machines and maintaining them, improving, and distributing them. It is difficult to understand how much Chief Engineer Keen knew at the time, just after the war had ended, as to how significant the Bombes had been in assisting the Allies.

America and the race to build the first digital computer

Due to the Official Secrets Act in Britain, it was not possible to state that Colossus was designed and built as the first semi-programmable computer. America would accelerate its electronics technology post-war, using solid state devices, and build an industry to dominate the world, with Japan and China close behind. This caused a great deal of frustration for Alan Turing and engineer Tommy Flowers. Flowers did go on to develop the Premium Bond random number generator, ERNIE, but that was little consolation for his remarkable achievements in designing and building Colossus. ENIAC would become the USA's first programmable computer in 1945, but not the first computer overall, as Colossus was available to be used in codebreaking in 1944. (The Mark 2 was available just prior to D-Day in June 1944.) ENIAC stood for Electronic Numerical Integrator and Computer. It would possibly be the first general-purpose digital computer. However, it was financed by the American Army and associated support organisations, and used principally for processing military calculation problems that needed vast processing power. ENIAC was used for ballistics calculations as well as hydrogen bomb calculations. It was considerably faster than electro-mechanical machines. The debate on who was really first in terms of designing and building the digital computer will be ongoing, as Colossus was only semi-programmable, but ENIAC was one step ahead and could be fully programmed more effectively. The early computers would still use thousands of vacuum tubes or valves, before the invention of the transistor at the end of 1947. The transistor would reduce the heat output compared with valves and improve reliability of the equipment.

Significance: The race to be first is usually a healthy form of competition between nations. However, those who are successful can also have an impact on the economy of their country in a positive way. This may also influence their competitors in reducing their market share due to them being late in marketing new technology. The Official Secrets Act in Britain appeared to tie the hands of many innovators and inventors in order to protect the state. The United States did not have quite the same restrictions, and would capitalise on this fact.

Turing goes to work at NPL (1945)

The National Physical Laboratory, which developed various innovative technological solutions and inventions was in Teddington, south London, and was established in 1900. A Government-funded research laboratory, it concentrated on physics and scientific research by a team of scientists. Alan Turing joined the staff of NPL in 1945 as a temporary senior scientific officer. NPL would later introduce and develop advances such as 'Data packet switching', which is used as the basis for the internet and modern computers today. Donald Davies developed this packet switching technology, joining NPL in 1947, and he was briefly an assistant to Turing. Turing would produce a paper on his ACE computer and work on the development of ACE until he left in 1948. This was shortly before he published his paper on Intelligent Machinery in 1950. 'Computing Machinery and Intelligence' would set out the 'Turing test' for intelligence. Today, the NPL has expanded its research programme into biosciences, environmental science, acoustics, quantum technologies, ionising radiation, medical physics, time and frequency, and others.

Significance: NPL would be an opportunity for Turing post-war and he continued to write technical papers. However, Turing became frustrated at his lack of freedom there to pursue his projects.

Establishment of the Eastcote Association (Post-war)

Post-war, Eastcote had many ex-employees who may have prepared, operated, or maintained codebreaking machines, or worked in a support role. The Eastcote Association was a social club to allow those people involved at the site during wartime to come together and share experiences. There would be poems written, plays performed, sometimes for local children, and an opportunity to talk about those darker days during wartime. An association news journal was also published. It is important to state that as their employment at the outstation was still under the Official Secrets Act, care had to be taken by individuals in talking of matters that might otherwise affect national security, including some of the procedures operated at the outstation. The Eastcote Association was disbanded after a time, probably due to dwindling numbers. Many who had worked there were scattered around the UK and even abroad post-war. Those who were Wrens or demobbed Wrens may have later joined the Association of Wrens to keep in contact with colleagues, but not all did.

Significance: A club of mainly ex-military personnel who had worked at Outstation Eastcote during wartime, and who wished to keep in touch with each other.

No evidence of the organisation is held within Eastcote as far as one can tell, but Bletchley Park has some documents and examples of its reports.

Post-war cynicism about Enigma and Lorenz weaknesses

After the war ended, it was still difficult to speak about the Bombe, Robinson and Colossus machines and the process at Bletchley Park to decode enemy messages. This was largely because the Official Secrets Act still applied for a considerable time after the war. It was only later, in the mid-1970s, when there had been some relaxation and declassification, that British codebreakers could tell some of the story to German officers and personnel about the weaknesses of Enigma and Lorenz. They could reveal that the British had built a machine, the Bombe, to decode the message settings of Enigma, and were successful in reading Nazi messages on a frequent basis across the services, and even the German Secret Service, the Abwehr. This met disbelief by some, both ex-Nazis and civilians who could not grasp the fact that the Allies had a system in place and machines to make Enigma impotent during wartime. Of course, it was not quite so easy as this, as there were long periods when Bletchley Park codebreakers failed to crack Enigma messages. Lorenz was only declassified a few years ago, and the Colossus and Tunny systems were seen as far more advanced than the Bombe machine designed to crack Enigma. Germany was under a false illusion that their encoding machines and systems were unbreakable. Perhaps the biggest shock was that Lorenz and the S40/S42 machines could be neutralised by the Allies with a combination of codebreaking machines and manual methods, almost like a production line in operation. Hitler's orders to commanders and generals on high command Fish communication links were read at Bletchley Park with some ease once Colossus had been made operational. There would always be some who would not believe this happened, and that it was nothing more than Allied propaganda.

Significance: Former Nazis may have not believed the possibility that the Allies had broken not only Enigma, but also Lorenz, and the secret writers which Hitler relied upon for his high command communication. They would need proof but it would have been a criminal offence to show them any at the time.

Bletchley Park closes post-war (1946)

After the war ended in 1945, it was not long before a new base for the development of GC&CS was established, in April 1946, at GCHQ Eastcote, Middlesex. Churchill's instructions to destroy and dismantle the codebreaking machines was implemented to a degree, although some machines were kept back and retained at Eastcote. Bletchley Park closed its gates and it was the end of an era. However, the importance of the site can be appreciated with the development of GCHQ over time, becoming the modern version of the Government Code and Cipher School. There are reports that the gates were locked at Bletchley by Denniston's assistant, Barbara

Abernethy, and the keys taken down to Eastcote, which would become GCHQ in April 1946. Bletchley would later be used for technical training on telecoms and associated training of personnel, before being established as a trust and a museum. The author has met several BT engineers who were trained at Bletchley Park or on various training courses. By the time that Bletchley had closed there would be in excess of twenty huts spread across the large site.

Significance: The end of an era in British codebreaking during wartime, and the start of a new period in east–west relations that then ignored that they were once allies. A reminder how quickly both politics and alliances can change in world history. Your friend one minute can quickly become your enemy the next. An example of this was Hitler's attack on Russia, Operation Barbarossa, him having previously signed a non-aggression pact with Stalin.

GCHQ Eastcote established (1946)

After the war ended and there was a period of reflection and re-evaluation for the organisations involved, it was decided that GC&CS should be relocated elsewhere than Bletchley Park and become the new GCHQ, or Government Communications Headquarters. This was established formally on 1 April 1946 at the old Outstation Eastcote base. It remained there for between six and eight years, when it relocated again to Cheltenham, the current home of GCHQ in Gloucestershire.

Barclays Bank in Eastcote set up a bank account for GCHQ Eastcote[70] but the public were not permitted to know what went on at the site. It was the early days of the Cold War, with plenty of threats and challenges to address, and intelligence to recover, monitor, and to decode. There were several codebreaking machines on site but the use of these was still classified. The Venona project to identify security breaches by intelligence agencies was one of the tasks for research at GCHQ Eastcote post-war, on an international scale. Modifications of Blocks 3 and 4 at Eastcote and further construction was carried out in 1947 for use by GCHQ. The Crown purchased the site in 1947, with occupants including the Post Office. The Americans also had a presence post-war, including a school on site for servicemen's children.[71]

Significance: A stage in the long journey to develop GCHQ to what it is now in the twenty-first century. Few would have known about Eastcote becoming GCHQ after the war ended. Even fewer people knew what GCHQ stood for or what its aims and objectives were, unless they were employed there, or perhaps at a senior level within the NSA, the American equivalent organisation.

Creation of UKUSA agreement (1946)

The UKUSA agreement was one of cooperation and sharing of key security and signals intelligence between nations and allies. It also included Australia, Canada, and New Zealand, so was considered as a multilateral agreement. It was officially signed on 5 March 1946 and evolved from earlier treaties and agreements, including the 1943 BRUSA agreement that Bletchley Park became involved in during wartime. While these were the principal countries sharing intelligence, associate members would include West Germany, Sweden and others. This would form the basis of common cooperation across allied nations in years to come.

Significance: An agreement that had evolved from earlier cooperation between Britain and the USA, and be built on with other nations in the post-war period.

Turing visits Eastcote as a consultant (1946)

Some reports indicate that Turing visited Eastcote GCHQ after the war as a consultant for a time. Eastcote had previously existed as the largest codebreaking outstation during the war. It is not known the dates that he was at GCHQ Eastcote. However, his ex-fiancée, Joan Clarke, also spent some time there post-war, as did Mavis Batey, a codebreaker under Dilwyn Knox at Bletchley. Other Bletchley codebreakers who moved to GCHQ Eastcote included Hugh Alexander and Hugh Foss.

Significance: While little is recorded on this matter, several famous persons from Bletchley Park did visit Eastcote, and added to the 'magic dust' that the Eastcote site had needed to make a difference in wartime and later in post-war Britain. Apart from Turing, one could argue one of the most remarkable people who went here was Tommy Flowers, the designer and builder of the Colossus codebreaking machine.

American presence at Eastcote post-war increases (1946 onwards)

The influx of Americans at Outstation Eastcote and post-war increased substantially. On the base there would be US Marines and US Army personnel, and a servicemen's children's school. They would have the Signals Intelligence Service, the Armed Forces Security Agency and the Special Cryptographic Advisory Group, or SCAG. The US Navy would be in Blocks 1 and 4. In 1974, Block 1 would be for the US Marines and would have to 100 men. Locals would witness many Americans wandering on Eastcote's high street and marching in Ruislip Woods and the vicinity. The evolution of the site via a codebreaking outstation, then into GCHQ into 1946, and later into RAF Eastcote, would be a metamorphosis of varied activities and supported via Britain's American allies. Some personnel would provide security duties for staff at the American Embassy in London.

Significance: It is important to recognise the history of the site and area around Eastcote, not only during the Second World War, but post-war as well. The close relationship with America during wartime as allies made such post-war links comfortable, and indeed advantageous for Britain and its Government.

EVENTS

Turing designs the ACE computer (1947)

Alan Turing designed the ACE computer, or Automatic Computing Engine, post-war. A pilot test machine was built at the National Physical Laboratory in Teddington in 1947. Turing's design was different to others but his logic approach was so different that his colleagues wanted to build a test machine first before committing to the project, which Turing was not impressed by.

Significance: The ACE computer would be another step forward in the development of computers. There would be disagreements as to how to proceed, which caused Turing frustration.

Crown purchases the Eastcote site (1947)

The Crown purchased Eastcote in 1947, enabling a variety of tenants to occupy the sites under various contractual lease agreements. These tenants included the Post Office, using Block 3. Americans would maintain a presence on the site for a good number of years, some providing support for the American Embassy in London. GCHQ would use Block 2 and some spurs in Block 3 prior to their relocation elsewhere in 1954. The Property Services Agency was on site in the 1970s and '80s. A US services school for children of American military personnel was established there during the 1950s. The site became extremely active and diverse over time. A dental clinic, veterinary clinic, mental health support, and a morgue would be necessary. The morgue was apparently used as an intermediate stop for fallen American personnel who had died in Europe prior to being flown home back to the USA for burial, and with their families receiving them.

The Census office would be based at Eastcote, transferred from Osterley. The Board of Trade also had a presence, and staff numbers increased significantly. Eastcote became crowded, even though it was a large site.

Significance: The acquisition of the site by Crown Properties may have oiled the wheels to allow closer ties with other agencies post-war. The engineering arm of the Post Office had provided a limited degree of support to Outstation Eastcote during wartime; after all, they were not that far away, at Dollis Hill. Now, post-war, the priorities had changed. The Americans on the base demonstrated the close relationship with Britain as allies and friends. This was even more important during the sensitive Cold War period.

Venona project established post-war by the West (1948)

The penetration of Western security services and government agencies post-war was an unpleasant surprise and needed urgent action to establish the damage that had been done by the Russians, and whether it was ongoing or not. Bletchley Park managers such as Commander Travis suspected Russia would be looking to conquer territory, both during and after the Second World War. Churchill was also not naïve in this respect. The origins of this security weakness had started during the war. So secret was Western intelligence project *Venona*, exposing the intelligence breaches of the West by the East, that initially presidents and prime ministers were not even permitted to access the confidential reports. In February 1943 the US Army's Signal Intelligence Service at Arlington Hall in Virginia made a pilot study of Soviet cryptographic work intercepted between the Soviet Foreign Ministry in Moscow and abroad. The key person engaged in this work and who made important discoveries in analysing Russian intelligence during wartime was Lieutenant Richard Hallock. His findings were of monumental importance, and would provide data that would be decrypted over several months and years. Five separate organisations were involved:

- Diplomats in countries within the Soviet embassy and consular business.
- Trade representatives including the Purchasing Commission.
- MGB (later becoming the KGB), being the Soviet espionage agency with Moscow, and with stations abroad.
- GRU – The Soviet Army General Staff Chief Intelligence residencies and attachés abroad.
- GRU Naval – being the Soviet Naval Intelligence Staff.

GC&CS, and later GCHQ, would become involved in assisting to recover intelligence relevant to the above, particularly after 1946. By 1948, there would be a leak of documents from Canberra, Australia, from the Russian embassy and diplomatic service. A formal team was then set up at GCHQ by 1950 to report on decrypted material recovered, and to investigate past messages during the latter stages of the war. The cover name 'Brie' was given to the operation, then later, 'Drug', and finally Venona. The parties worked closely together, and funding became available to resource the team working on the analysis of encrypted messages going back for some time. Joint UK–US reports to UK authorities consisted of translations of decrypted messages via the Soviet Foreign Ministry and abroad. The diplomatic and trade messages were also of interest. Some of the messages translated and decrypted are now held in the files at the National Archives. The first release of intercepted messages includes:

- MGB (i.e., later KGB), GRU and GRU Naval messages including destinations.
- MGB messages, to and from Canberra.
- MGB messages passing between Moscow, New York, Washington, and Mexico City.
- GRU messages passing between Moscow and New York.

A second release of documents included remaining MGB and GRU locations in the Americas, plus some messages between Ministries of Foreign Affairs and Foreign Trade. Some reports of particular interest went back to 1940–42. Historical intelligence was therefore still relevant in the context of the modern post-war world. Cover names used by the Russians were incorporated within messages, and we list below a few examples of interest:

> President Roosevelt – Kapitan
> Winston Churchill – Boar (MGB cover name)
> Great Britain – The Colony (GRU)
> Manhattan Project atomic bomb – Enormoz
> Guy Burgess – Hicks [A spy in Britain working for the Russians]
> Donald Maclean – Gomer [A spy in Britain working for the Russians]

That the Russians had intelligence of the Manhattan project via their spies and agents in America helped them on their way to achieving nuclear supremacy, or at least a formidable world nuclear power, which was their ultimate goal.[72]

Significance: The Canberra intercepts of Russian intelligence would result in a significant increase in activity in Western security agencies, and this included a Venona project team at GCHQ in Eastcote. Selected historical intercepted decoded Russian messages during wartime were of interest to the security agencies to help put the jigsaw together. Russian influence, security monitoring and espionage were threats to the USA, the UK, and Western allies. The fact that Russia had been one of the west's allies was now only history, and the rules had changed quickly post-war.

Russia changes its codes and ciphers post-war, blocking out the West (1948)

For some considerable time after the Second World War, the West had been struggling to intercept Russian encoded transmissions and decode them. However, post-war, at a time termed 'Black Friday', suddenly the intelligence agencies drew a complete blank as Russia changed its systems. The date was Friday, 28 October 1948. This action was triggered by agents and spies, who tipped the Russians off as to their potential exposure to Western powers accessing their intelligence communications. It was of significant concern at the time, as it was the Cold War where neither side, both nuclear powers, trusted each other. Each country needed intelligence as to whether the other side was getting prepared for a nuclear attack. As the Second World War came to an end, the Russians most likely acquired abandoned Nazi teleprinter attachments based on the Lorenz S40 and S42 models. They tried to use these to send and receive messages, not realising that the British and others in the West had the potential capability and machines to decode their messages once intercepted over the airwaves. To which degree, and for what duration this was successful by the Western allies, is unclear, and it became significantly more difficult to make progress as the Soviets moved away from the Lorenz encoding systems to other technology and designs. With the nuclear advancement of both sides, more secure systems would be required. The early 1950s was then considered by some personnel at the CIA in Washington as 'the dark ages for communication intelligence'. Indeed, by 1962, the discovery of Cuban missiles supplied by Russia a few hundreds of miles from the US mainland, was via an American reconnaissance aircraft and *not* by US Army SIGINT intelligence intercepts over the air or via landlines. This was a major weakness for America and its Western allies at the time.

Significance: The golden rule in codebreaking has to be, 'Don't assume that if you can break the enemies' codes and ciphers today, you can do so tomorrow.' Just as the Nazis produced a completely different encoding system to Enigma during wartime, the Russians were looking to throw a curveball to the West and block them out. It was only a matter of time, yet the NSA and the Western intelligence powers were unprepared for it when it happened.

GCHQ transfers to Cheltenham (1952–54)

Between 1952 and 1954 the GCHQ site at Eastcote in Middlesex was transferred to its new home in Cheltenham, Gloucestershire. This was principally because of a lack of space at Eastcote for all the personnel and facilities required. By 1954 the move had largely been completed. The site at Cheltenham would be upgraded later to form the new 'doughnut-shaped' modern building. Eastcote remained for a number of years after the move, for a variety of different uses, some administrative, but maintaining an American military presence until just after the turn of the century. The last contingent was from the US Navy in 2007.

Significance: The commencement of a new era in intelligence gathering and analysis post-war. Few would have realised the process of development and transition to arrive at the Cheltenham site via the earlier years, and the relevance to the predecessor of GCHQ, being GC&CS.

Eastcote GCHQ becomes RAF Eastcote post-war

When Eastcote was considered too small for housing GCHQ in the early 1950s it was decided to relocate it to Cheltenham to the new GCHQ. This process commenced around 1952 and by 1954 was largely complete. Eastcote still had a role to play but in a different capacity, and this included supporting American servicemen and women in operating in Europe, provision of an American school for servicemen's children, work related to several civilian activities, such as Post Office logistics, a morgue, etc. For a while it was designated RAF Eastcote and still maintained as a relatively secure site. The number of Wrens on site would be a tiny fraction of the 800 plus who operated Bombe codebreaking machines in shifts during wartime. Indeed, the Wrens diminished to near zero as they were demobbed after the war ended, sent abroad, or relocated to other WRNS shore-based facilities. This can be evidenced by studying the official Wren officer-based registers, where some were listed as previously belonging to HMS *Pembroke* V or HMS *Pembroke* III.

It is not known how many Wrens remained in the early years of GCHQ to operate the two transferred Colossus machines from Bletchley Park before the machines were sent to Cheltenham and then dismantled. Note that Tommy Flowers attended Eastcote to help assemble and set up the machines with a small contingent from his Post Office Engineering team. There would be some RAF staff and personnel for engineering duties at Eastcote during wartime, but most likely decreased after the war ended. American Marines would be in substantial numbers on the base, so it is perhaps surprising that it was not allocated an American base name. The Eastcote site had a wide range of names and designations over its lifetime until the site was eventually sold for residential development in the early twenty-first century, becoming known as Pembroke Park.

Significance: The metamorphosis of the site at Eastcote during both wartime and post-war was complex. It took on a number of roles, mostly linked to codebreaking, intelligence and support for Bletchley Park and other sites. The transition to RAF Eastcote was but another stage in the timeline. This was the beginning of the end of Eastcote as a military support base, often with American input.

Turing dies a tragic death (1954)

The coroner recorded a verdict of suicide, with Alan Turing taking his own life at a time when he had been condemned for his homosexuality by the authorities and narrowly escaped going to prison. He died officially on 7 June 1954, a few days before what would have been his 42nd birthday, in Wilmslow, Cheshire. This was at a time in history when it was unlawful to be a homosexual. He had been forced to accept chemical castration and it is possibly the stress this caused that contributed to his premature death, when he had so much more to give the world in ideas and technology. Turing, like many others, was not permitted to speak about much of his wartime work at Bletchley Park as it still was classified under the Official Secrets Act. A royal pardon was given to Turing some years later and the injustice was formally recognised. He remained friends with his ex-fiancée, Joan Clarke, a linguist, and codebreaker who worked at Bletchley Park with him during the war. Turing's image is on a modern £50 note as recognition for his contribution to British history. Several properties in London and England have blue plaques to commemorate Turing being there.

Significance: A sad and untimely death, with Turing being alone and not really understood. Turing had so much more to give the world and would have been fascinated with the development of personal computers, smartphones and A.I.

Post-war hybrid decoding machine built and operational (1955)

By 1955, a hybrid decoding machine had been developed combining Colossus and Robinson designs. This would be termed Colorob and be operational for a time. It may have been used at GCHQ Cheltenham. The Australian Government established a signals agency in 1947, The Defence Signals Bureau. It would develop its first computer called Infuse, from the UK's Colorob machine. Many Australian women worked as computer programmers for these early computers.

Significance: A design that utilised two different machines for codebreaking, each with certain advantages and disadvantages. As electronic components became more readily available and reliable in modern times these may have been incorporated in the machine. The hybrid machine was an experiment and stepping stone to better computers.

Two Colossus machines sent to Cheltenham GCHQ (1956)

With the winding down of GCHQ Eastcote, equipment had to be transferred to Cheltenham, the new home of the GCHQ, on a much larger site that would expand considerably in size. Colossus machines Red and Blue, being the last two remaining advanced Colossus codebreaking machines, would be sent to Cheltenham together with other equipment. It is unclear what they were used for at the new GCHQ, but both were dismantled and destroyed in the early 1960s. Eastcote would make way for an Elliot 405 Computer. This was the age of new technology, new machines, and the application of computer programming.

Significance: The transfer of the Colossus machines was the final stage prior to dismantling them a few years later. By 1960 the last Colossus had been dismantled. Other machines and equipment would eventually take their place and be even more advanced. Punched paper tape would be replaced by magnetic tape, and then magnetic drums or discs for storage.

BTM merges with others post-war (1959)

Prime Minister Attlee, and Harold Wilson, were shown a demonstration of a Hollerith machine at a British Industries Fair in May 1950. BTM would become involved in stored programme computers and the Hollerith Electronic Computer, HEC1, would be built in 1951, with HEC2 following in 1953. HEC4 would later be suitable for business data processing. In February 1959, BTM would go on to merge with competitor Powers-Samas Accounting Machines Ltd. The new company arising from it would be International Computers and Tabulators Ltd (ICT). They would employ 16,000 people and assets were valued at £24 million. Later, it would become ICL.[73]

Significance: The expansion and merger of BTM with other competitors would make the new company powerful in a developing market of innovation and new technology. Powers-Samas was once a competitor to BTM in a commercial sense, and a merger with it, was an important stage in the company's history.

EVENTS

Gary Powers' U-2 spy plane shot down by Russians (1960)

The U-2 spy plane was used to fly at extremely high altitudes, far above enemy missile range, until it was eventually intercepted by the Russians as it photographed Soviet installations on 1 May 1960. The plane was built by the top-secret United States Lockheed 'Skunkworks', under designer Kelly Johnson.[74] Its sole purpose was to gather intelligence photographically for military reconnaissance for the CIA and the US military, well before the age of satellites and drones. Pilot Gary Powers, who had flown the U-2 and was shot down, managing to eject from a stratospheric height, was paraded as an American spy, and was eventually exchanged for Soviet spies after a lengthy period of humiliation for the Americans. Lockheed would go on to build the SR-71 Blackbird high-performance military plane and later design the F-117 Stealth Fighter.

Photographic evidence is, of course, needed of enemy installations and equipment. The use of drones is increasing in modern warfare. Camera resolution with high-capacity sensors can almost read a car registration plate from many miles above in the right conditions. This is but one way of gathering intelligence, but drones are still vulnerable to missile attack, even from hand-held missile launchers. Modern times in 2023 have seen examples of 'scientific weather balloons' from China and other foreign powers passing over American soil and having visual and photographic access to military and other installations from above, at least, allegedly. Some of those have also been shot down as having suspect intentions. Spying by different methods is well and truly active on both sides of the world fence, and will not be going away anytime soon.

Significance: While the U-2 was extremely successful for a period in the 1960s, viewing installations in Cuba and elsewhere in the Cold War period, it was bound to be shot down sooner or later, and the Americans became more than a little complacent. Modern reconnaissance systems will rely more on pilotless drones that can be operated remotely.

Professor Michie leads on Artificial Intelligence

Donald Michie worked alongside Alan Turing at Bletchley Park as a codebreaker and played chess with him frequently. Michie had made certain modifications to the Colossus Mark 2 machine a few days prior to D-ay to improve its efficiency. Post-war he had built a system for problem solving called Menace, which was demonstrated a few years ago for students in a Royal Institution Christmas lecture. Surprisingly, Michie was not even credited by the lecturer, nor by the BBC producers, for designing it, which was a travesty. As a scientist, Michie had a remarkable career, after the war studying anatomy and working with his wife on in vitro fertilisation, poles apart from mathematics and codebreaking. However, Michie was also fascinated about the idea of machine intelligence and A.I. (Artificial Intelligence) and would carve out a niche in this area, post-war, speaking on the subject, writing papers and chairing various committees. Michie understood the difference between a machine being 'clever' and one with intelligence. Machine learning is, of course, essential to achieving the goal of intelligence, but just because a system or machine learns from experience, does not mean it 'thinks' like a human brain, or even an animal brain. Professor Michie worked at the Turing Institute in Glasgow for a time. He became the founder of the Human Computer Learning Foundation, a charity. The modern world now has scientists and others in the field of computers worrying about the rapid advancement of A.I., and the impact on society, in a negative way. Michie could have added significantly to the discussion if he had the opportunity to do so. The driver of a modern car, with much of its automation and move to the concept of automated driving, and the car electronic brain being aware of its surroundings, has much to be thankful to Michie's research of years ago. His untimely death in a major road traffic accident in July 2007 brought this all to an abrupt end. An old schoolfriend of mine once met Professor Michie in a business meeting and remarked to me what an unassuming and kind person he was. Michie had a variety of interests spanning medical science, mathematics, games of logic and A.I.

Significance: Some of the codebreakers at Bletchley Park were extraordinary individuals, achieving so much in a short timeframe under a wide variety of specialisms. Professor Michie was one such person. Clearly, he had much in common with Turing, but also looking to expand his knowledge in the fields of medicine, biology, and artificial intelligence. His achievements, along with Turing's, were curtailed only by their premature passing from this world.

Information released post-war on codebreaking (mid-1970s)

It was the mid-1970s before the lid was lifted on codebreaking, Bletchley Park and the outstations. Machine names such as Bombes were unfamiliar to the British public, and there was a cloud of secrecy surrounding the personnel, equipment and systems. Some still remain secret today, and Lorenz was only declassified in around 2002. With the removal of restrictions under the Official Secrets Act, those involved at listening Y-stations, at one of the codebreaking sites or the Post Office engineering sites could finally tell their family and friends what they did during the war. However, many still chose not to say anything as that was the culture and discipline they had been brought up with. Over time, there would be news stories, documentaries on television and interviews of selected people about the codebreaking era. However, not everyone was willing to talk on the subject.

Those involved in intelligence, codebreaking and in a support role during wartime had to sign the Official Secrets Act, making it a penalty for sharing such information with unauthorised persons or states. Even after the war had ended, staff were reminded not to talk about what they had done, and that they were still considered to be under the legal powers of the Act. This was all classified until

Front Entrance of Watergate House off the Strand in London. This was the closest to the start of the organisation which later developed into GCHQ. Inset shows Commemorative Plaque unveiled by HM Queen Elizabeth II in 2019. *(© 2019 Ronald Koorm)*

Enigma Machine with keys being pressed to illuminate the lampboard, which is above the keys. The steckerboard, or plugboard is immediately below at the front of the machine. *(Photo from a private collection, by kind permission of Damien Horn, Jersey, Channel Islands)*

Three Rotor wheels from an Enigma machine. Note German swastika and manufacturers number at top of the wheel. Rotors had to be inserted in the correct sequence from a selection of boxed rotor wheels, and identical rotors had to be inserted at the receiving end machine and positioned in accordance with code book instructions to form part of the encoding 'settings'. Enigma Settings were changed every 24 hours, so decoding messages by the allies had limited time frames before further decoding processes had to be applied to discover the settings for the next day. *(Photo from a private collection, by kind permission of Damien Horn, Jersey, Channel Islands)*

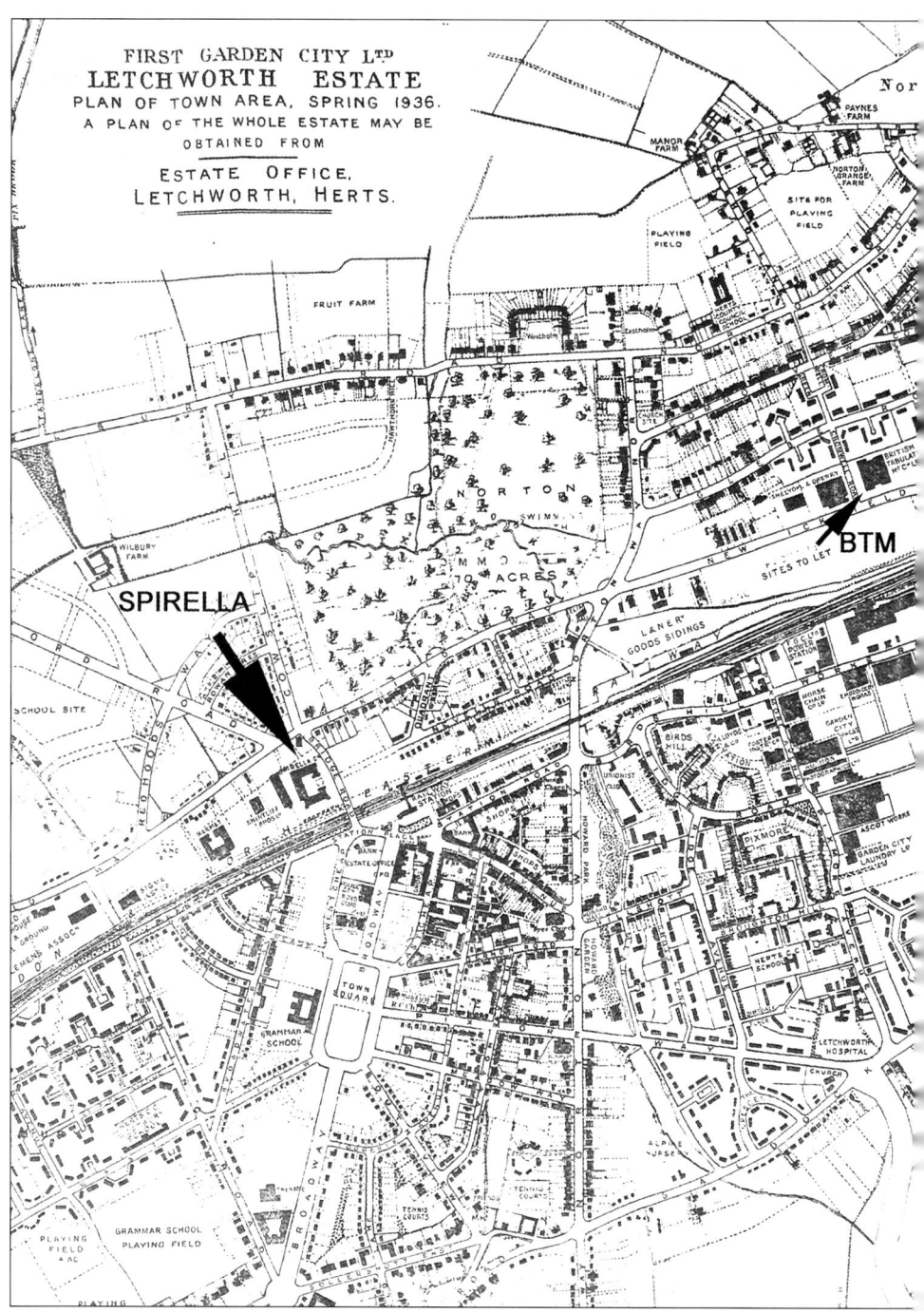

City of Letchworth shown with indication of Spirella and BTM in 1936. Spirella would play a major part in the second world war in helping to manufacture components for the BTM Bombe codebreaking machines. BTM also had a long factory building nearby to the rectangular building shown. Annotation by Ronald Koorm. (*Courtesy of City of Letchworth and Garden City Heritage Collection Museum in Letchworth, Hertfordshire*)

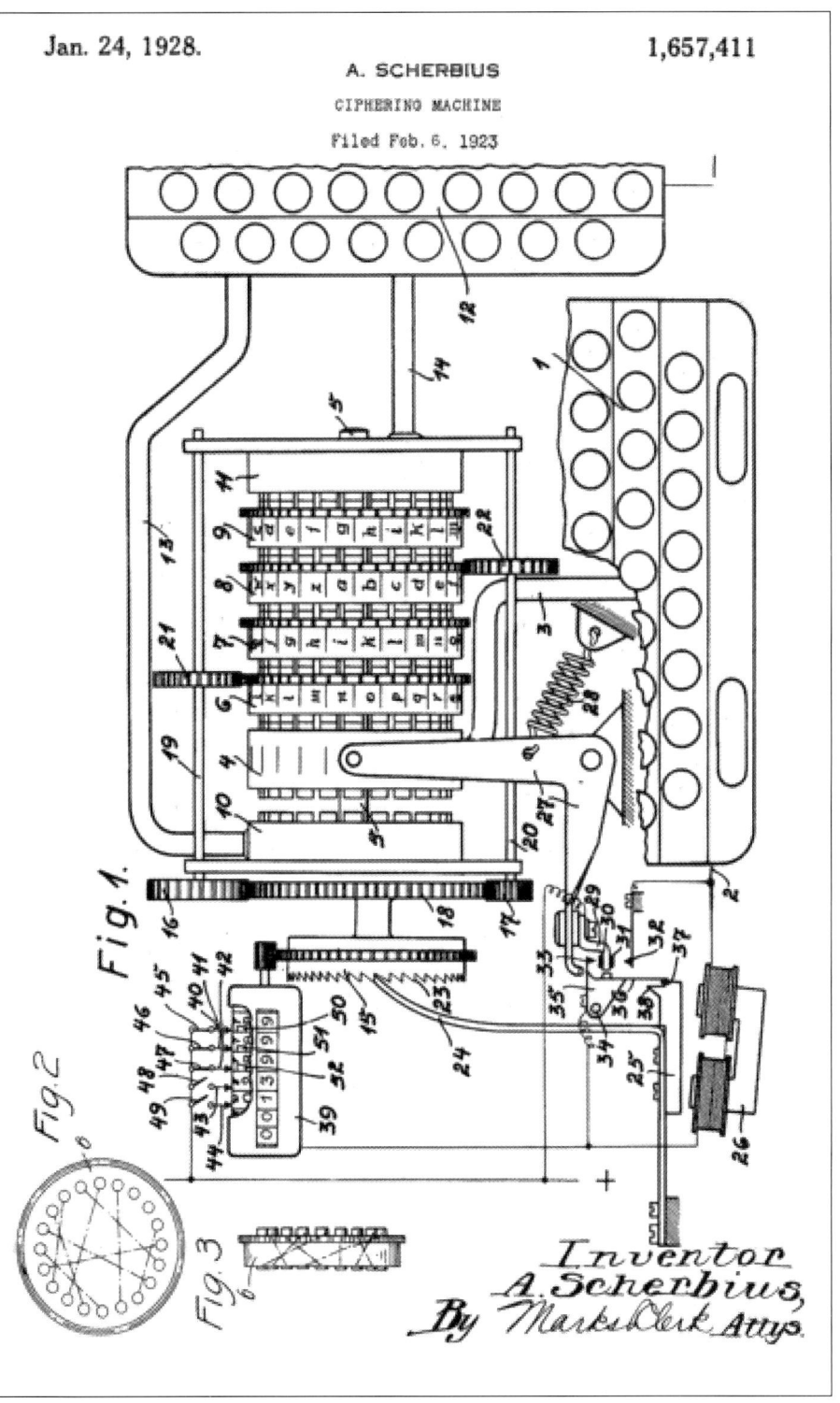

Extract of patent drawing in 1928 of encoding machine designed by Arthur Scherbius, inventor of the Enigma.

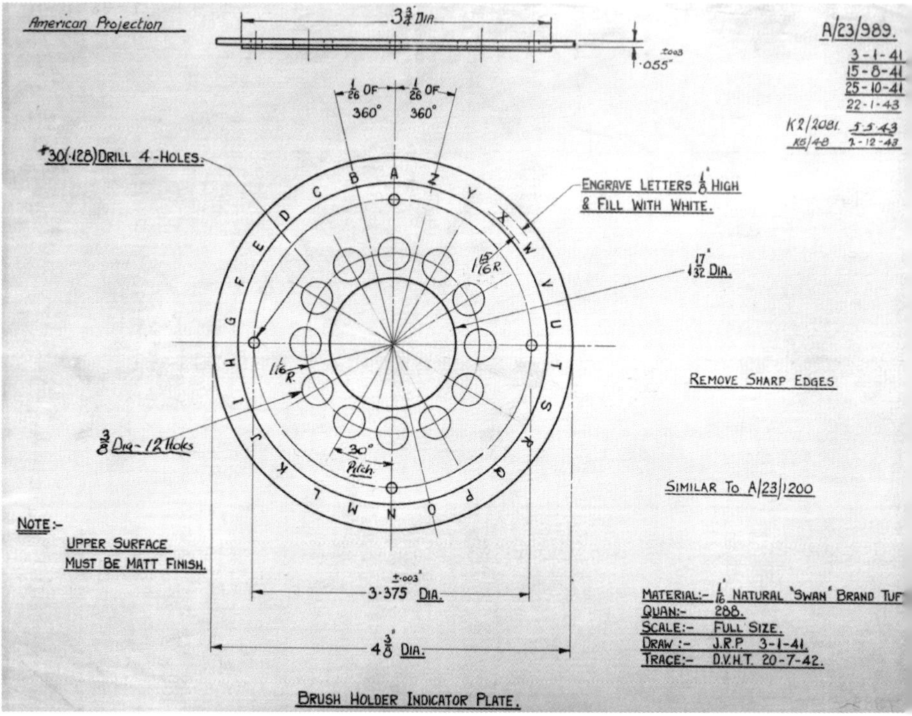

Bombe Brush holder indicator plate drawing. (© Crown Copyright by kind permission Director of GCHQ)

Colossus codebreaking machine in action operated by Wrens. Wheels had perforated punched paper tape read by an optical sensor, which had to be kept clean by the operator. Colossus was more advanced technically, than the Robinson machine, the latter needing duplicate sets of pulleys, and paper tapes to be synchronised. (© Crown copyright by kind permission Director of GCHQ)

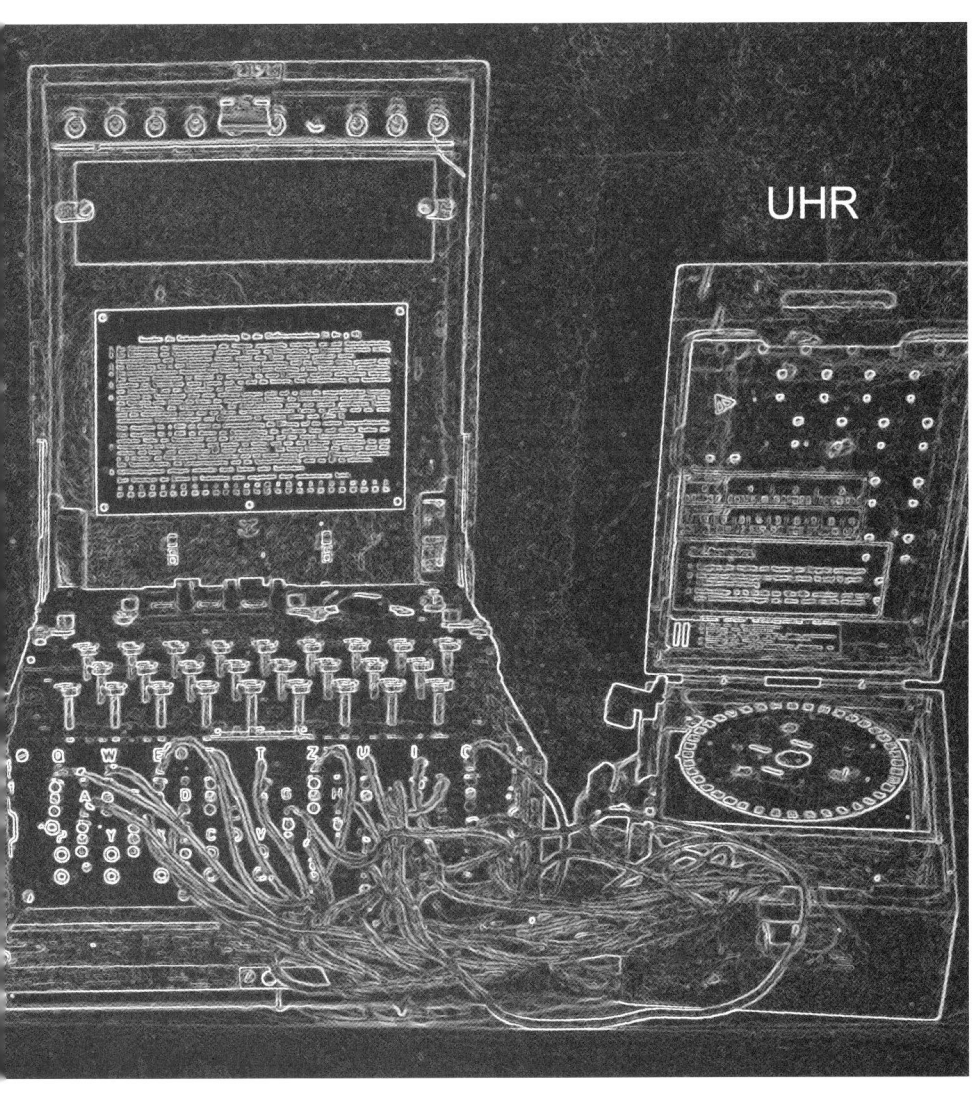

Enigma with separate Uhr scrambler attachment, to increase difficulty for the allies to crack the Enigma codes. The attachment was connected to the machine with cables from the Enigma plugboard, and was in a separate box. It was also termed the 'Plug clock' or 'Stecker Uhr', and used by the Luftwaffe. Manufacturer *Konski and Kruger*. The author's thanks to www.chiffiermaschine.com for some of the background information. *(Photo enhancement graphic work – Ronald Koorm)*

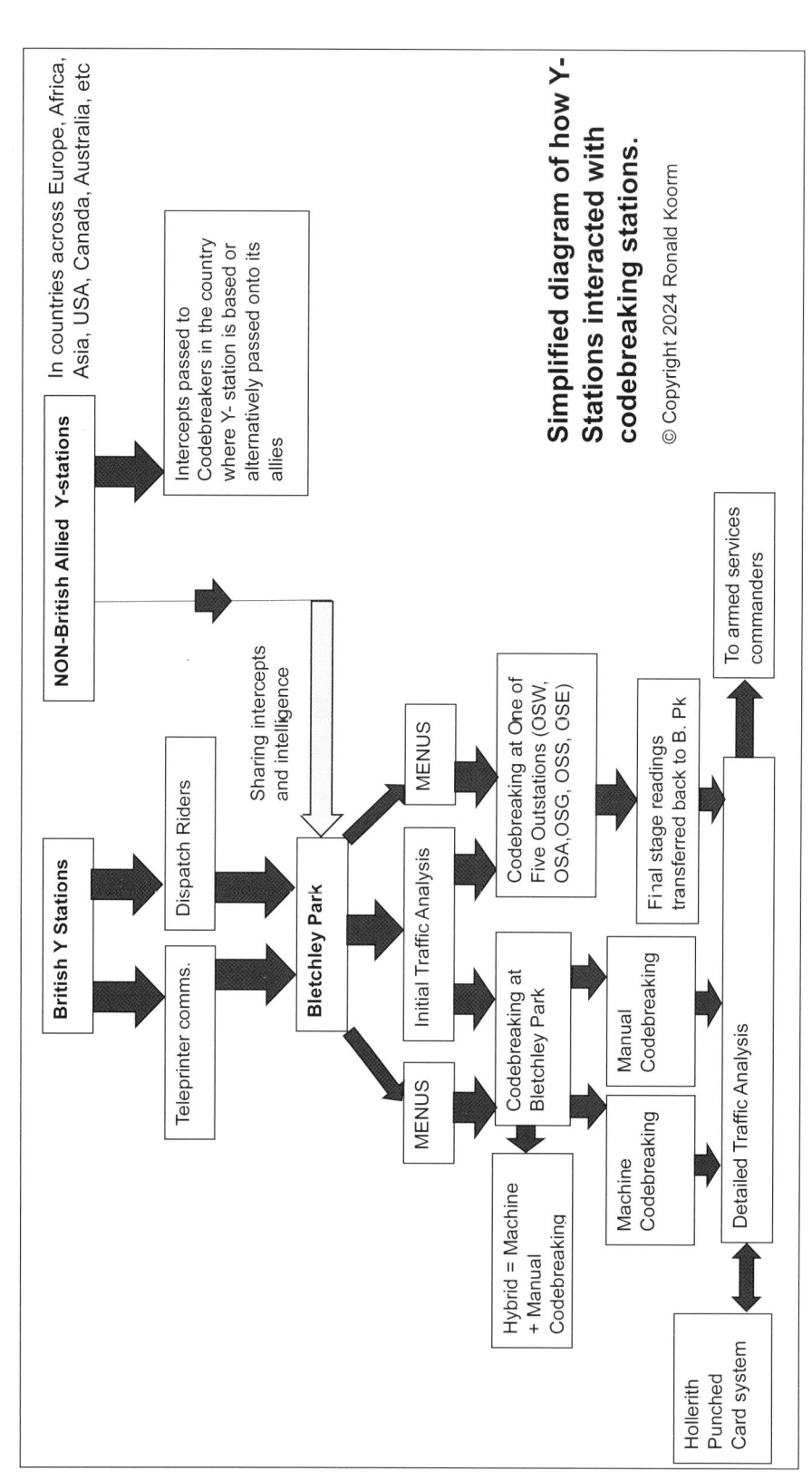

Diagram of Interaction of Y-stations with codebreaking stations. (Note: Diagram does not specifically show *Typex* final decoding stage prior to translation of decoded message.) (© Copyright 2024 Ronald Koorm)

Recruitment Poster for the WAVES in the United States of America, several who worked on building and operating codebreaking machines. *(Courtesy of The National Cryptologic Museum, Maryland, U.S.A)*

WAVES personnel in uniform. Only a small percentage of them worked on four – wheel bombe codebreaking machines. *(Courtesy of The National Cryptologic Museum, Maryland, U.S.A)*

WAVES women working along side male personnel on component assembly for the American four-wheel Bombe. *(Courtesy of The National Cryptologic Museum, Maryland, U.S.A)*

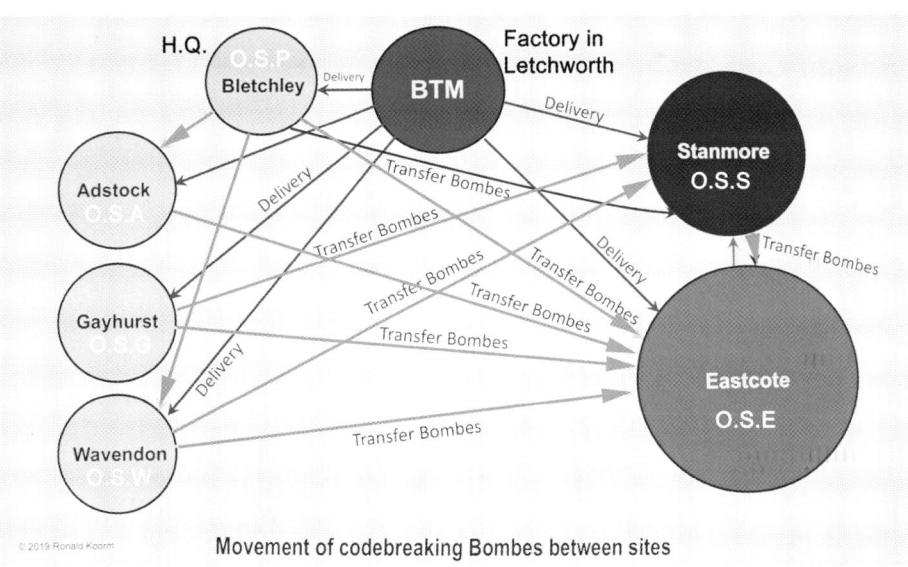

American four-wheel Bombe codebreaking machine, built to attack the Nazi U-Boat Enigma messages which impacted on shipping in the North Atlantic during wartime. *(Courtesy of The National Cryptologic Museum, Maryland, U.S.A)*

Schematic diagram showing movement of Bombe codebreaking machines between outstations, Bletchley Park, and the BTM Letchworth factory. Several machines would start off at smaller outstations and be transferred to Outstation Stanmore and Outstation Eastcote. *(© 2019 Ronald Koorm)*

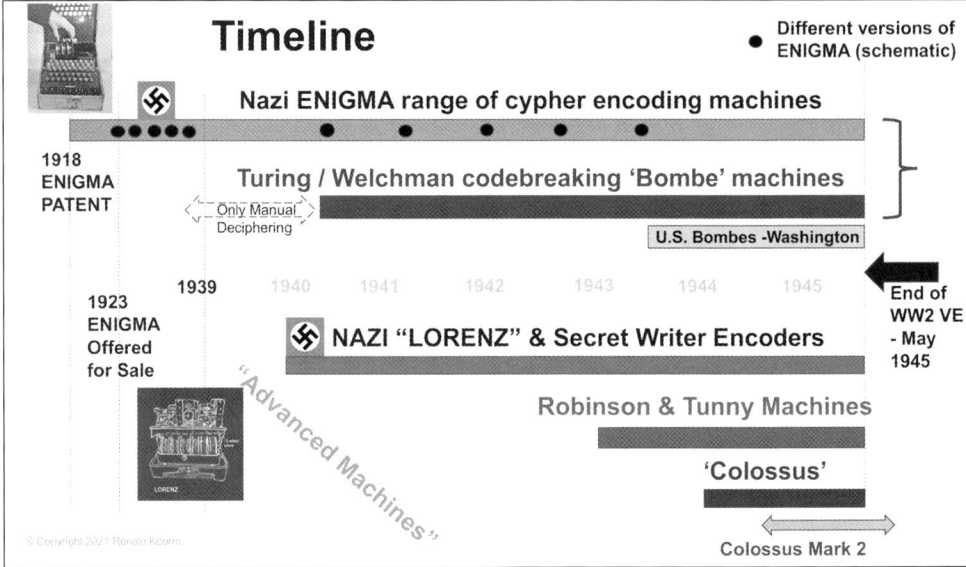

Timeline showing the main parallel encoding/decoding systems during world war two and showing the advanced machines. Note bar line for U.S. four-wheel bombes. *(© 2021 Ronald Koorm)*

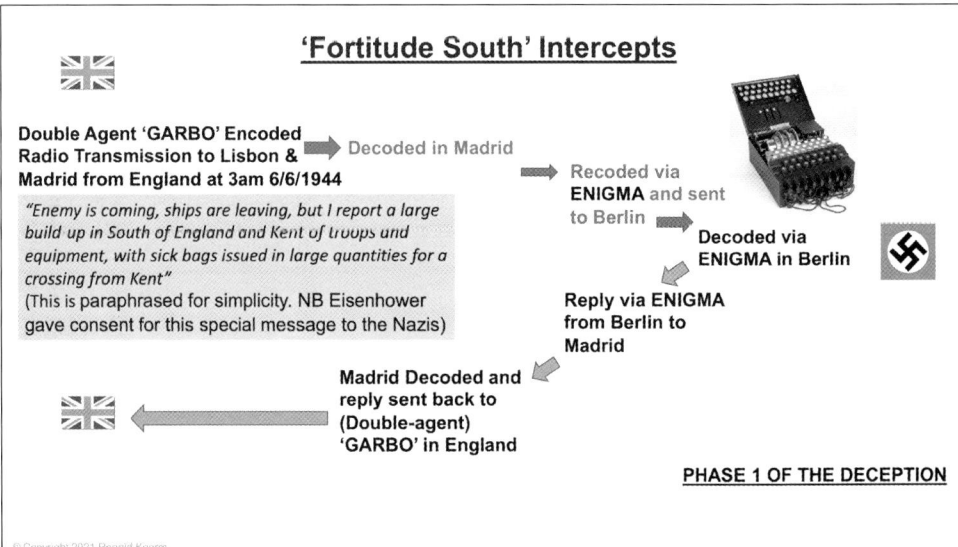

Fortitude South Deception, Phase 1. Double-agent Garbo sends a message to the Nazis with special consent from General Eisenhower. The Nazis responded at around 8 am in the morning and apologised for the delay to Garbo. The response was but the first stage in the deception regarding FUSAG. *(© 2021 Ronald Koorm)*

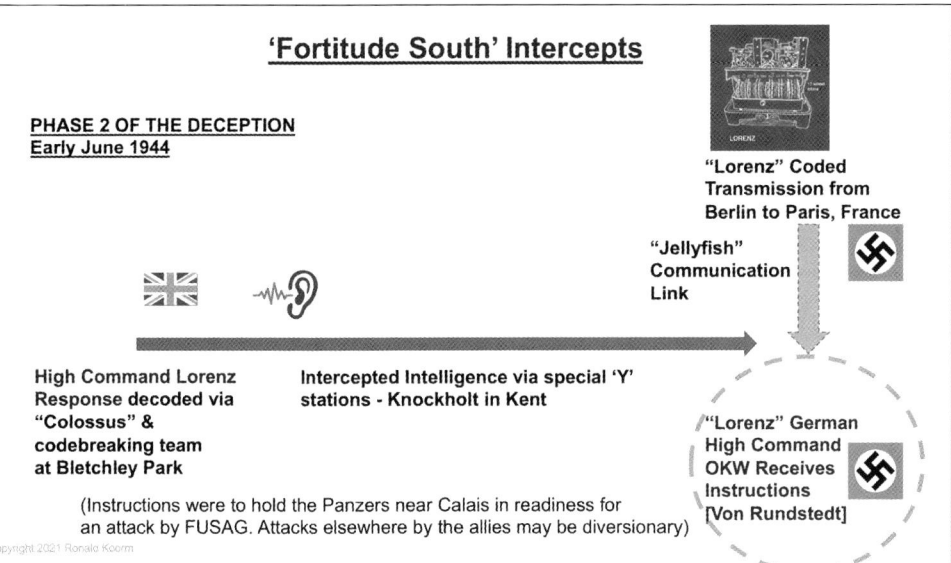

Fortitude South Deception, Phase 2. The prize for the allies was intercepting the Nazi German High Command messages via communication links such as 'Jellyfish'. Knockholt in Kent played an important part in this intercept which was passed to Bletchley Park. (© 2021 Ronald Koorm)

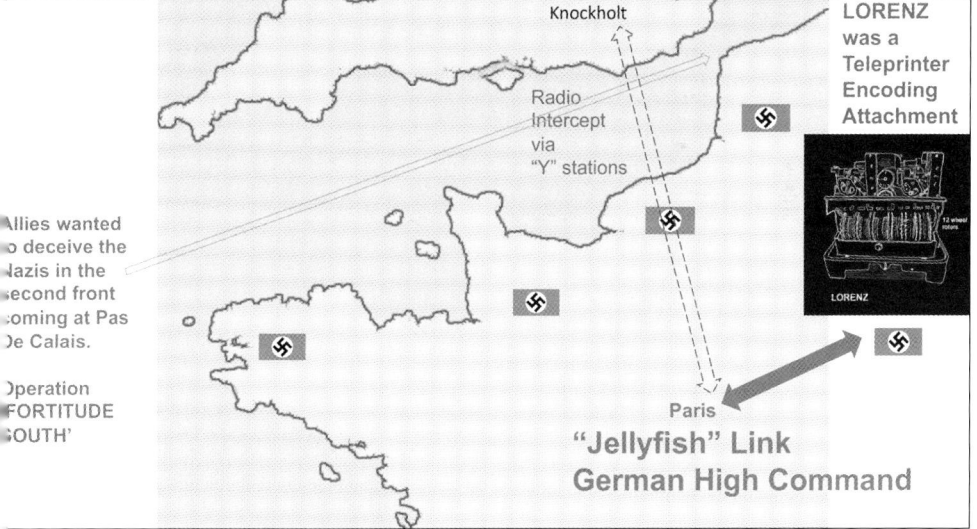

Fortitude South deception intercepting 'Jellyfish' communications link from German High Command in Berlin to Paris, France. Knockholt Y-Station in Kent, would become essential to intercept the Nazi messages via the Lorenz encoding attachment. (© 2019 Ronald Koorm)

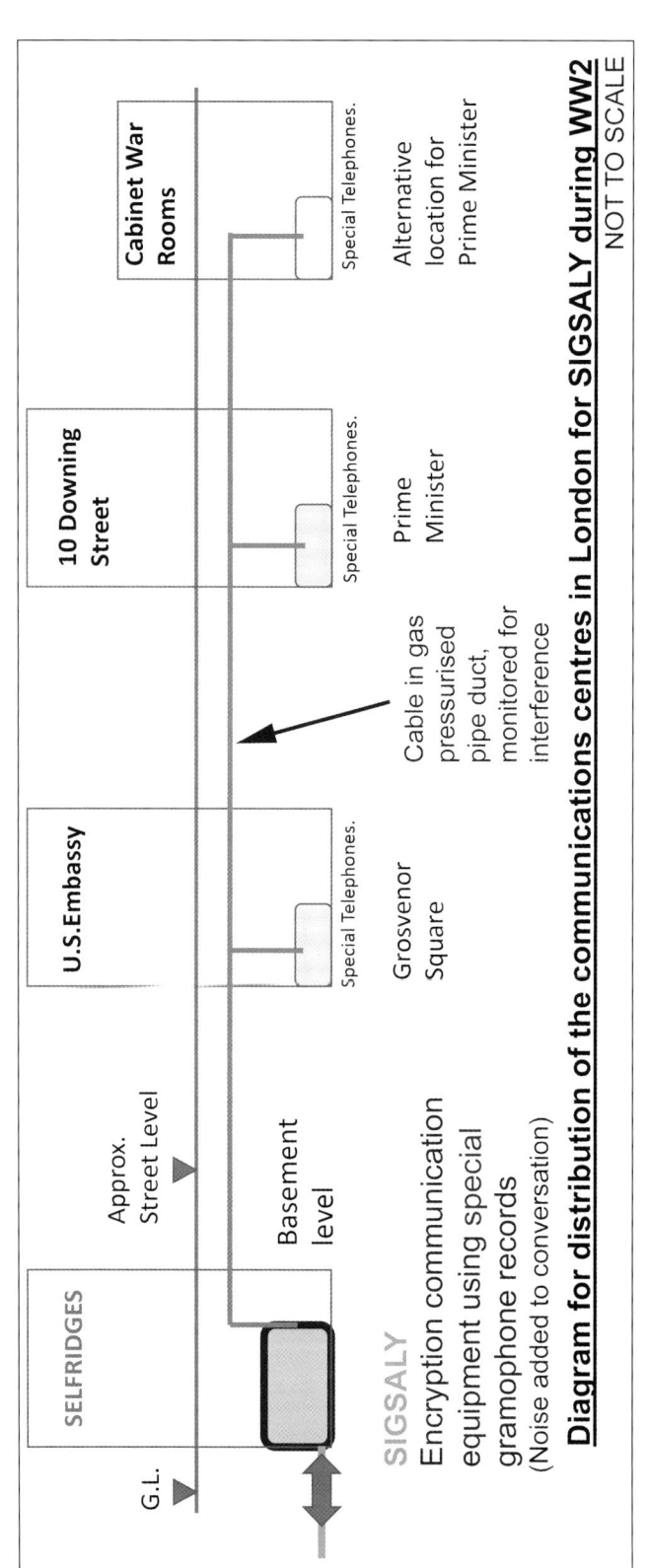

Encryption system of SIGSALY, designed and installed by the Americans during WW2 in the basement of an annexe to Selfridges, the Oxford Street famous department store. This was top secret and used by Prime Minister Winston Churchill to communicate with American presidents Roosevelt and later, President Truman. Techniques included Pulse Code Modulation or PCM, which was advanced for the time. Churchill mainly used the Cabinet War Rooms in Westminster for transatlantic conversations. (© 2019 Ronald Koorm)

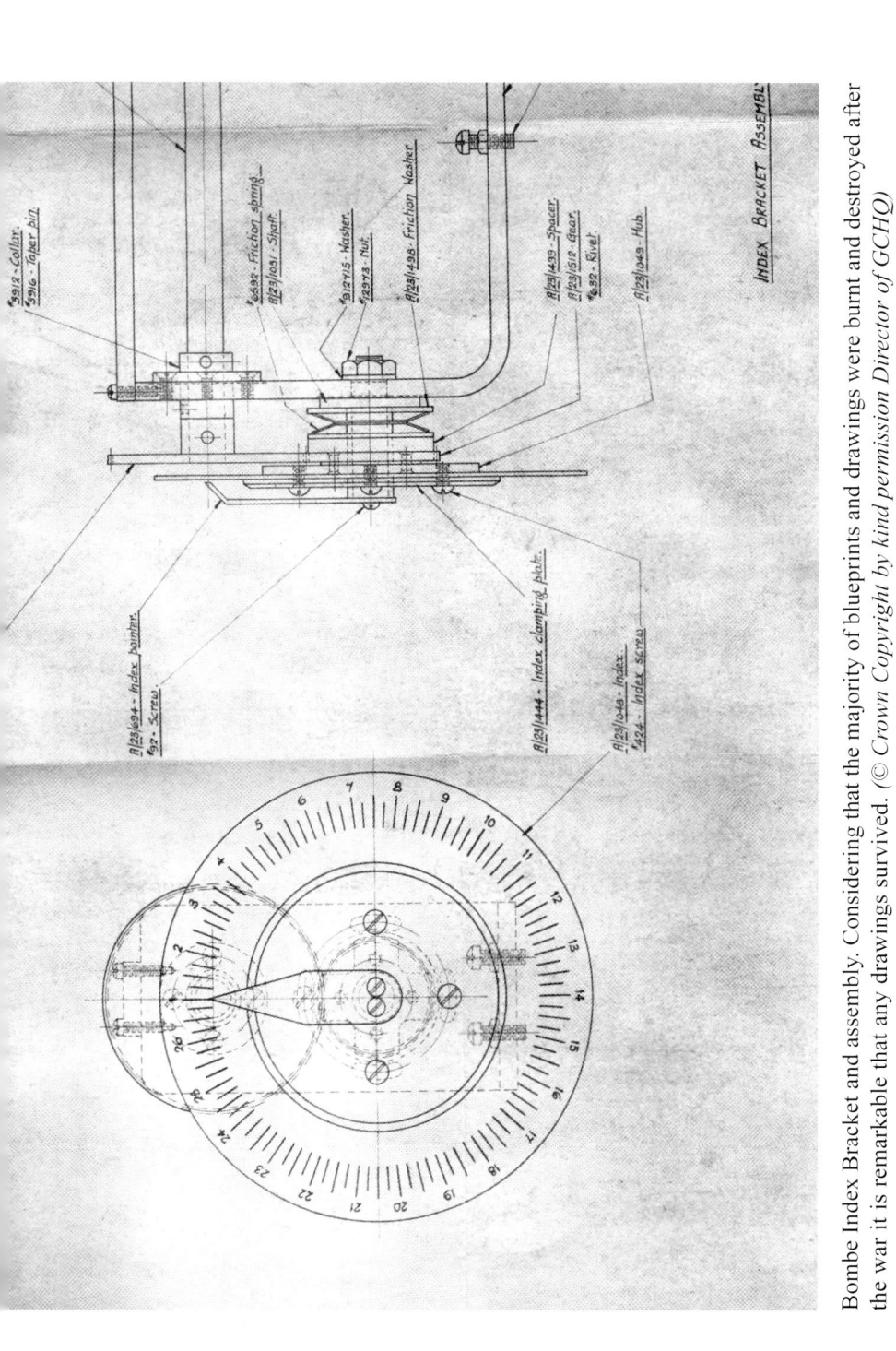

Bombe Index Bracket and assembly. Considering that the majority of blueprints and drawings were burnt and destroyed after the war it is remarkable that any drawings survived. (© Crown Copyright by kind permission Director of GCHQ)

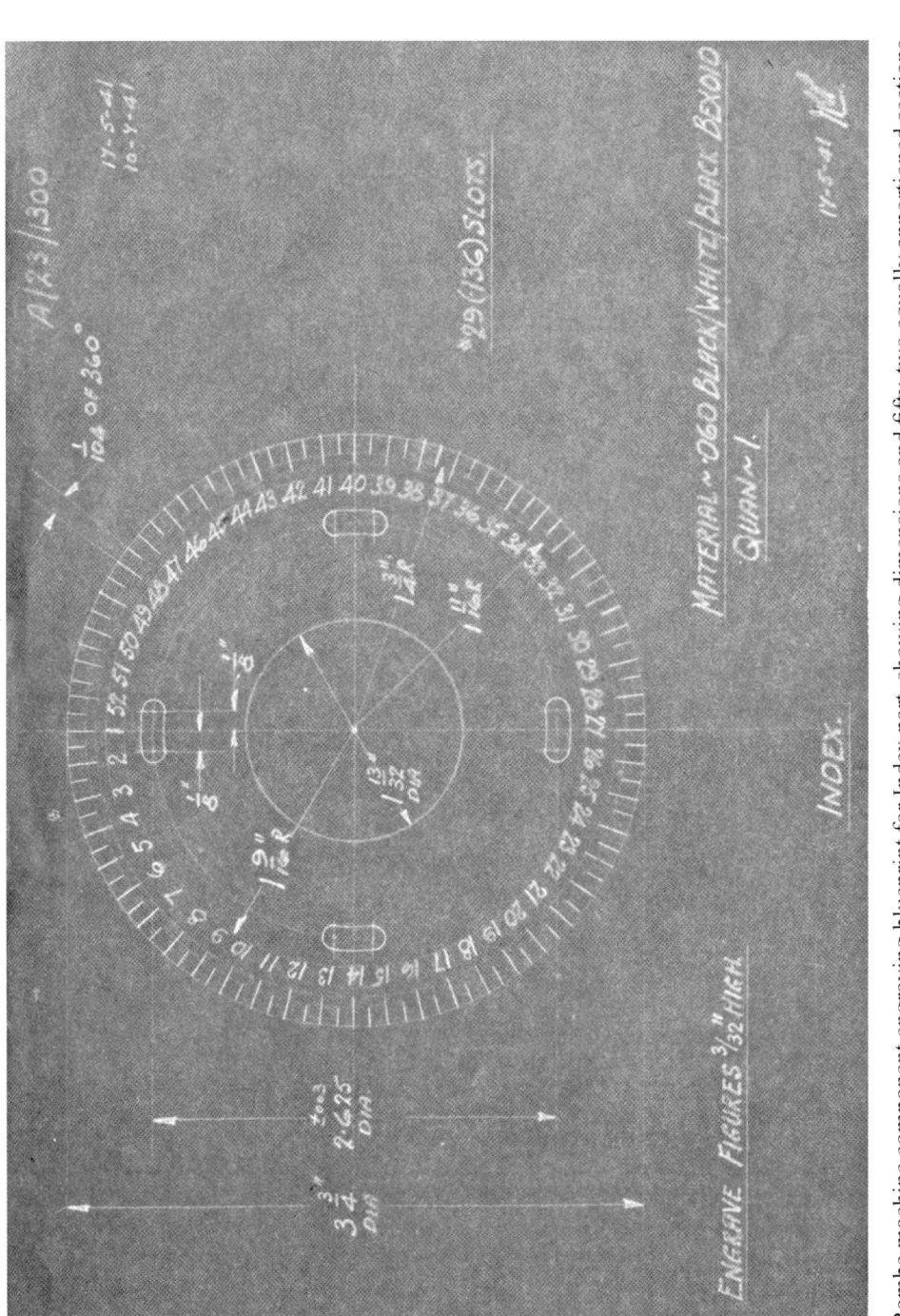

Bombe machine component engraving blueprint for Index part, showing dimensions and fifty-two equally apportioned sections

the mid-1970s. Frederick W. Winterbotham was permitted to publish *The Ultra Secret* in 1974. While some who had worked at the Y-stations, at Bletchley Park, the outstations, and elsewhere told their families what they did when there was declassification of the specialist work, many did not, and went to their graves with their secret intact. Additionally, most of the equipment had been dismantled and destroyed by then, so one only had the odd photograph or drawing to suggest the machines and processes that were involved. Several books were written on the subject with *The Hut Six Story*, written by Bletchley senior codebreaker Gordon Welchman in 1982, but this got him into a great deal of trouble with both the British and Americans for allegedly giving too much of the detail. He did not consider that he had done anything wrong, but lost his American high-security clearance overnight, damaging his post-war career considerably. Few modern politicians would be able to keep secrets for almost thirty years, so it is testament to the stoical individuals who worked on codebreaking and support duties to have kept silent for so many decades.

Significance: Based on the 'thirty-year' rule, the codebreaking story of wartime was largely declassified, and open for scrutiny after many years of profound secrecy.[75] After I had given a talk on codebreaking at a junior school in north-west London, an 11-year-old girl in the school audience came up me and asked, 'If all this was so secret under that Act, how could people later be able to talk about it and you give this talk on wartime codebreaking?' A good question. Some, but not all classified information can be released by the government after an appropriate passage of time has elapsed. But the fact is that some family members may have passed away by then, and would not have known or understood what their children were involved in all those years ago.

CESG relocates from Eastcote to Cheltenham (1977)

Some of the last support sections relocated from GCHQ Eastcote to Cheltenham, the home of the relocated GCHQ, in the late 1970s. CESG was the Communications Electronics Security Group. It is now part of the Government's National Cyber Security Centre. The UK Government's National Technical Authority for Information Assurance, including cryptography, advises organisations on how to protect their information and information systems against today's threats from external cyberattack. CESG evolved from CESD in 1969, when it merged with GCHQ.[76] While CESG did not manufacture equipment or products, it worked closely with industry to ensure appropriate services, equipment and products were available. GCHQ then funded specific research for organisations, such as to certain universities undertaking relevant projects.

Significance: An important section that had evolved and developed over time to find a relevant place in Government and national security protection that has an impact on technical advice to organisations within the state.

Northwood Hills support for GCHQ closes (1978)

A secret office base in Northwood Hills, Middlesex, closed in 1978 after supporting GCHQ in Cheltenham for several years post-war. These were rented offices at the junction of Tolcarne Drive and Chamberlain Way, since demolished for housing. The sub-section here was the Services Communication Development Unit, or SCDU.

Significance: The end of GCHQ support in north-west London.

Bletchley Park establishes a memorial for the three pioneering Polish codebreakers

A memorial of an open book on a plinth in stone is situated within Bletchley Park to commemorate the three principal Polish codebreakers who helped Britain and its allies before and during the Second World War to crack the Enigma encoding machine. These were Marian Rejewski, Henryk Zygalski and Jerzy Rozycki. Relatives of these men visited Bletchley Park museum many years after the war ended, and were guests of the CEO. One lady was the niece of Henryk Zygalski. They were able to lay flowers at the memorial. Without the work of these three cryptographers and mathematicians, the progress made by the Allies would have been much less than was actually achieved. Alan Turing and his colleagues benefitted enormously from their contribution.

Significance: Recognition of the contribution made by three Polish mathematicians who became codebreakers, and who helped the Allies defeat Nazi Germany with their work. The design and building of the Bomba machine provided the first codebreaking machine to attack Enigma, and this was achieved by the three specialists working together to prove that it was possible to use machines to reduce time in manual codebreaking.

Welchman writes *The Hut Six Story* and has it published (1982)

With Gordon Welchman going to America post-war, his expertise was useful for the NSA and those involved in codebreaking strategy. His security clearance in the USA was at a high level. However, in writing his memoirs in *The Hut Six Story*, he upset both the US security services and those in the UK too. They jointly prevented him from marketing his book. However, there is no evidence that copies of the book were destroyed or banned. It is, however, likely that the NSA security team interviewing Welchman in America would have confiscated copies from his home. Without advertising, reviews, marketing opportunities and talks on the book, sales dwindled very quickly. However, copies were sold in both America and Britain. US President Ronald Reagan and British Prime Minister Margaret Thatcher agreed there was a potential security breach and were not prepared to compromise national security, although Welchman considered he had done nothing wrong. His book was later republished with some amendments. It is available today in the museum bookshop at Bletchley Park at the time of writing.

Welchman narrowly escaped being imprisoned, and his American high-security clearance was withdrawn. The impact of the incident, together with profound suspicion of him by the authorities on both sides of the Atlantic, broke him as a person.

Significance: Some saw this publication as Welchman 'breaking cover' and spilling the beans as regards Bletchley Park and the codebreaking methods used during wartime. The authorities were not impressed, even though Welchman considered he had done nothing wrong. He wrote the story at a time when he had high-security clearance in the United States, and was a consultant on intelligence. That was taken from him virtually overnight and severely limited his future employment prospects as an adviser and expert.

Flowers passes a course in personal computing (1993)

Tommy Flowers, the Post Office Engineering mind behind the Colossus semi-programmable computer that helped reduce the length of the Second World War by a couple of years, decided to learn more about modern technology post-war. He enrolled on a course in Hendon to study personal computers. He passed that course with flying colours and received a certificate at the end, in 1993. His fellow students may not have been aware how important and significant he was, and what he had achieved during wartime under considerable pressure. Flowers had also designed and built ERNIE, the random number generator for the National Savings Premium Bonds.[77] The computer course would take students through the practical aspects of the PC operating system, effectively how to communicate with the personal computer in practical terms, and the different aspects that make up the computer and their functions. Modern computers tend to be more user friendly now, and much more powerful in terms of processing power, speed and memory. We tend to take this for granted, compared with systems of fifty years ago. When Flowers carried out his computer course, smartphones had not been invented, and the internet would have been hardly a trickle of activity. Flowers ended the course with a piece of paper to confirm his competence in operating and understanding personal computers. From his enrolment at Woolwich Polytechnic back in 1922 to study electrical engineering he had come a long way.

Significance: The codebreaking machine designed and built by Flowers, Colossus, an early computer based on valves, did not have that much in common with modern personal computers of the 1990s. Yet, perhaps Flowers could see the logic behind personal computers in the operating system, and the miniaturisation of components, transistors, and integrated circuits used. Time and technology had moved on, and Flowers wished to be competent in the new technology available. Clearly, he was keen to learn new things, and being probably the oldest student in the class did not bother him.

Bletchley Park established as a museum (1994)

Escaping a proposal to demolish and redevelop Bletchley Park and provide housing on the site, it became a trust and a museum specialising in codebreaking. It was opened as a museum in 1994 by HRH the Duke of Kent, its chief patron. Bletchley Park had been officially made into a trust the year before. The site has expanded considerably in terms of educational facilities, and with additional funding provides a unique experience for visitors both from the UK and abroad. Google contributed more than £500,000 to the trust to further its development and for restoration of the site in 2011. The focal point of the Park is perhaps, the mansion, which has architectural features of interest, and the many huts that surround the site. The huts housed many famous individuals during wartime, trying to crack the Enigma and Lorenz ciphers and codes: Alan Turing, Gordon Welchman, Bill Tutte, Donald Michie, Roy Jenkins, Hugh Alexander, Mavis Lever, and many others.[78] There exists a Roll of Honour listing people who contributed to codebreaking at or linked to Bletchley Park, whether actual codebreakers or alternatively in a support role, such as many of the Wrens or engineers. Bletchley Park relied substantially on the listening or Y-stations to be effective in codebreaking. These would intercept and write down the encoded Morse code messages on the radio, across many stations both home and abroad. They would have the added challenge of variable atmospheric conditions affecting the quality of the radio reception.

Significance: The possibility of Bletchley Park opening as a museum was only possible because it managed to escape major redevelopment as a housing estate. Secrets during wartime and post-war could now be shared with the public, and stories told of how the Park helped Britain and its allies win the Second World War in the area of interception of enemy intelligence.

Replica Colossus built at Bletchley (1994–96)

Following the destruction of the Colossus machines post-war upon Churchill's instructions, none remained of the ten built. The National Museum of Computing was established at Bletchley Park as a separate trust. Under the direction of Tony Sale, it was decided to build a replica working Colossus II machine for the public to see. This would be a mammoth undertaking as the machines had all been destroyed, most of the drawings and plans burnt, and many who had worked on the machines or built them were not around any longer. With perseverance and a group of enthusiasts and volunteers, a replica Colossus was built, which took almost ten years to complete. Those working on it had limited access to a few basic photographs, and some memories from those who had involvement during wartime on the construction and operation of the machine. Sale managed to obtain eight monochrome photographs and some copies of fragments of circuit diagrams of parts that had been kept illegally by engineers. The new machine reads data at 5,000 characters per second. While HRH the Duke of Kent officially inaugurated the Colossus II in 1996, the working machine was unveiled to the public in June 2004.

Significance: As all Colossus had eventually been dismantled and destroyed after the war, there was now a challenge to see if it could be rebuilt and put into use for demonstration purposes. It would be a long process, but with the passion and determination of the volunteers, it was achieved after several years of hard work and testing.

Enigma machine stolen and sent to media presenter (2000)

An Enigma machine was stolen from Bletchley Park museum in April 2000 and eventually mysteriously delivered to Jeremy Paxman, a BBC news and current affairs presenter. He was perplexed as to why the encoding machine was sent to him. The thief had demanded a ransom for the Enigma, or he threatened to destroy it if this was not paid. The machine, G312, is thought to have been worth around £100,000 to the right collector. The Bletchley Park Trust offered to negotiate with the thief. The perpetrator had claimed he was acting for a third party who had bought the machine in good faith but was not aware it was stolen. The ransom deal fell through, and in October 2000 it was sent from the north of England to Paxman at the BBC *Newsnight* office at Television Centre, intact and apparently undamaged, although with a strong smell of oil when opened. It had been in the post room for several days prior to being opened. Specialists from Bletchley Park went to the BBC studios to verify its authenticity as the one that had been stolen.

Significance: A publicity stunt, perhaps? No one will truly know the background behind this event, but there are several different versions. No one was more surprised at receiving the Enigma than Jeremy Paxman.

Visit to Outstation Stanmore post-war for some Wrens (2000)

While Outstation Stanmore had ceased operations after the war, a visit was arranged for a limited number of Wrens and a very small number of RAF personnel on 1 June 2000. This was a nostalgic trip for those who were able to visit the derelict site, and to bring back memories. Soon afterwards, the site was sold off for housing. The same happened to Outstation Eastcote, which no longer exists due to development. English Heritage has recorded the monument number and location of both codebreaking sites, indeed of all the five codebreaking outstations, online. The Stanmore site was not far from Stanmore station, and at a crossroads that leads to Elstree to the north and Edgware to the south. A total of 629 Wrens and fifty-seven RAF engineers worked at the site. The author has researched the organisation of the site and prepared a block diagram of the different departments and sections that worked there, based on information from the National Archives.

Significance: The revisit to Stanmore must have triggered memories for some who had the opportunity to attend on that summer day, and would be a last look before the site was demolished and developed. It is understood that a quantity of photographs were taken, both internally and externally of the buildings and site.

GCHQ builds new premises in Cheltenham (2002–03)

Following a period of management review, and with considerable Government interest, a new building was constructed at Cheltenham, Gloucestershire, for GCHQ. This would be referred to as the 'Doughnut' due to its circular shape. GCHQ had evolved from Room 40 at the Admiralty, to Watergate House in The Strand, to GC&CS at Bletchley Park and to Eastcote in Middlesex, prior to its current location in Cheltenham. The new centre was opened in 2003. The cost was around £450 million, but may have been even more.

Significance: The need for expansion and new technology to help support the objectives and aims of GCHQ in the modern world.

NSA decrypts and translates material relevant to the Holocaust (post-war–2004)

By 2004, around 600 documents had been decrypted and translated by the United States NSA on matters relating to the Holocaust, via the National Archives and Records Administration.[79] In 1999, the United States Inter-Agency Working Group on Nazi war crimes was established (IWG). It would be their role to identify and seek disclosure of as many relevant documents as possible, assisted by the Nazi War Crimes Disclosure Act of 1999.

Significance: This information added to the history of the Holocaust during the war, making it available for study to all who wish to view it.

TNMOC established (2007)

The National Museum of Computing opened to the public in 2007 in Block 'H', with a large quantity of exhibits and equipment relating to codebreaking, computing, and associated items. It houses reproductions of the Bombe codebreaking machine and of Colossus. The latter machine was reconstructed from scratch by volunteers led by Tony Sale, taking many years of hard work to create a working machine. None of the original machines exist. TNMOC is on the same site as Bletchley Park but is now a separate charitable trust. The aim of the museum, based on its mission statement, includes education, information and working demonstrations of British codebreaking equipment and computers, with a programme of learning for schools and others. The museum is run by a dedicated team of volunteers with a passion for the subject. Its demonstrations have been witnessed and seen by a number of ex-codebreaker veterans, some of whom may have worked at Bletchley Park or the outstations during the Second World War. Many of them are listed on the Roll of Honour at Bletchley Park.

Significance: That it took until 2007 to open this museum demonstrates the journey that has been taken in separating out computing and its history, from codebreaking, and machines associated with it. TNMOC is on the same site as Bletchley Park, albeit as a different charitable trust.

Michie dies in a road accident (2007)

Professor Donald Michie, mathematician, codebreaker, medical scientist, and pioneer in Artificial Intelligence, tragically died with his wife in a major road accident in England in July 2007. He had been a close friend and colleague of Turing, and they had shared many ideas and objectives. Michie had made a name for himself in the field of *in vitro* fertilisation post-war with his wife, and went on to chair various committees in AI, attending and speaking at conferences and producing technical papers that are still being referred to today.

Significance: The loss of Michie was, arguably, as significant as the tragic death of Turing relatively early on in their careers.

Eastcote site demolished (2008)

The codebreaking base at Eastcote, once Outstation Eastcote and later GCHQ, was eventually demolished in 2008 after the land was sold to a developer for housing. The development was initially opposed but went through as approved, and is now known as 'Pembroke Park'. The public footpath dividing the site into two still exists, and the origins of that go back to the sixteenth century. The site has had numerous different names, including Outstation Eastcote, HMS *Pembroke* V or PV, GCHQ, RAF Lime Grove and RAF Eastcote. A plaque now exists behind green railings to commemorate the base and uses, which was unveiled around fifteen years ago by the Mayor of Hillingdon in the presence of military and RAF officers, some civilians, and the local press. Many of the roads have names commemorating either people or organisations who contributed to the codebreaking activities during wartime. Few persons have seen the plaque due to its tricky position, and are genuinely surprised when it is pointed out to them. Those who wish to study the commemorative plaque should first locate the pedestrian crossing next to the housing development on the Eastcote Road, and the railings and plaque are close by. The official monument listing of the site is HOB UID 1222785. It housed 103 codebreaking Bombes at its peak at the end of the war. The plaque mentions 110 machines, but that was not the number of Bombes at the conflict's end.

Significance: The end of an era, and a sad time when such an important site in Britain's wartime and post-war heritage was abandoned as considered to be insignificant, and replaced by a modern housing estate. It was the equivalent of selling the *Cutty Sark* ship off for firewood, but providing a commemorative plaque instead. The loss of such sites can only be partly compensated for by museums such as Bletchley Park in Buckinghamshire, by written accounts by operators of Bombe codebreaking machines, and other equipment, and by the Roll of Honour at Bletchley.

Bletchley Park Roll of Honour established

The Roll of Honour was established at Bletchley Park to commemorate those who worked at or in support of Bletchley on codebreaking and those assisted with the specialist work. The roll includes many men and women, including those from the WRNS, civilians, mathematicians, cryptographers, RAF engineers, Post Office engineers, factory workers, and others. It can be viewed online, and some personnel are listed with photographs. Women can also be searched using their maiden names as well as married names. A commemorative wall is also in existence at the Park. Those who apply to be considered for the Roll of Honour and accepted receive a certificate from Bletchley Park and a GCHQ medal referring to GC&CS, its predecessor. Wrens who are on the roll may have been selected for 'Special X Duties'.

The Roll of Honour lists people who:

- Were employed by the Government Code and Cypher School (GC&CS) at Bletchley Park or its outstations.
- Served in the Armed Forces at Bletchley Park or its outstations.
- Served in the Y services of the armed forces intercepting enemy radio communications.
- Served in Special Liaison Units or Special Communications Units.
- Served in the Radio Security Service.
- Worked for the GPO at Bletchley Park, in the Colossus team at Dollis Hill, or at Y stations.
- Served in signals intelligence in the armed forces of Commonwealth countries.
- It also includes US signals intelligence personnel who were stationed in the United Kingdom.[80]

Significance: The Roll of Honour is about recognition of specialist service during wartime, and in an area that relatively few people were party to. It is for the public and family members to study the roll and be proud of what was achieved years ago.

Commemorative plaque unveiled at Pembroke Park (2014)

On 20 November 2014 at Pembroke Park in Eastcote, Middlesex, a plaque was officially unveiled of the summary history of Outstation Eastcote and of GCHQ by Catherine Dann, Mayor of London Borough of Hillingdon.[81] It was attended by local people and councillors, as well as representatives from the Royal British

Legion and the RAF. The Eastcote Residents Association reported on the event in the autumn edition of their publication, as did local papers. The site had been demolished and redeveloped for housing. Some of the road names reflected the history of the site, which were proposed from a large list by local residents and the Ruislip, Northwood, Eastcote Local History Society. Some of the road names include: *Flowers Avenue; Blagrove Avenue; Wren Lane; Ellis Close; Aitken Close.* Pembroke Park, the name of the development, reflects HMS *Pembroke* V, which was the name of the outstation during wartime. Blocks of flats also have significant names, such as Flowerdown Court, Denmark Hill House, Bletchley House, and Alexander Court. Susan Toms of the RNELH Society helped coordinate the names for the benefit of the developer.[82]

Significance: It is important to reflect and record historical sites during wartime, and those that had an influence during the Second World War in the areas of codebreaking support and GCHQ/intelligence activities. Few would appreciate that GCHQ did not commence in Cheltenham but on the outskirts of London, and with a little help from Bletchley Park as GC&CS.

The Queen unveils GCHQ plaque at Watergate House (2019)

In 2019, Queen Elizabeth II unveiled a wall plaque on Watergate House, near The Strand in London. This was to commemorate the centenary of GCHQ, now in Cheltenham. The origins of GCHQ is complex and it was previously termed GC&CS, being the Government Code and Cipher School. Watergate House is now used as office premises, and is a listed building. The plaque outside incorporates a cipher/coded message in the panel.

Significance: Recognition that the origins of GCHQ began over a hundred years ago, under a different set of personnel and a different organisation that was to be GC&CS.

Enigma makes record sale at auction (2020)

A rare wartime Enigma machine sold at auction at Christie's in 2020 for $440,000 (£347,250). However, in December 2019, the record was set at Sotheby's with an Enigma sold for $800,000 (£630,000). The model was an M4 Enigma. To date it is the highest price for an Enigma but there is always a possibility the record will be broken again, and an Enigma could possibly sell for a million dollars or more. Several sites have Enigmas for sale and contact details of the owners. Some machines have been fully refurbished and are in working condition.

Significance: Rarity of an object usually results in increased demand and high prices being paid. Enigma machines are no different, although many tens of thousands were built, few survive, and even fewer of them survive in good condition and in working order, complete with rotor wheels and steckerboard cables.

Enigma discovered by marine archaeologists in the Baltic (2020)

In November 2020, a team of German World Wide Fund for Nature conservation divers discovered a wartime Enigma machine covered with sea-encrusted barnacles on the seabed in Gelting Bay in the Baltic while on a project looking for discarded fishing nets. They thought at first it was an old typewriter, but then quickly realised the significance of the find and that it may have been thrown overboard by a Nazi submarine or ship during wartime. It was brought ashore to be restored, a project that may take several years. It is probably the case that numerous Enigma machines are littered under fields, buried below ground or on the seabed, as many tens of thousands were made and used by not only the Germans, but also the Italians, Swiss, and others. Reports indicate that prior to the German surrender in May 1945 around fifty U-boat crews sailed into Gelting Bay, to scuttle their submarines and destroy encoding equipment and cipher books. Therefore, there could well be more Enigmas lying on the seabed. The Enigma found by the divers is to be donated to the archaeological museum at Schleswig. Archaeologist and diver Florian Huber discovered the machine and realised its significance. It was the strangest find in his research dives, and unlike anything else he had come across.

Significance: The finding of an Enigma on the seabed will probably not be the last. Several machines may have been dumped by the German military as the war came to an end, along with code books.

Plaques commemorate Alan Turing, mathematician, codebreaker, and pioneer of computer science

Since his tragic death, various blue plaques have appeared on the external walls of buildings where Alan Turing had visited, worked, or been educated in his life. Some of these are summarised here as follows, although there are other tributes around the country including a road named after him in Manchester and a seated statue on a park bench in the city centre:

(a) 2 Warrington Crescent, London, W9 birthplace of Turing. He lived there in 1912–1954. Warrington Crescent is in Maida Vale, north-west London. The plaque says 'Codebreaker and Pioneer of Computer Science'.
(b) Sherborne School. Codebreaker and Pioneer of Computer Science Boarded Here 1926–1931.
(c) Baston Lodge, St Leonards (on sea). Spent his childhood here.
(d) Trumpington Street, Cambridge.

EVENTS

(e) The University of Manchester, Coupland Street. Reader in Mathematics 1948–1954, ALAN MATHISON TURING, A Creator of computer science, Code breaker, and mathematics.
(f) Copper Folly, Wilmslow, Cheshire. '… lived and died here'. This was Turing's home for several years and where he tragically died.
(g) Rainbow 'Pride London' plaque at 2 Warrington Crescent, 'Love Lived Here'.

Significance: Several commemorative plaques of this most extraordinary man who made such a difference in the Second World War, with his codebreaking machines. We must not forget the numerous papers and articles Turing also wrote, many of these being referred to as relevant today.[83] I believe most people who have studied Turing and his work consider that he was ahead of his time. Technology had to catch up with his ideas and concepts. Bletchley Park also commemorates Turing, and includes him on its Roll of Honour.

AI safety summit held at Bletchley Park (2023)

With former Bletchley Park personnel including forward-thinking, brilliant academics such as Turing, Michie, and others, who were intrigued by machine learning and artificial intelligence, it was appropriate that a specialist conference on AI was held on the site. Bletchley Park is, arguably, one of the key birthplaces of early computer science, with Second World War input and both mathematical and technical developments. This was classed as an Artificial Intelligence safety summit, to discuss questions on the control and development of AI, and ensure it is developed responsibly by both individuals and organisations across the world.[84] The explosion of the internet, the worldwide web, and its many implications have brought considerable benefits to society, but also negative aspects. The rate of progress of AI systems is such that it will dominate society in years to come, sooner rather than later. The summit covered aspects of safety, security, economic growth linked to AI and other topics.

Significance: Welcomed by the British Prime Minister Rishi Sunak and others, the summit brought together great minds, organisations and ideas, to help set future policies and regulatory frameworks for AI to ensure it is used for the common good. The responsibility of those who will go on to develop AI machines, programmes, and systems will become a significant challenge to help prevent a future catastrophic failure.

Links, Events and Sequencing

This part of the glossary outlines some of the links, connections, and sequences of events relevant to deception, intelligence, and codebreaking. Thus, the links and sequences can be shown in the form of a listing to better understand the history of smaller events leading to a more significant event. As an analogy and example, the invention of the wheel ultimately led to the motor car, and changed the landscape of most countries with roads, and vehicle infrastructure. However, there were multiple stages before that was achieved, with various experiments, failures, redesign, and different fuels used to power the motor car, from steam to petrol, diesel, and electricity.[1] Similarly, the Second World War activities in encoding machines, decoding and codebreaking started many years prior to the conflict. While the First World War principally used hand methods for encoding and decoding, the significant change in the second war was the introduction of specialist machines and, later, early valve-based computers, to assist in the process. Manual codebreaking was still part of the equation, but much time could be saved with machines designed to aid data processing to establish encoding machine settings. Indeed, a whole industry of skilled and semi-skilled personnel would operate codebreaking machines across the outstations, with relatively few mathematicians and cryptographic experts based at HQ in Bletchley Park working on the more complex parts of the decoding problem.

While there may be some debate among historians as to the exact sequence and timing of certain activities and events, we provide here a basic outline of some links to events. Due to a lack of space these have largely been simplified for ease of reading. More detail can be found in the glossary volumes under the relevant headings.

1.0 Tunny, Lorenz identification and decoding

- Non-Morse transmissions received at Denmark Hill Y-station.
- Bletchley Park advised of unusual transmissions received.
- Bletchley Park personnel listen to transmissions and agree these were not traditional Morse.
- Bletchley Park tries to analyse the structure of the non-Morse transmissions.
- William Tutte, mathematician, analyses the Lorenz structure despite never having seen the advanced Nazi teleprinter attachment machine.

LINKS, EVENTS AND SEQUENCING

- Fish/Tunny communication links identified across Europe.
- Robinson Mark 1 designed and built.
- Robinson Mark 2 designed and built.
- Max Newman approaches Tommy Flowers regarding designing and building a more sophisticated codebreaking machine.
- Colossus Mark 1 designed and built.
- Colossus Mark 2 designed and built, being five times more efficient than Mk 1 Colossus.
- Colossus Mark 2 used just prior to D-Day in June 1944, and modified by codebreaker Donald Michie.
- Tommy Flowers designs and builds Colossus with input from Max Newman of Bletchley Park.
- Colossus dismantled and destroyed post-war apart from two machines, 'Red' and 'Blue', which are sent to Eastcote, the new GCHQ.
- Eventually all machines are dismantled, although for a time the last two machines are held at GCHQ Cheltenham.

Clearly, there would be many sub-stages between William Tutte's work and the design and construction of advanced decoding machines. The monitoring of Nazi Tunny communications links would be ongoing. Fortunately, the majority would be transmitted by radio, allowing Allied interception via Y-stations, although a small number were landline-based also.

Relevant links: Tunny, non-Morse, Denmark Hill, Robinson, Colossus, Bletchley Park, GC&CS, William Tutte, GCHQ, Fish, Teleprinter, Lorenz, secret writers, Max Newman, Tommy Flowers.

2.0 Codebreaking outstations established

- Bletchley Park considered to be vulnerable to enemy air attack, and needs to spread the risk.
- Three country house estates identified near to Bletchley for possible outstations: Adstock, Wavendon, and Gayhurst.
- Bombes transported from BTM to Bletchley Park and to the three outstations.
- Bombe production increases and more space required.
- Stowe School in Bucks becomes an option for another codebreaking outstation.
- It is decided that Stowe School should not be used as an outstation, exact reasons unclear.
- Stanmore identified for an outstation, established in 1942.
- Stanmore seen as geographically close to Dollis Hill, and not too far from Letchworth and BTM.
- More space required to keep up with BTM Bombe production; also resources of operating personnel at the outstations becomes of serious concern.
- Eastcote identified for an outstation, the largest and established in September 1943.

- Eastcote is geographically close to Outstation Stanmore, a few miles away.
- Five outstations in total. Note that Bletchley Park was not considered to be an outstation but was GC&CS Headquarters, and also had some Bombe codebreaking machines on site.
- WRNS personnel, or Wrens, would operate the Bombe machines.
- Machines would be transferred across to the largest codebreaking outstations as they came operational.
- All the codebreaking outstations closed down after the war, although Eastcote is redesignated GCHQ in April 1946 and has a reprieve, albeit in a different operational role.
- The two largest sites, being Stanmore and Eastcote, later demolished for housing.
- Monument Reference numbers exist on the English Heritage websites in respect each of the five codebreaking outstations, acknowledging they existed.[2]

The total number of outstations established was five, abbreviated as OSA, OSW, OSG, OSS, and OSE. Bletchley Park hut with Bombes is given OSP as the equivalent abbreviation, although technically Bletchley is the headquarters, GC&CS. Therefore, six sites in total including Bletchley would have British Bombe codebreaking machines.

Some of the country house outstations would close down after transferring machines to Stanmore and Eastcote as the war progressed. The outstations were used for data processing using Menus of instructions sent from Bletchley Park.

Relevant links: Bletchley Park, GC&CS, Bombes, Alan Turing, Dollis Hill, PORES, Adstock, Gayhurst, Wavendon, Stanmore, Eastcote, outstations, Stowe School, Special Duties X, WRNS, Wrens, Royal Navy, Pembroke V, HMS *Pembroke* V.

3.0 BTM background leading to manufacturing Bombes

- In 1902 intellectual property rights and licensing obtained from US Tabulating Machine Company to form a British company, BTM, to sell Hollerith machines.
- Hollerith pays £10,000 for the rights to sell the machines in Europe and Britain.
- In 1903 C.A. Everard Greene sent to the US to learn about the Hollerith machines as regards assembly and maintenance.
- In 1904 the Tabulator Limited formed as a company but there are financial problems.
- In 1907 it is then renamed the British Tabulating Machine Company Limited, or BTM.
- In 1908 BTM acquires a licence from the Tabulating Machine Company of the US to market punched card machines both in Britain and the British Empire.

LINKS, EVENTS AND SEQUENCING

- In 1911 BTM makes tabulating machines under licence for statistical processing.
- In the same year it installs machines in central London for census processing and analysis. Additional machines are provided in Scotland for the Scottish census.
- By 1920 BTM manufactures its own equipment and machinery, not just relying on the resale or hiring out Hollerith machines. The profitability increases.
- By 1924 the American company becomes International Business Machines or IBM, and contractual relations with BTM decline over the years as the companies go their own way.
- BTM involved in census processing for various countries, including Egypt. Data-processing experience on a large scale.
- BTM produces the Rolling Total Tabulator machine in 1940, and the design is completely independent of US licensing. This also increased sales and profits.
- British Government looks to find a manufacturer of Bombe codebreaking machines following work done by Turing and Welchman.
- Government learns about BTM's census experience and data processing.
- Cantab contract signed with BTM for manufacture of Bombes.
- Harold Keen, chief engineer at BTM, responsible for production.
- Bombes produced in Letchworth, Hertfordshire.
- BTM refers to Bletchley Park as 'Bureau B' for administrative purposes.
- Bombes transported from Letchworth factory by a lorry with a tarpaulin cover and only a driver, who was unarmed.[3]
- 211 British Bombes produced by end of the war.
- Churchill gives instructions for codebreaking machines to be dismantled and destroyed at the end of the war.
- Philpotts, CEO of BTM, holds a special staff dinner in 1945 for those involved in the production of Bombe machines.
- Philpotts knighted after the war for his services in Bombe production, although the exact wording on the citation would not have mentioned the Bombes, which were still under the Official Secrets Act at the time. Keen was also awarded an OBE.
- Some Bombes remain at Eastcote for a time.
- All Bombes eventually dismantled, none remaining.
- BTM goes on post-war to develop commercial computers, some with other companies.
- In 1959 BTM merges with Powers-Samas Accounting Machines, who were previously a competitor to BTM. It is later merged into International Computers Limited, or ICL, in 1968.
- The Fujitsu Company acquires ICL in 2002.[4]
- Replica Bombe built and displayed at Bletchley at TNMOC by volunteers.

NB: The Americans produced at least 121 Naval four-wheel-based Bombes to supplement the British Bombes later in the war, based in Washington for operational use. BTM had no known involvement in manufacture of these, as far as can be ascertained at the time of writing.

Relevant links: BTM, Hollerith machines, H. Keen, F. Freeborn, Bletchley Park, Bombes, GC&CS, Alan Turing, Gordon Welchman, Drayton Parslow, Philpotts CEO, census work, Cantab contract, British Empire, London, IBM, tabulating machines, the Second World War, Letchworth, Hertfordshire, Powers-Samas, Spirella, US Bombes, WAVES.

4.0 WRNS background (i.e. Wrens)

- WRNS first formed in 1917.
- At end of First World War WRNS closed down, officially closed in 1919.
- WRNS re-established during Second World War in 1939.
- Following basic training, a proportion of WRNS are selected and used on 'Special X duties' on Bombe codebreaking machines and later on Robinson and Colossus machines.
- Most 'Special X' duties Wrens are employed at the codebreaking outstations, some at Bletchley Park too.
- Hut 11a and Hut 11b used at Bletchley Park for training Wrens in operating Bombe machines, and the outstations carry out their own training on site.
- Some WRNS personnel relocated to different outstations during wartime, and provide operational expertise or training for others.
- Wrens train the 6812th US Signals engineers on operating the Bombe codebreaking machines at Eastcote.
- A proportion of WRNS personnel sent abroad to support the war against the Japanese; after VE day, many at Y-stations in tropical countries.
- WRNS demobbed at end of the war.
- 74,000 WRNS personnel in total covering a wide range of duties in wartime.
- Operational Special Duties 'X' WRNS amounted to some 1,676 personnel, or approximately just over 2 per cent of the total, a relatively small number.
- Trained WRNS for such specialist duties exceeded 2,000 personnel.
- WRNS disbanded in 1993.
- Several Wrens involved in codebreaking or support in codebreaking activities are recognised on the Bletchley Park Roll of Honour for their wartime services.
- At the Bletchley Park Veteran's day, several Wrens attend the event along with others.

Note: In modern times, all naval occupations in the Royal Navy are open to both men and women.

Relevant links: WRNS, Wrens, Special X duties, Pembroke V designation, HMS *Pembroke* V, Bombe, Robinson and Colossus machines, Bletchley Park, codebreaking outstations, 6812th US Signals and ETOUSA agreement, Mill Hill training, Scotland, First and Second World Wars, conscription of women, and the Royal Navy.

LINKS, EVENTS AND SEQUENCING

4.0 TRE Background

- The predecessor to TRE had previously been located in Dundee, Scotland. It was known as the Air Ministry Experimental Station, or AMES.
- The name is changed to TRE in November 1940.
- TRE was then based on the Dorset coast as a radar research station, near Swanage.
- Nazi *Würzburg* radar captured in France and brought back to TRE in England for study.
- Concern of potential air attack on TRE by the enemy in Dorset as retribution for capturing the radar.
- Malvern College identified to be the new base for TRE for relocation.
- Malvern College relocated to Blenheim and later to Harrow School in anticipation for TRE.[5]
- TRE relocated to Malvern College site. Mainly civilians as employees. Physicists, scientists, electronics engineers and support staff.
- TRE expanded in terms of size and personnel over time to several thousand personnel.
- Specialist support to Bletchley Park, PORES, and BTM by physicists and scientists, including Wynn-Williams on codebreaking machines.
- In 1953 TRE changed to the Radar Research Establishment.
- In 1957 changed again to the Royal Radar Establishment.
- Several employees of TRE become famous people or invent specialist equipment.[6]

Note: The matter of TRE leaving the Malvern site after the war ended was formally raised in Parliament, as the Malvern College staff and pupils wanted to go back, but TRE wanted to remain on the site. Malvern College in Worcestershire today occupies the site once again, as a public fee-paying school.

Relevant links: TRE, Dorset, Malvern, Malvern College, Worcestershire, Scotland, Bletchley Park, codebreaking machines, radar research, Wynn-Williams, PORES, BTM, *Würzburg* German radar.

5.0 Churchill and the outstations

- In 1908 Churchill spends time on part of his honeymoon in Highgrove House, Eastcote, a stone's throw away from what would become Outstation Eastcote in later years.
- Churchill elected Prime Minister in 1939, heading a coalition party for the war.
- Churchill visits Bletchley Park, the codebreaking HQ.
- Churchill receives a request for resources from four Bletchley Park codebreakers, who have concerns.
- He stamps the letter and file 'Action this day', agreeing to provide whatever resources were needed for Bletchley Park.

- He agrees the risk of attack by the Luftwaffe on Bletchley needs to be managed, and three initial codebreaking satellite outstations are identified: Adstock, Wavendon, and Gayhurst.
- A further two outstations are identified and implemented, Stanmore and Eastcote, as the war progresses.
- Churchill receives summaries of the message intelligence at Downing Street, from Bletchley Park and supported by the data processing of the outstations, which enables Bletchley to keep abreast of the messages.
- Churchill gives the instruction to dismantle all the codebreaking machines and to burn all the drawings of the machines after the war.
- Churchill's instruction is principally to avoid the technology coming into the hands of the Russians.
- Some machines remain for a time post-war at Eastcote, which becomes GCHQ in 1946.[7]

Relevant links: the First World War, the Second World War, Bletchley Park, Eastcote, Prime Minister during wartime, Paddock at Dollis Hill, Cabinet War Rooms, Westminster, GC&CS, SIGSALY, codebreaking outstations, request for resources from codebreakers.

6.0 Flowers' path to building Colossus

- Thomas Flowers studies engineering at night school in East London.
- He joins the Post Office engineering branch, and is based at PORES, Dollis Hill, north London.
- Flowers works on telephone exchange equipment and has an interest in valves, reading and learning about their potential.
- Flowers signs the Official Secrets Act together with his boss Radley and his colleagues, and is tasked with working on codebreaking components and parts for GC&CS at Bletchley Park.
- He works on the Robinson machine designing parts for it and is critical of the design.
- He works on a Mark 2 Robinson, more sophisticated but still not very efficient or reliable.
- Turing introduces Flowers to Max Newman of Bletchley Park, who wishes to have a new machine built to tackle the Lorenz Nazi teleprinter attachment, or Tunny.
- Welchman dismisses Flowers' concept of a valve-based machine as wasteful of resources in wartime. Newman, however, has faith in the engineer.
- Flowers convinces his boss, Radley, that he can build the new machine, Colossus, given the right team and resources.
- Flowers designs and builds Colossus, with many hundreds of valves as digital switches, and takes it to Bletchley Park to be reassembled. It works and is put to use.

LINKS, EVENTS AND SEQUENCING

- Flowers designs and build Colossus Mk. 2 just in time before D-Day in June 1944. It is considerably faster than the Mk. 1 model.
- Colossus is used by Bletchley Park in a two-tier system for decoding message settings, firstly using Colossus in the Newmanry section. Then the results are passed on to the Testery team to hand-break the cipher key.
- Flowers is out of pocket by £1,000 to finish the Colossus. He is later given a prize of £1,000 and a medal.
- Post-war he tries to obtain a bank loan to fund another machine. The bank refuses, on the basis that they don't believe such a machine could work or be built successfully. Flowers is unable to advise the bank that he has designed and built several machines previously. The Official Secrets Act stops him from talking about this, so the new machine is never built.

Relevant links: Colossus, Robinson machines, PORES, Dollis Hill in north London, Post Office engineering, Max Newman of Bletchley Park, Gordon Welchman, Alan Turing, Valve technology, GC&CS, Tunny.

7.0 Poles help develop codebreaking base in France

- Marian Rejewski, Henryk Zygalski, and Jerzy Rozycki are three Polish mathematicians and cryptographic experts who have worked on cracking the Enigma machine back in Poland.
- Before the war commences, they have managed to crack Enigma and work out the wiring circuits. By 1932 they have a good understanding of the Enigma.
- Prior to start of the Second World War they arrange replica Enigma machines to be passed to the French and the British, together with vital information on codebreaking of the Enigma.
- As the Nazis invade Europe starting with Poland, they manage to escape. Initially they flee to Paris.
- They relocate into Vichy France, to a château in the town of Uzès, in Provence. This is a temporary location for a time, between 1940 and 1942, until the Nazis progress deeper into southern France and the risks are greater. It will be used as a cryptographical intelligence base.
- There, they work alongside French and Spanish codebreakers at the Château des Fuzes, and continue to work on cracking Enigma enemy intelligence communication links.
- When the Nazis get closer and invade southern France, they have no alternative but to escape in November 1942 to Algiers, North Africa, to continue their work.
- The codebreakers later return when the conditions are more suitable, with less risk.
- Jerzy Rozycki dies at sea in January 1942, crossing from Algiers to France intending to continue his work at Uzès.
- Bletchley Park later commemorates the three Polish mathematicians and cryptographic experts with a memorial.

Relevant links: Poland, France, Spain, England, Bletchley Park, GC&CS, Vichy France, Uzès, Château des Fuzes, Algiers, the Second World War, Bomba machine, mathematicians, Rozycki, Rejewski, Zygalski, Turing.

8.0 Letchworth becomes critical to success of Bletchley Park

- Letchworth Garden City hosts several separate manufacturers prior to start of the Second World War.
- Irvin's is an American-owned parachute manufacturer.
- Spirella is an American, then later British, foundation wear manufacturer.
- BTM is making, repairing, modifying machinery for calculations and data processing.
- The Letchworth workforce is made up of men and women, but as the war commences and conscription for men starts, more roles are taken on by women.
- Irvin's approaches Spirella to assist with parachute manufacture. This works successfully for both firms.
- BTM wins the contract for making Bombe codebreaking machines.
- BTM has to distribute the work around Letchworth, not just in their main factory building.
- Spirella are approached by BTM to use their factory and some of their workers as the volume of Bombe manufacturing increases significantly.
- Spirella moves their corset manufacturing to London, to make more space. BTM sets up the Spirella factory and its workers to make Bombe rotor-wheel brushes, wiring, connectors and cabling related to the Bombes.
- A modular form of mass production is produced to build the Bombes and is highly successful.
- BTM invite Bletchley Park codebreaking specialists to their factory to see the Bombe production in progress. Turing attends several visits to help iron out problems.
- BTM coordinates the personnel on Bombe production including the workers around Letchworth on assembly in various locations.
- BTM builds the super-Bombe, the 'Giant', in their factory.
- BTM constructs 211 Bombe machines in total, sending a few of them to Bletchley Park, but the vast majority go to codebreaking outstations.
- Between one quarter and one third of BTM's factory in Letchworth is given over to Bombe production during wartime.
- The BTM factory is no more, but the Spirella building was refurbished in the 1990s and is now used for commercial purposes.

Relevant links: Hertfordshire, BTM, Spirella, Irvin's, Bombes and Bombe production, Bletchley Park, Alan Turing, Gordon Welchman, Giant machine, US Hollerith company, census work, Hollerith machines, data processing, Letchworth Heritage Garden City Collection and Museum, female workforce, H. Keen, F. Freeborn, British Empire.

LINKS, EVENTS AND SEQUENCING

9.0 GCHQ develops post-war

- The establishment of GCHQ (officially) at GCHQ Eastcote, Middlesex in April 1946 is the start of a new era, post-war.
- Outstation Stanmore is considered for GCHQ but is not as large as Eastcote, and is therefore dismissed.
- Over time, the need for further expansion is identified to cover the range of sections, tasks and operations required. Eastcote is running out of space and land to expand further.
- Eastcote becomes involved in the Venona operation to identify the scale of threat to Western security services, and penetration by the Eastern countries such as Russia and East Germany.
- Cheltenham identified in the early 1950s for relocation of GCHQ from Eastcote.
- Between 1952 and 1954 sections of GCHQ gradually relocate to Cheltenham from Eastcote.
- Two Government-owned sites in Cheltenham used initially, from 1952; Oakley and Benhall. They are around 46 acres each.
- Combined, the sites have almost a quarter of a million square feet of building space, but there could be potential to expand a further 100,000 square feet of area.
- The expansion is considerable, and initially is underestimated by management. The Communications Electronics Security Group or CESG is moved to Cheltenham in the 1970s.
- The Signals Intelligence service, or SIGINT, is developed as a civilian section in Cheltenham by 1965. Outstations can be manned by both a combination of military personnel and civilians.
- GCHQ relies on clerical and industrial staff, with many specialists to cover the range of duties and operations.
- The initial organisation of GCHQ is across five groups: Technical, Traffic Analysis and Task Control, Cryptographic, Intelligence and Cypher Security.
- The old site at Benhall is demolished in phases, and the development of the modern GCHQ is advanced by constructing the radical 'doughnut' design.
- The new GCHQ premises opens in 2004.
- Several outstations support the headquarters.
- In 2016, the National Cyber Security Centre is established as a part of GCHQ. The headquarters of NCSC are in London.

NB: In 2019, a commemorative plaque for the centenary of GCHQ (1919–2019) was unveiled by HM Queen Elizabeth II at Watergate House in The Strand, London.

Relevant links: GCHQ, GC&CS, Bletchley Park, Admiralty and Room 40, the Second World War, Russia, Venona, Eastcote, Northwood, Cheltenham, Watergate House, HM Queen Elizabeth II, NCSC.

Commentary on Events

From the range and scope of events listed, both significant and minor events, one can appreciate the complexity of war and how interception of intelligence did not just happen, it required organisation, technical expertise, knowledge, logic, and sometimes a bit of luck too. The range of personnel involved was substantial and covered a broad church. Listed below are some of the sources of those personnel:

RAF
Army
Royal Navy
Diplomatic corps
Post Office engineers
WRNS
WAAF
ATS
Mathematicians, linguists, classicists, physicists
Y-Station radio operators, telegraphers, aerial engineers
Factories such as BTM and Spirella
Freelance workers around Letchworth, assembling Bombe components
Research stations such as TRE and PORES
Government War Cabinet selected personnel
Bletchley Park and the five outstations
WAVES personnel (USA)
NCR in Dayton, Ohio
Bell Telephone Labs, USA
Polish, French, Spanish codebreakers
Allied personnel across the USA, Canada, Commonwealth, Russia, Poland, France, Netherlands, North Africa, etc.

This list could easily extend over several pages, but that is not the intention. People had to identify the problems, prioritise them quickly, decide how best to achieve effective results, organise people and create targets and objectives using the appropriate skilled and semi-skilled people, while constantly monitoring the progress and the impact of the enemy. Those in charge needed to adapt strategies where necessary, to compensate for new threats, new machines, new ciphers, and keys, plugging weaknesses, locating resources, and not losing sight of the key objective: to make a difference and win the war in terms of intelligence. The records held at the National Archives at Kew show memos and reports with great concern about possibly running out of both space and personnel to operate codebreaking machines. Men were being allocated to train and fight, to be at sea and in the air, and prepare for the invasion of France, Sicily, Italy, Crete, and North Africa. Women had to fill a lot of the resource gaps, and at relatively short notice. There was an appreciation that one needed to train staff before they would become effectively useful, such as when operating Bombe machines or operating Robinson codebreaking equipment. There would be basic training, such as for the Wrens, but only a relative few would be selected for the role of 'Special X' duties, and those skills would have been trained by competent staff in an intensive course either at the outstations or at Bletchley Park. Even the ETOUSA-enabled US signals engineers would need that specialist training, in Britain, and that had to be factored in before any of them could be let loose on setting up and operating Bombe machines. So, delays in the training process had to be allowed for. New methods would come in, along with modifications to machines, changes and adaptations. All had to be communicated to the operational personnel, so that they were aware if their procedures or settings had to change compared to those on older machines or equipment.

Power supplies and spares in wartime

One point rarely mentioned in the range of books and articles on codebreaking and intelligence gathering is that a large amount of electrical power was needed to run things like codebreaking machines, Hollerith tabulators, and auxiliary equipment. There might be disruption to electrical supplies in air raids, but there must be back-up generators in case of power failure, and those generators needed testing and maintaining by engineers. Spare parts had to be made available. How did the postal service cope with delivery of spare parts to an outstation if there were bomb craters in the road courtesy of the Luftwaffe? Some spares may have come directly from engineering workshops or direct from factories, but someone had to catalogue the parts, check them, package them, address them, transport them and someone had to sign for them, as a receipt. That was before they could even consider using the part in the machine. It is no good having advanced codebreaking machines and trained personnel if a tiny part is needed to replace a faulty component, to make the machine work, and that is stuck at a port, hundreds of miles away. The logistics alone must have been a constant headache for operational managers, engineers, factories, and others. Tube valves were necessary for radio receiving equipment, and for specialist machines such as Colossus. The Philips company, with a large factory in the Netherlands, had managed to secure a number of tube valves, tooling equipment, and expertise and ferry it all to England just as the Nazis were beginning to occupy the country. Valves were particularly difficult to make and materials would be less available in wartime unless imported from the United States, and that had its own challenges with the U-boats. As 211 Bombes were constructed by BTM, there were economies of scale, and an opportunity to make the machines modular and easier to repair. But there would be modifications, changes, and items like the diagonal board circuit added. Those all needed logging, so there was a proper record on the machine both at the factory and at the outstation and Bletchley Park. This was, of course, years before computers could be used for tracking an inventory of components, or tracking the training of Wrens who might be working on codebreaking machines. Everything had to be done manually, accurately, and with precision.[1]

High command communication

The pressure on Adolf Hitler and his generals would also drive their obsession for secrecy and to find ways of infiltrating Allied intelligence during the war. The move from using Enigma to a new advanced teleprinter encoding attachment was not made to replace Enigma, but more to provide another layer of confidentiality for the German high command. Enigma would still be used in their tens of thousands for general communication for the German armed services and the Italians too. Lorenz, in comparison, would only be used by the elite, the most senior officers who had Hitler's approval and confidence. What is surprising is that while Lorenz and the secret writers were intended to be used in fixed locations, such as buildings and permanent structures, they would later be utilised by field marshals, operating in the field in mobile caravan trucks with sleeping bunks for the operating personnel. Some would even be captured by the Allies and transported to England for further investigation by the codebreakers. Such equipment would be sensitive to shocks, vibration, and impact, so hardly ideal for the battlefield, or when under attack from American P-51 fighter-bombers. The aerials used by the enemy must have been both robust and substantial to send the encoded messages across many miles of variable terrain, with hills, trees, vegetation, and physical features affecting the transmissions, as well as variable atmospherics. Missing characters of the Baudot code would confuse the German recipients as well as the Allies intercepting the messages, but was all part of the challenge.

Reality and myth in codebreaking history

The brilliance and perseverance of William Tutte at Bletchley Park in unravelling the teleprinter attachment configuration and design made a huge difference to the war effort and in intercepts of Nazi high command messages. However, this did not happen overnight. In documentaries, books, films, and drama productions, it is all too easy to get carried away to purely concentrate on and identify heroes and clever people such as Turing, Welchman, Tutte, and Flowers, among others. However, there would have been many failures, disappointments, disagreements, arguments, and poor morale at times. There were long gaps of little or no progress, mistakes, making incorrect assumptions, trial and error, particularly using cribs and clues,

COMMENTARY ON EVENTS

but not always obtaining a successful result. The armed forces and Churchill relied on results, successes, and needed examples of them to boost the morale of the British people. The pressure on not just those at Bletchley Park, but at Letchworth, Spirella, Dollis Hill, TRE in Malvern, the codebreaking outstations, the Y-stations, training centres at Mill Hill and elsewhere, would have been considerable to produce output, a resource of skilled personnel, with results, and information that could help defeat Hitler that bit faster.

If a Wren or Y-station operator had the opportunity to be able to read the entries in this glossary back in the early to mid-1940s, they would have become aware of the bigger picture and how everything fitted together; how their small contribution was a small cog in an enormous machine that was assembled with multiple cogs to make the machine work. However, at the time they would have been only given information on a 'need to know' basis. A fear of the enemy, or enemy agents finding out what the Allies were doing behind closed doors at Bletchley, Dollis Hill and elsewhere, frightened Churchill and the management at Bletchley Park. One slip could put back the war by months, if not years, and make the concept of D-Day a pipedream. The average Y-station listening operator may become quite skilled in identifying an enemy Morse key operator, and may use that skill to obtain additional information that could at times, help the Allies. But unless employed at a senior level of management, that Y-station operator just took instructions and orders from a superior, and they did not ask too many questions. There may have been a bit more teamwork in some of the more specialist Y-stations, but rarely would they be privy to the eventually decoded message content that they spent hours listening for on crackling earphones under difficult atmospheric conditions. The decoding of the message would have to take place elsewhere, unless it was unencrypted and plain Morse code. Even those operating Bombe codebreaking machines at the outstations would not know what the content of the messages were they were helping to crack. Some would say that was an added layer of secrecy and reduced the risk of careless talk. Codebreakers, by comparison, operating manually from first principles, may have had more opportunities to contribute to defining methods and systems to break enemy ciphers and codes efficiently, particularly when working in teams with a common objective. Indeed, such development was actively encouraged. If advanced cryptographical methods and systems could be devised that might result in faster processing of messages, use fewer staff, and be taught to newer recruits, who would learn from the more experienced codebreakers. Mathematician Bill Tutte was a bit special in his approach. Where others at Bletchley had tried and failed, he persevered over several weeks and came up with the solution of the configuration of the Tunny machine, the new Nazi secret writer. Yet, he was relatively young as a mathematician. A combination of new blood and experience would be a constructive combination in making progress over time. The real enemy was 'time', or lack of it.

The change of message settings every twenty-four hours by the enemy put additional pressure on Bletchley personnel. Adding new non-Morse messages with new machines that had never been seen previously by the Allies added another layer of uncertainty during wartime. Two parallel encoding and decoding systems. Totally separate systems, with the Bombe machine useless against non-Morse messages but still essential for cracking Enigma messages, and those would be on a much larger scale in terms of quantity and output.

Strategic intelligence

Planning for strategic operations such as Operation Torch relevant to North Africa, or attacking Sicily with a large amphibious force, required feedback of accurate intelligence prior to the action. That was not always forthcoming. Bletchley had gathered an enormous number of trivia as intelligence from numerous intercepts of messages. However, it all had to be recorded, sorted and catalogued, such that the data could be recovered by date, by names, by geographical places, by events. That is where the control of Fred Freeborn came in, who was seconded from BTM in Letchworth, Hertfordshire. His team of data processors using Hollerith machines would be crucial to help in piecing together snippets of information based upon requests from Bletchley Park codebreakers and support staff. The organisation required to accommodate this operation was substantial and complex. Different machines and staff carried out different activities in the Hollerith section, and the staff numbers grew over time to many hundreds of mainly, women. The largest potential strategic prize was in deceiving the enemy at D-Day, to save thousands of lives and convince the Germans that they should retain certain Panzer divisions near the Pas-de-Calais to await an attack across the Channel. This was a complex plan and required careful coordination of men, women, equipment, Y-stations, Bletchley Park, codebreaking outstations, double agents, all the way up to Eisenhower and Churchill. D-Day was more than just a battle. It was a significant event that incorporated several different assaults on the enemy, in different locations, as well as introducing deception before and during the battles, and the gathering of intelligence. Eisenhower and Churchill knew that it had to work first time or the consequences for both the West and Europe would be dire. The experiences of utilising Ultra intelligence for events such as Operation Torch would prove to be invaluable for the Allies, many years prior to D-Day.

Analogy of data processing

Imagine a transport network where there are hundreds of thousands of journeys by customers each day, many millions in a year, and data is required as to the habits, times, and routes of the travelling public, but without the use of computers, using a card index. A senior manager requests urgent feedback of events on a particular series of dates at short notice, but the team with the information is under pressure to provide statistics on a range of other important requests. How to priorities those requests? Does the manager in charge of the team workers just instruct to stop work on numerous database searches halfway through, disrupting the flow of information? There is a limited number of skilled staff and equipment available. What effect would such a change have on the morale of the workers?

COMMENTARY ON EVENTS

Apply this now to Bletchley Park, and the Hollerith team, and it is very similar in principle, but with potential consequences of life and death added into the equation. Of course, nowadays, information can be obtained almost instantly in 'real time' with computers. Type in a search, press return or enter, and the information is listed in front of you ready for emailing someone or printing it off. But during wartime they did not have the luxury of computers. It was card-based, a sort of sophisticated Rolodex, helped by punched cards and crude instructions given to machines by women operators using electro-mechanical equipment. There were noisy, dusty, and unpleasant working conditions. There were disagreements on priorities of searches for information between the enquirer and the Hollerith section. There was interference by Bletchley managers, causing frustration to people who were under-resourced, poorly paid as a whole, and could hardly hear themselves think over the noise of the machines processing, sorting, stacking the punched cards. However, the reports were provided and allowed Bletchley personnel to identify links between items that might be considered and classed as mere trivia in a group of enemy messages. A sort of jigsaw puzzle of enormous size with various people trying to link together certain parts of that puzzle. Sometimes it would bear fruit, but at other times it would lead to a dead end.

The machines would need constant and regular attention and maintenance as they were electro-mechanical. Parts would have to be repaired and some replaced. New machines were brought in, including sorters, tabulators, and other specialist machines. Each member of staff would have to be trained to operate one or more machines, and carry out specific tasks in a specific sequence. There would need to be cover for those falling sick, or being absent for whatever reason. There could be no reduction in efficiency, as otherwise that would quickly be noticed by Freeborn, and those at Bletchley. BTM would have to purchase the cards, and test batches so they would run through the machines. They would be used in the tens of thousands, even hundreds of thousands into the millions. Storage of the cards would be an ongoing challenge as regards finding adequate space for them. They would also be a potential fire risk, with so much combustible material in the buildings and huts. There would be different machines for different stages, the punch, sorter, and tabulator. Staff would need to be trained on operating each machine and then given tasks to perform. Many of the machines would require power supplies and electrical power to operate. Maintenance would be necessary, and breaks for staff would be permitted for short periods. Some cards would become damaged or lost and affect the processing. All this would have to be managed by Freeborn and his senior team, with the utmost efficiency.

Typex Machines manufactured by Powers-Samas

A competitor to Hollerith was the Powers Company and it eventually changed its name to *Powers-Samas Accounting Machine Limited*, with a UK division. In wartime, it would go on to manufacture a substantial number of Typex machines, which were British versions of the German Enigma machine but with some technical improvements. Typex would be used at Bletchley Park as the penultimate stage of processing the enemy messages after the settings had been determined via Bombe codebreaking machines. The final stage would be translation from German into English, assuming the message settings had been correctly determined. Typex machines were also used elsewhere, including at some of the Y-stations abroad. Women operators usually operated Typex at Bletchley Park. Powers-Samas was also a competitor to BTM in Letchworth, who made the codebreaking Bombes. That there were around twenty-three or so versions of Typex, or Type-X machines, indicates the development over time for different organisations.

Confusion and competitive rivalry in Nazi circles on intelligence

One aspect of Allied intelligence in the Second World War that must be credited is the excellent structured and focused coordination of the intelligence services and systems used. That is not to say there were no problems. There would, of course, be disagreements, mistakes, errors, mishaps, and so on. In contrast, the Germans had Adolf Hitler to contend with; a power-hungry megalomaniac who prioritised certain aspects of the war in a less than logical approach, leaving the Nazis exposed, particularly in terms of organisation in intelligence. Hitler allowed seven intelligence agencies to spring up and fight between themselves, the antithesis of a coordinated approach. This could only benefit the Allies.

On balance, one must consider that the enemy were first class in coordinated attacks using U-boats for a long period of the war. They had some practice in the Spanish Civil War to fine tune their military strategy. They also had ruthless armaments, such as the Mk V Tiger tank, which picked off Allied tanks as though it was a side-show at a fairground, shooting ducks on a wall. The British, however, had the edge in terms of coordination of intelligence from the Y-listening stations to the logging of encoded messages, the use of machines to strip away the permutations of Enigma message settings, and the translation of the messages and submission to senior military commanders. Even more incredible is how the introduction of more advanced enemy encoding machines did not faze or trouble Bletchley Park too much. They found a relatively young member of staff, a mathematician, who worked the problem for several weeks and cracked Lorenz and the structure of it. A more advanced decoding machine was eventually designed and built, and a team approach used to utilise skilled cryptographic experts in conjunction with the decoding machines. The Nazis were efficient in direction finding using both fixed and mobile listening stations, but it took a lot more than just direction finding to make a difference in wartime. One might argue that if a leader other than Hitler had been in post then perhaps a better, coordinated approach by the Nazis would have occurred with more productive results. Fortunately for the Allies, this did not happen.

The race to recover codebreaking equipment in 1945

As the war developed in Europe, there were penetrations of the German lines in the east, west and south, with the Allies advancing, sometimes slowly. However, there was a particular interest to recover as much signals intelligence, cryptological equipment, and knowledge of the enemy whether it was in machines, technology, documents, maps, diagrams, or other material. While this largely commenced in the latter part of 1944, it would be 1945 that would bring forth the greatest spoils for the Russians, and the British and Americans. Indeed, some of the finds would be Nazi equipment that could attack Russian Fish signals intelligence and teleprinted-based messages. Seven and a half tons of specialist equipment would be captured and examined. Anything of this category would be like gold dust to the experts at Bletchley Park. Abandoned or captured Enigma machines, code books, call sign listings, abandoned wheel rotors, training manuals, and similar would be extremely valuable. There were so many Enigmas made and in different versions, it would be impossible to conceal them all, or even destroy all of them. Some would be thrown overboard from U-boats or spy ships, but only a fraction of the numbers would be on the seabed. Where the Russians captured Lorenz machines or secret writers, in their advance, they may have been tempted to use the equipment for their own military communications. But that would have its risks. They would not have been aware that the British had Robinson and Colossus decoding machines that could strip away a large part of the permutations of machine settings, leaving the remainder to be worked on by humans at Bletchley Park in the Testery section and read the messages. With this equipment, advanced for its time, the Allies would be able to read any Lorenz transmissions sent via the airwaves, at least in theory.

Codebreaking can be a lonely existence in wartime

We, as students of history, have one big advantage over those that performed duties as codebreakers and support personnel during the war. We have the record of what happened, the people involved, the events, organisations and action taken at various stages. Those actually there never knew the outcome until it happened. D-Day was an enormous gamble, and yet it had to be planned years ahead, with an assumption of mass casualties on the day, and a hope for the best under difficult circumstances. Cracking a cipher or code was a big deal, but that had to be seen as part of the bigger picture. If you were in a hut at Bletchley, you were probably given information on a 'need to know' basis.[2] You may not understand or appreciate the consequence of your success or failure in breaking codes, message settings, and deciphering messages, as many others would be involved. Time was crucial for generals, Churchill, Eisenhower, and senior commanders. No use delivering a translation of a decoded message late, as your troops or ships might have been attacked by then, with significant losses. Working in teams of specialist personnel must have helped, as one could share ideas, systems, successes, and failures. The more senior you were, such as the head of a hut or section, the more responsibility would lie on your shoulders and give you sleepless nights. Hearing of merchant and naval ship losses in the Atlantic at a time when the U-boats were running circles around the Allies, and Bletchley codebreakers were temporarily impotent in enemy naval codebreaking, must have been soul destroying. Working on a Typex machine, or perhaps setting up and running Bombe codebreaking machines, was no less traumatic. Equipment would break down, connectors would break from attached cables, and people would go off sick, or need compassionate leave to attend a close relative's funeral. But the job still needed to be done and appear seamless to the management.

William Tutte would have to work largely on his own to crack the design configuration of the twelve wheels of the Lorenz advanced enemy machine.[3] Some of his colleagues may have even thought he was time wasting, as it would be some weeks before he had achieved his breakthrough with the Lorenz/Tunny challenge. Tommy Flowers would have the responsibility to design and build the Colossus machine, and still lead his team of engineers, reporting to his boss, Radley. He knew there were those at Bletchley Park who had little faith in him and his valve-based ideas, but he had to put that aside. At least Max Newman at Bletchley believed in him. One needs to have a particularly strong character to continue working on an important project for many weeks, and months, working long hours, confident and believing in yourself, and in overcoming technical hurdles. All this had to be done with the fear of enemy air raids, and the constant worry of family members fighting in the armed services or training, for the big assault in France yet to come. Material shortages, power cuts or fluctuations in power supplies, rationing; it is a wonder that anything got designed or built in wartime. The one thing driving Britain (and its allies) was the fight to maintain the freedom of the country and the objective of defeating Hitler and his cronies, who wanted to interfere with that freedom. Churchill, of course, played a huge part in maintaining leadership and morale in the UK during wartime, and was a statesman respected by both the US presidents, and possibly to a degree even by Stalin later. But we can state that whatever one's job or occupation in wartime, at least part of it would be a lonely existence, mainly because one never really knew until the last hours of the Second World War what the outcome would be.

Coordination of intelligence

Once the Allies landed in France at D-Day, Bletchley Park remained busy decoding the intercepted Fish link communication messages, as well as those sent via Enigma. Yet, other sources of intelligence were used too 'in the field'. This included interrogation of captured enemy prisoners of war, the use of tactical radio signals intercepts, the use of resistance fighters in the area providing information, and others. The gathering of all this intelligence in all its various forms was a huge undertaking for the military commanders. One had to filter through the intelligence and establish priorities of importance. Which intercepts were false or intentionally misleading, which were low priority, and which would become the highest priority. Those latter categories had to be passed through to senior officers and then to commanders, or sometimes the other way around. Bletchley Park would also be interested in intelligence gathered in the field by different Allied units and divisions as this could support other intercepts obtained via Enigma or on the Fish communication links. So much information would have been passed through, and much of the Enigma-based intelligence as trivia, it needed to be categorised, filtered, prioritised and summary reports produced for the top brass. Traffic analysis would be a major part of the intelligence loop. The Hollerith processing teams at Drayton Parslow, a few miles from Bletchley, would have been extremely busy, and this is reflected by the long hours the personnel would work on the data and the increase in staffing to maintain the service for Bletchley Park. Freddie Freeborn of BTM, managing the Hollerith section with many hundreds of staff, would be earning his money, but working hard for it.

Training bases in England for the American Allies

Preparation for the Normandy invasion and beyond for penetration into France, Belgium, Holland and Germany, included the training of US signals detachments in England. This would occur across different locations, and then units were sent to France or elsewhere. For example, US signals service companies were trained and stationed in places such as Wincham Hall, Cheshire (K-19), also at Burton Bradstock, Dorset, and Marbury, Cheshire, in May 1944, and Ringwood, Dorset, and Lymington, Hampshire, just prior to D-Day. The 3255th Signal Service Company were transferred to Omaha Beach on 12 August 1944, to become operational in the combat area several weeks after the successful landings in Normandy. It was important to locate and track enemy movements in the area, and pass the information promptly back to commanders. The Nazis had effectively been caught with their trousers down at Normandy, but were retaliating and regrouping to slow the Allied advance as best they could. As far back as April 1944, the 118th Signal Radio Intelligence Company assigned to the Third Army had been intercepting enemy military traffic at their base in Dartford, Kent, in particular information about German troop movements along the Atlantic Wall. Some of the intelligence enabled them to identify German units using radios and radio transmissions. The unit arrived in France on 15 July 1944 and worked alongside the Third Army HQ.[4]

Codebreaking – to share, or not to share?

In wartime, when one has allies, the question will be raised as to whether one should share key intelligence on documents, systems, equipment with them, and if so, how much to share? This is relevant as if there is a security breach and your ally is careless with the information provided by you, that could have significant consequences in the war, and weaken you compared to the enemy. On the other hand, sharing crucial intelligence with your friends and allies can help win battles, weaken the enemy and reduce the length of the war. A balance needs to be struck here and there is no right or wrong answer. One must make careful judgements before acting. Britain was careful with providing intelligence to the Russians, allies working together against Nazi Germany and the Axis powers. The country could not afford to release all its sources, or information about the codebreaking machines and systems it was using. However, a Russian spy working at Bletchley Park, John Cairncross, was feeding the Soviets intelligence, some of which was left carelessly lying on the floor of the codebreaking huts. Perhaps, Russia then distrusted Britain even more than previously when it had these secrets passed to it?

Britain did share great quantities of intelligence with the United States during wartime, and possibly with Canada and Australia too. That proved to be beneficial to Britain, and quickly led to improvements in both systems and equipment, even resulting in the American Navy building their own version of the Bombe for Washington. There would be visits of skilled personnel and officers in both directions over the Atlantic, to further military and political ties between the nations. The Lend-Lease agreement organised by the US helped significantly to oil the wheels of politics. It is arguable that with Lend-Lease benefitting Britain as allies, it could not have refused to cooperate, and sharing information on the Bombes and Ultra would be the least it could do to return the favour.

Vulnerability of ciphers and codes

One must always be alerted to seek where there may possibly be vulnerability to the security ciphers, codes, and systems that leave you exposed to the enemy to exploit those vulnerabilities. It can be stated that all nations engaged in the Second World War at some stages were left exposed to varying degrees. Identifying those weaknesses, and being informed by your allies to act, is an ongoing process. One can never become complacent and believe that your systems are 100 per cent secure. The Russians were certainly exposed to enemy intercepts of their messages and Bletchley Park had written a number of reports to highlight this. The question was how to approach the Russians with this information while not disclosing all the sources of the reports. A tricky situation. Of course, the most famous exposed system was that of the Germans' Enigma, followed by Lorenz, and the advanced machines. But there were periods when the Allies were stumped, and made little progress, with substantial losses of shipping and resources in the Atlantic. Modern-day organisations employ specialist experts to try to hack their own security systems, to discover and plug the weaknesses.

Speech synthesis and development

The impact of research in speech synthesis, and development into what would later become the vocoder, should not be underestimated. Encryption of speech conversations was essential in wartime, particularly for leaders of countries speaking to their allies on a semi-regular basis. Bell Telephone Laboratories would be up there with the best, developing systems and equipment such as the SIGSALY machine and others. Homer Dudley of Bell Labs had worked on the basis of speech synthesis and the origins of the vocoder in the 1920s and '30s. The early development of speech synthesis clearly goes back to pre-war years. Analysis of speech and investigation of frequencies would eventually bring about equipment to prevent the jamming of torpedoes being fired at the enemy, and the application of radio waves and radio frequencies to problem solving. These did not happen overnight, but were relatively slow burners in the areas of physics, science, and communications. The Americans were largely ahead, but let us not forget that Alan Turing in England was also developing speech-encryption systems in the latter part of the war and into the post-war era. Without effective speech-encryption systems the scrambler telephone systems would not exist, and the enemy may have gained advantages in compromising Allied conversations to a far greater extent than was the case in wartime.

Photographic reconnaissance

It is appropriate to add something on photo-reconnaissance as it formed a significant part of the intelligence gathering, an essential piece in the overall effort of data collection based on aerial photography. The use of aircraft fitted with specialist cameras in models such as the De Havilland Mosquito, Supermarine Spitfire, and many others, was widespread throughout the war, and gave the Allies essential information on both land and sea, from the air. This included feedback and evidence of damage from bombing raids on installations, target identification in advance of attacks such as before D-Day in Normandy, and many other situations. In the Cold War period the shooting down of Gary Powers' U-2 spy plane was a blow to the American Government and the CIA. However, the U-2 was one of the most successful reconnaissance aircraft before it was lost. The reader is advised to read the book *Skunk Works* by Ben R. Rich, which traces the development of this amazing aircraft, and leads us into the development of the stealth aircraft that now form the backbone of modern air forces, if you can afford the astronomical cost. The Skunk Works was a secret research and development unit within the Lockheed company, designing ground-breaking new aircraft for the US Government. Kelly Johnson was the chief engineer, and enabled his team of highly skilled designers to change aircraft design history with innovation and by taking risks. All this at a time largely before modern computers, although the stealth planes developed did have them. The average stealth fighter is really nothing more than a flying brick with weaponry and electronic guidance. Switch off the computer guidance in the aircraft and it really will fall to earth like a brick, as it is aerodynamically unstable. It won't really glide in the same way as a Boeing 747 if you switch off the engines. More a case of a vertical drop to earth. Better keep those computer batteries charged then? Drones are, of course, more commonly used now, both for attack and reconnaissance. The cost of drones will reduce over time, allowing even less wealthy enemy states and countries with terrorists to acquire and use them. Those will need to be monitored by Western defence systems.

The Official Secrets Act limits innovation in post-war Britain

When Tommy Flowers, the PORES engineer who had built Colossus Mk1 and Mk2, applied for a bank loan post war to develop further his ideas on machines, he was stopped from doing so due to the Official Secrets Act tying his hands. There was nothing stopping you from designing and building new machines, but the problem was if you wanted funding, then organisations and institutions like banks and finance houses wanted evidence you were up to the job and had a successful track record of this work. It was not possible to state that you made a valuable contribution to the war effort by designing and building similar machines. The drawings of the machines had been destroyed, as had the machines themselves. The legislation stopped you talking about what work you had done during the war. There was therefore a vacuum in respect of the technology and innovation, with nothing to show for it. The bank managers treated Flowers like some hare-brained inventor, who had ideas for something new, but nothing to show them as a demonstration, and they saw this as extremely high risk, and a potential loss of their money.

This was not the only example of legislation stifling innovation in Britain post-war. The Americans captured the computer market, and their main competitors were Japan, ironically, their previous enemy but now driving forward developing transistors, microprocessors, computers, and associated items. A sad state of affairs. The analogy might be with British-designed military aircraft that would be taken on board by the Americans and developed further due to a lack of UK funding. The Harrier jump jet is but one example. Frank Whittle's jet engine would change the world, but Britain would be left behind, except for firms such as Rolls-Royce, which would have its own challenges. Competition would dictate who developed what and when. Add to this the copying of intellectual property, which enabled Russia and China to make leaps and bounds in technology, saving much of the development costs and time by 'borrowing' ideas from principally Western powers.

Spies, agents, double agents and more spies ...!

Throughout history and certainly in the twentieth century, agents and double agents played an important role in helping to pass secrets from one nation to another. The West was rather complacent and allowed Russian spies such as George Blake and others to penetrate British security services with considerable ease. Few of the spies were caught. John Cairncross spied for the Russians at Bletchley Park, although he was being monitored to a degree. The most successful double agent was, arguably, Pujol Garcia or 'Garbo', who assisted in the Fortitude South operation approaching D-Day, and fed the enemy a pack of mistruths and lies about what was going on in southern England.[5] Garbo had the knack of creating a false network of agents to fool the enemy, and they sent substantial funds across to maintain this network, money that was passed to MI5 and the British Government. Whatever Garbo did seemed to work and deceive the enemy. After the war Garbo moved to Venezuela to escape a potential backlash from any remaining Nazis. He did eventually collect his OBE in London but could not say too much about the detail of the services he excelled at in wartime.

Interaction of the services in intelligence and codebreaking

We know that the codebreaking machines were largely operated and set up by WRNS personnel, but there would be others who would contribute greatly to codebreaking, and to intelligence support. These included RAF, WAAFs, and ATS, some of whom were based at Bletchley Park, and others at listening stations or elsewhere. Three quarters of personnel at the Park were female. Therefore, many women were instrumental in the process of deciphering enemy messages, or in collecting and processing enemy intelligence. Whichever service you were in, you were expected to wear their uniform and be loyal to them. That did not mean you would not work alongside other services if required to do so. It is rather sad that there are no new 'Wrens' in the services, due to the WRNS being disbanded some years ago. However, it is now possible for a Royal Navy recruit to apply for any job in the service, and none are excluded to females. This was not the case in the First or Second World War.

Films on Enigma and Turing

The interest in the Second World War and codebreaking resulted in two important films, firstly *Enigma* (2001), and secondly *The Imitation Game* (2014).[6] The latter film was largely about Alan Turing and his contribution to cracking Enigma using a combination of manual methods and codebreaking machines, the Bombe. *Enigma* was based upon the challenge to break Enigma with the Shark encoded enemy messages that were sent to and from enemy U-boats. It was also about uncovering within the coded messages a plot of the unlawful killing of Polish soldiers by the Russians. Of the two films, the author much preferred *Enigma* for the tension it produced. The excellent mood music by composer John Barry enhanced the film considerably. By contrast, *The Imitation Game* was trying to inform and educate the public about how Turing influenced the outcome of the war with his brilliance, innovation, and autistic character. However, it had large gaps in the story, and that may have given a false impression to those that were not well up with the history of the period. For example, only a prototype codebreaking machine was shown, and some have commented afterwards there must have only been one in use, which is both misleading and untrue. Some people are shocked when one informs them that there were actually more than 200 machines. There is no mention of the Wrens, or of the codebreaking outstations, or of the substantial and varied support teams that made the Enigma decoding process work. Neither is there any mention of the more advanced German machines that came into use, or that the 'Turing' Bombe was of no use in tackling those advanced machines due to its limitations in design. It is accepted that there are limitations in trying to compress a lot of historical facts into a movie of limited duration, and in a way that will not turn the viewing public off. Not everyone is enthused by Enigma, or of codebreaking as a subject. It had to be entertaining as well as educational. Of course, any film on Enigma and Second World War codebreaking is going to potentially help Bletchley Park Museum with increased attendances, interest in the subject and an opportunity to learn more. That is a constructive outcome, even if the director compressed history for the movie perhaps just a little too much for my liking. A third film, not so well-known, was *All the Queen's Men* (2001), which is about trying to recover the Enigma machine.

Other film productions may also have had a link to codebreaking over the years. Even the James Bond film *From Russia with Love* had the plot revolving around a cipher machine, 'The Lector', which looked rather different to an Enigma machine but was roughly the same size. It had a modern press-button keyboard. At least it was in a hinged wooden box and could be carried around, so was portable. Also note that 'Lector' rhymed with Spectre, the target enemy organisation in the film. Whether that was intentional or not, we will never know. Ian Fleming, the author of the James Bond books, had worked for naval intelligence and for MI5, so had a relevant background in writing his novels.

Has the wartime codebreaking story been covered in sufficient detail in those two films? Probably not. There are ample opportunities for film producers and media studios to explore further subjects related to codebreaking in a constructive and entertaining way, such as the story of the Polish mathematicians cracking Enigma, of the codebreaking outstations and the WRNS, of the story of Lorenz and Colossus, to name but three. I suspect that most members of the public have never heard of machines such as Typex, Lorenz, Robinson, or of Colossus, and their significance during the last war. Directors and producers out there are spoilt for choice in capturing parts of wartime history with a good scriptwriter. Dramatic films can sometimes get the message across to the general public far more effectively than just with a documentary.

HM Queen Elizabeth II unveils plaque at Watergate House in London

In February 2019, HM Queen Elizabeth II unveiled a plaque at Watergate House in The Strand, London. This was to commemorate the centenary of the origins of GCHQ in 1919. The plaque incorporated a coded message, which was unique for such an item. Watergate House was part of the evolving GC&CS, the Government Code and Cipher School, used for analysing intelligence and decoding messages. This was before eventually the Headquarters of GC&CS was established in 1939 at Bletchley Park in time for the start of the Second World War. During the author's visit to the Watergate House site in 2019, on the window sill at the front of the building was a boxed Monopoly board game, the Alan Turing edition. The interior designer had provided a simulated rotor wheel design near the entrance internally, emulating the Bombe codebreaking machines, but with digital technology. Note that no Bombe machines were actually in existence at Watergate House during the war, or at any time. It was far too early for that in terms of the history of codebreaking.

Science Museum in London holds exhibition on intelligence

In 2019 the Science Museum in London collaborated with GCHQ and held a special exhibition, 'Top Secret – From ciphers to cyber security'. This was open to the public to enable them to learn about the subject of ciphers, codes and intelligence, with spies and spying also playing an important part. A Lego model of the GCHQ 'doughnut-shaped' building was displayed, as were diagrams and drawings of codebreaking equipment. Cabinets displayed a variety of cipher machines, being part of 100 displayed items in total, some of a highly specialist nature. An envelope could be seen that had Government Communications Headquarters as the start of the address, which was intended for Bletchley Park before it closed down at the end of the war. This indicates that GCHQ was sometimes used instead of GC&CS, which was the official name of Bletchley Park during wartime. However, the exhibition did not indicate the relevance of codebreaking outstations and their role, or how they were managed with WRNS input. It would possibly have been a challenge to decide which items and information to include and which items to leave out, as space and time would have been limited. One of the more unusual displays was a piece of the Colossus machine in a glass case presented to the Americans in celebration of the UKUSA agreement for cooperation on ciphers, codes, and intelligence. Part of the display illustrated aspects of the Krogers, who worked from a suburban house in Ruislip, 45 Cranley Drive, passing state secrets to the Russians. The Krogers, who claimed to be Canadian but were Americans, were eventually arrested by the British authorities and prosecuted for spying. Their cover was to be rare book dealers in England. The Krogers' real names were Morris and Lona Cohen.

The GCHQ National Cyber Security Centre (NCSC) was represented and showed examples of a 'Ransomware' attack that affected many organisations including the NHS in 2017. A secure briefcase telephone used by Prime Minister Margaret Thatcher during the Falklands War was also on display. The exhibition ran for almost eight months until late February 2020. It was clearly timed carefully to mark the centenary of GCHQ in 2019.

Venona project and the implications for the Western alliance

For most the aim of the Second World War and participation in it was to defeat Nazism and defeat the Japanese in the Pacific. For some world leaders it was but a stage in the chess game for strategic planning to either acquire territory, or prevent others from acquiring it. What might have been apparent to leaders such as Roosevelt, Churchill, and Truman is that one did not want to end one world war only to start the next. The race for nuclear power was one of the catalysts to achieve strategic military advantage as a world power, and the Manhattan Project had secrets and technology that both sides would be keen to access for themselves. Keeping the technology on the A-bomb, on advanced jet engine technology and on rocket missiles was paramount, and yet it did not work out that way, thanks to several Russian agents and spies infiltrating Western intelligence networks and organisations. America and the West became seriously exposed in the technology race, and this saved the Russians (and perhaps even the Chinese) some time in development of military systems and nuclear arsenals. That warning bells were being sounded at Arlington Hall in Virginia in 1943 through their work on Russian intelligence, played through to the post-war period, and the Canberra embassy discoveries in Australia caused grave concern as to how fragile the Western intelligence services were, having been seriously compromised by the Russians. Analysis of thousands of encrypted messages identified more weaknesses, and the use of agents to smuggle valuable information back to Moscow. Many of these agents had senior positions in British and American agencies, while others were much more under the radar but doing immense damage to the Western states. Carelessness and sloppiness contributed to many of the intelligence breaches. McCarthyism was one of the knee-jerk reactions that would target communism in whatever form it was found in American society. The political fallout was not pleasant, but the NSA still had to work with GCHQ, Canada and Australia, and share information. Venona, as a project, took up valuable resources and opened the eyes of the Western leaders when they were eventually informed of the security breaches. Russia had time to bring their most trusted agents back to Moscow, relatively untarnished, and develop their weapon systems using information supplied to them. There would be exceptions to this, such as Klaus Fuchs, who would be exposed as an enemy agent by GCHQ, prosecuted in Britain and sent to jail. He would serve little more than nine years in prison, afterwards emigrating to the GDR. The Russians would also, by then, have a good understanding of NATO capabilities, and how to organise their Order of Battle should a conflict with the West be necessary. The Cold War was well and truly at a very low temperature. The Cuban missile crisis was not far away, and was the most dangerous time for the world in the early 1960s. The Venona project eventually fizzled out but other priorities took its place eventually.

The morality of spying on prisoners of war for intelligence

Both sides of the war spied on prisoners of war, mainly on officers but occasionally general enlisted men. While sometimes this may have been to identify planned escapes from prisons, the biggest prizes were in identifying and secretly recording conversations from generals and senior officers. These may cover a broad range of topics, from their thoughts on how the war was going, to disagreements between officers, to details of men and equipment under their control, and military strategy against the enemy. The Geneva Convention on prisoners of war could be conveniently overlooked when such clandestine attempts were made to listen in on private conversations. After all, some intelligence might be gained that could give the Allies an advantage tactically or strategically. It might even help shorten the war. The question here is whether such tactics were really necessary during wartime, morally sound, or not. Conversations of Nazi officers sometimes revealed horrendous details of human slaughter, almost as a game, including the shooting or execution of unarmed civilians, men, women, and children. War has a habit of bringing the very worst out of some human beings, and rules appear to be set aside for the sake of convenience. However, despite there being thousands of hours of audio recordings and transcripts from the recordings taken by the British of Nazi officer conversations, not one single person was prosecuted as a direct result of that evidence of serious wrongdoing and acts of atrocities in wartime.

A lawyer might challenge such evidence with arguments that the information was not provided formally in interview, and could therefore be considered as purely trivial conversation, misleading, exaggerated, or plainly untrue. They may say it would be inadmissible in court. It might be one officer demonstrating to another how they could prove to be a good Nazi and officer of the Third Reich by telling exaggerated stories of conflict and control over the enemy, even if the enemy was perceived as unarmed civilians and a threat to the state. That some of the listeners were Jewish refugees who spoke fluent German and would spend hours listening to the accounts of murder, rape, and other atrocities, must have had a detrimental effect on their mental health in the longer term. Such clandestine eavesdropping on prisoners of war is most likely common in wartime in world conflicts, and will remain as a potential tool for either party to consider as an option to gain intelligence.

The Holocaust and use of encoding machines by the Nazis for communication

While one expects an enemy to design, manufacture and use cryptographic machines and systems for communication in wartime, it is surprising that such technology and systems would be used for the horrors of mass extermination of Jewish and other innocent people. Yet this did happen, and reports were sent to and from divisional commanders, the German Police, the Gestapo, and other agencies, outlining the statistics and 'progress' made in Hitler's master plan for the Third Reich.[7] The deciphering and translation of such reports and documents by the Allies and post-war observers and historians exposed accounts of mass murder on a scale that was truly horrific. Enigma was but a tool for the enemy. It was how you used that tool that became important. The Nazis would have assumed that the Allies would never be able to decipher the Enigma-based encoded messages relating to extermination of human beings. They were wrong. One wonders how a Nazi soldier would have reacted when he was instructed by an officer to encrypt a message on an Enigma machine based on a report of mass killings of men, women, and children, and to send that message via Morse code to divisional command? What did he feel emotionally? How could he have enabled himself to press those Enigma keys, given the horrific nature of the report? But he was just a messenger. He did not write the rules. Adolf Hitler and his henchmen like Heinrich Himmler wrote those rules.

Loss of codebreaking sites and places of interest

The loss of several codebreaking outstations that operated during the Second World War included those at Stanmore, and at Eastcote, in Middlesex. Both were demolished to make way for much-needed housing. However, in hindsight, this was a hasty decision, as at least part of the sites could have been retained, with some of the hutting perhaps set aside as a museum or similar. The consequence of this loss of historic buildings and sites means that only books, articles, written accounts, and perhaps the odd video or film of wartime veterans such as Wrens and other personnel who worked at the sites remains as a record that something significant and important went on there. Some surviving personnel kept folders, articles, newspaper cuttings and even the odd photo as a memento. This could be passed on to their children and grandchildren for safekeeping. Bletchley Park still has the occasional veterans' day, bringing together surviving people who worked on wartime codebreaking, or in a support role, for a lunch. Some of these may even be on the Bletchley Roll of Honour, but there are some out there who never made it on to the Roll, possibly because they were not aware it existed or for other reasons. The outstations were effectively satellite stations serving the HQ, Bletchley Park, at the time. Their contribution to the war effort was enormous, and made a difference to the outcome of the war. In essence, apart from the country houses, they were a collection of basic huts and finger blocks, freezing cold in winter and boiling hot under the summer sun, quite unpleasant places to have to work long shifts on temperamental codebreaking machines. The Stanmore and Eastcote outstations have disappeared for good, but the public footpath that divided Eastcote into two is still there, and estate road names do have a link back to people who worked there or were involved in codebreaking. We have the local residents together with members of the Ruislip, Northwood, and Eastcote History Society to thank for that. The estate developers too, should be congratulated for allowing a commemorative plaque on the site so others could be informed about the history of the site pre-development.

We have a duty to keep the story alive for the younger generation, and to tell them what life was like before smartphones, laptop computers and iPads. This glossary or part of it, may assist the reader in that task, to a small degree. History societies should take the opportunity to learn more about what went on, who did what, who invented which machine, when did certain events occur, what were the outcomes at the time, and which mistakes were made by both sides. What can we learn from those times? In my view, it was all about bringing lots of different people together with very different backgrounds and skills, and making them work as a team, to a common objective, in helping to defeat the enemy. The Bombe machines and equipment did not always work well, equipment broke down, people became frustrated, but they persevered. There was a need to design and build ever more advanced codebreaking machines, and to train operators to set them up, run down checklists on clipboards, as though it was a pre-flight check for an aircraft, and set up the machines for a 'run'. The handbooks to operate the machines were still being written at the time and some of it would be trial and error. How on earth was a Wren who had spent years operating Bombe codebreaking machines now expected to operate a completely different animal, a Robinson or Colossus?

Bletchley Park and TNMOC at Bletchley have a responsibility to convey a balanced picture to the general public as to what went on during the war as regards intelligence and codebreaking. It is as much about conveying and informing the public and visitors about the immense drudgery and boredom of naval and other personnel setting up and operating equipment on very lengthy shifts, as is glamorising the subject of codebreaking and putting Alan Turing on a metaphorical pedestal. But people don't really want to hear about the less glamorous bits of the subject. Ironically, it may well be the close family members of codebreaking veterans that might be told more of what really went on, by their mother or father who worked on the machines, or in a support role, say at a listening station. That is, if they were at all willing to give their side of their stories as many did not, and never will. Bletchley has a process of procuring interviews of veterans where they can, as a record for the future. That is a good use of their time. When the veterans are gone, those interviews, photos and recordings may be the only things left, particularly as many of the sites involved during wartime have now been destroyed, dismantled, sold off to developers, or otherwise disposed of. While not all historical sites can be kept for posterity, great care should be taken in the future before such sites are eliminated for good.

Organisations

Abwehr

The German counter-intelligence agency and secret service of the German high command, prior to the Second World War and during wartime. The Abwehr possessed Enigma encoding machines, as did the armed services and others for communication. Decodes of the Abwehr messages were eventually successful by the British.

The Abwehr were organised as six groups broadly as follows when Captain Canaris took over command:

    Army Espionage
    Cipher Centre
    Counterespionage
    Sabotage and Uprisings
    Naval Espionage
    Air Force Espionage

Canaris would remove the Cipher Centre for others to manage, and concentrated on mainly espionage. The Abwehr would become a division of OKW and its status raised considerably. The largest section of the reorganised agency became Abwehr I, comprising nine groups: Army East, Army West, Army Technical, Marine, Air Force, Technical Air Force, Economic, Secrecy (Forgery/espionage), and Communications. The principal posts in the main cities were known as Abwehr posts or *Asts*. There would be one *Ast* to each of the military districts within the Reich. Each adopted a Roman numeral designation:

Koenigsberg	I
Stettin	II
Berlin	III
Dresden	IV
Stuttgart	V
Muenster	VI
Munich	VII
Breslau	VIII
Kassel	IX

ORGANISATIONS

Hamburg	X
Hanover	XI
Wiesbaden	XII
Nuremburg	XIII
(Area probably did not exist)	XIV–XVI
Vienna	XVII
Salzburg	XVIII
(Area probably did not exist)	XIX
Danzig	XX
Posen	XXI

There would also be units called Combat Organisations or KO, which operated across a range of countries. The Hamburg *Ast* was involved with naval activity against England and America, and had monitoring bases in South America, Greece, and the Iberian Peninsula. Wiesbaden *Ast* would take control of Abwehr operations for the invasion of France in 1940.[1] Dresden would take an interest in identifying enemy targets for aerial bombing, which is ironic considering that in the latter stages of the war Dresden was fire-bombed in February 1945 and largely destroyed by the Allies. The Abwehr would use Enigma machines extensively for communication.

The Admiralty

The British Admiralty joined forces with the War Office and army to establish the London-based 'Room 40' team of intelligence and codebreaking personnel back in 1919. This developed to become GC&CS, and an important base at Bletchley Park became the headquarters just prior to the start of the Second World War. The origins of the establishment would be the germ of a seed of the intelligence organisation GCHQ, which still protects Britain from terrorism and other acts against the state.

AFSA – Armed Forces Security Agency

This US organisation developed a specialist group termed SCAG in the early 1950s, and followed on with SCAMP (Special Committee Advising on Academic Problems) and NSAAB (National Security Agency Advisory Board.)

Bell Laboratories

The company that arose from the invention of the telephone and became crucial in the Second World War to design and build specialist equipment such as SIGSALY, which was used for encoded transatlantic communication between Britain and America. In the 1940s it was relocated to Murray Hill, New Jersey. Alan Turing would visit Bell Labs during the war. The company would go on to change the world in 1947 by developing the modern transistor, which would replace valves.

Bletchley Park

Established in 1939 with just a handful of specialist personnel, it would develop over wartime into a strategically important intelligence-gathering and codebreaking establishment, on a remote site in Buckinghamshire. Alan Turing, Gordon Welchman, and others would be recruited from universities to help attack the Enigma German encoding machines using a combination of mathematics, logic, and developing various systems over time, including electro-mechanical machines. Bletchley Park was under the jurisdiction of the Foreign Office, and expanded to involve several thousand skilled and semi-skilled personnel; linguists, mathematicians, classicists, military personnel and civilians, personnel from the WRNS, RAF, ATS, Army, and others.

Strictly speaking, Bletchley Park was born out of an earlier organisation, originating from the British Admiralty and the War Office, then later via Watergate House in The Strand, many years prior to 1939. The growth in departments, personnel, systems, and operations across the site and the later five satellite codebreaking outstations became a separate organisation based around GC&CS. There would be links back to Government intelligence agencies such as MI5. Three quarters of the personnel at Bletchley would be women. Some would be actual codebreakers alongside Turing and others, but many of them would also be in a support role, operating specialist machines, becoming data processors, Hollerith tabulating machine operators, or in administrative support. After the war ended, Bletchley Park would close down for a period. It was used as a training base for telecommunications engineers post-war, and was later established as a museum open to the public. The Mansion House dominates the site overlooking a large lake and extensive grounds. Many of the huts used for codebreaking operations still exist. At its peak more than 10,000 men and women worked at the site in a variety of roles, from typists, mathematicians, cryptologic experts, linguists, translators, radio telegraphers, Typex operators, some being military, and with many civilians too. The mix of civilians and military was unusual, and some Wrens were criticised for being out of uniform when a senior officer visited Bletchley. Three quarters of the staff on site were female.

The unique site at Bletchley Park and its history during the Second World War may sometimes give less well-informed people a misleading impression that it all happened at Bletchley, and that Britain and the Allies would not have won the war without it. While the contribution of personnel such as Turing, Welchman, Alexander, Tutte, Denniston, Michie, and others certainly made significant contributions to the war effort, the reasoning behind the Allies winning the war against the Axis powers and Japan are many and extremely complex. The cracking of Enigma and later the non-Morse codes using specialist codebreaking machines and codebreakers at Bletchley did save time and almost certainly shortened the war due to the gathered and decoded enemy intelligence. The distribution of information was not always efficient, and there would be various disagreements between management personnel and staff at times. It appears that the management of some of the naval code books used by the Admiralty was quite sloppy, and could be used to the enemy's advantage.

ORGANISATIONS

The changing of British naval and shipping codes and code books at the right time, and with the intention of preventing them being broken by the Nazis, had as much to do with reducing the impact of the U-boats on the Atlantic convoys as the decoding of 'Shark' intelligence via Enigma. Nevertheless, the complexity of the site and ongoing changes at Bletchley Park during wartime and afterwards, needs to be explored further. Therefore here is some basic information regarding some of the buildings, huts and blocks and their use:

Block A. Naval intelligence.

Block B. Italian air, naval, and Japanese codebreaking.

Block C. A hut that contained Hollerith tabulating punched card machinery and processing of punched cards. This was managed by the head of the Hollerith section via BTM, Frederick Freeborn. The punched cards processed, filtered and sorted data and intelligence as well as information relevant to the Bombe codebreaking machines for Bletchley Park. Prior to being contained within Block C, the equipment and Hollerith punched card activities were located in Hut 7 until November 1942. A further relocation was eventually arranged of the entire Hollerith punched card section to Drayton Parslow, a few miles from Bletchley Park. The reason for the relocation was that Bletchley needed the space occupied by both the machinery and vast volume of punched cards, which would be in the high hundred thousands, perhaps even millions. The cards would be an aid to record keeping, cryptanalysis and intelligence reporting, with data flowing back and forth between Block C or Drayton Parslow, and Bletchley Park.

Block D. A brick-built building at Bletchley Park that eventually housed the personnel of Huts 3, 6 and 8, relocated from the original wooden huts. Hut 8 was established to deal with the Nazi Naval Enigma traffic, such as U-boats and similar. It was cryptanalysts in Hut 6 that would convince management that codebreaking machines, the Bombes, would save much time in the decoding process. This used an electro-mechanical system that would be 'programmed' with plugging in lengthy connecting wires at the rear of the machine and using rotating wheels to simulate Enigma wheeled rotors. The term 'Ultra' was used to identify and categorise intelligence decrypts from Hut 6, and from Hut 8 initially. Welchman would devise a phrase 'Hut Six Ultra', to differentiate it from other hut-decrypted output.[2] Churchill would be kept informed of a summary of the important Ultra decrypted messages.

Block E. Radio transmissions and Typex machines.

Block F. It housed both Colossus and Tunny machines.

Block G. Traffic analysis and deception.

Block H. Tunny and Colossus machines. Now the basis for TNMOC, a museum on the site.

Hut 1. Until November 1939 this hut housed a SIS wireless station. It later also housed the first codebreaking Bombe machine, No. 1, called Victory, for testing in March 1940.

Hut 2. This was constructed in around May 1939 close to the north end of the mansion. It would house a lending library and later be used for German and Italian language classes from mid-1942. It was demolished in 1946. At times it would be used for recreation and tea.

Hut 3. Constructed in August 1939. This hut would become the main reporting centre for German Army and Air Force Enigma messages until summer 1940, including translation. A much larger Hut 3 would be built later, and the original was then relabelled Hut 9, probably causing some confusion initially.

Hut 4. Hut 4 was constructed in August 1939. It is situated south of the mansion and was one of the largest huts to be built on site, organised by Captain Hubert Faulkner. It had two later extensions. This hut housed the German Naval Section, which dealt with non-Enigma messages from the early part of 1940. In 1942 this moved into Block A and Block B. From then until the end of the war Hut 4 housed Military Intelligence, the Japanese Military Section, and parts of WT coordination. It is now a cafe and bar run by the Bletchley Park Trust as part of the Bletchley Park Museum.

Hut 6. Arguably the most famous and significant hut containing codebreaking experts in Bletchley Park during the war. It was also the subject of a controversial book, *The Hut Six Story*, written by Gordon Welchman after the war. The book was not widely publicised as there were threats from the American and British authorities regarding the content, which they claimed potentially compromised the security of the West. Hut 6 contained mathematicians, academics and codebreakers such as Alan Turing, Gordon Welchman, Hugh Alexander, James Aitken, Stuart Milner-Barry, Dennis Babbage, David Rees, Mair Russell Jones, John Jeffreys, and many others, who were tasked to break the Nazi Enigma machine codes and enable Britain and its allies to read the German messages once translated into English. Hut 6 would be established as an idea by Welchman, and run by Jeffreys for a time. Data would come in via listening stations across the country and abroad, and there would initially be hand decryption of the Enigma messages, followed by attacking the settings with the Turing/Welchman Bombe codebreaking machines at Bletchley Park and the outstations. The instructions given to the outstations for setting up the Bombe machines would be based on a 'Menu', a strange diagram with lines linking letters, which was determined by the codebreakers at Bletchley Park based on their analysis in the huts. The combination of the Menus plus the setting up and

ORGANISATIONS

running of the rotor-based Bombe codebreaking machines would help determine the settings for the Enigma machine. The aim was to eliminate the permutations of the settings as far as possible to arrive at the correct solution, which could then enable the message to be read once the settings had been programmed in.

Stuart Milner-Barry would succeed Welchman in September 1943 as the Head of Hut 6. There would be several hundred people involved in Hut 6, some carrying out manual codebreaking, others working with data received by Bombe codebreaking machines from other huts and the codebreaking outstations elsewhere. 'Typex' machines at Bletchley, operated mainly by women, would convert the decoded messages into German text ready for translation. There would be liaison with other huts and sections to make all this work effectively. While there would be some teleprinter machines available to communicate messages from Y-stations, the volume of these outpaced the number of machines. Dispatch riders were heavily relied upon on motorcycles to transfer the encoded messages and data to Bletchley Park. Many of the dispatch riders were Wrens, working in all weathers and travelling to and from the listening stations and the outstations. Listening stations would collect and write down the message data in groups of five letters or 'words', including the preamble the German Enigma operator transmitted prior to the main message for setting up. It was these forms that would be so crucial to the occupants of the huts at Bletchley Park. They would need to be filtered down and prioritised for decoding/processing. Gordon Welchman devised a system to help the efficient prioritisation of certain Enigma-based messages, which were teleprinted to Bletchley for speed. Let us not forget that the purpose of decoding the enemy Enigma and other encoding machines was to establish what they were planning, their order of battle, their build-up of resources, requests for supplies and information. The decoded messages would be passed to the chiefs of staff and the armed forces, and many were summarised for Churchill, who took great interest in them.

Hut 6 at Bletchley Park is now formally listed Grade II as reference 1391795 by Heritage England, which reflects its significance in British wartime history and places of particular specific interest, based on its use during the war for codebreaking and associated activities. It was within Hut 6 that Harold Fletcher kept a record of each of the codebreaking Bombe machines, liaising with BTM in Letchworth, the factory producing and manufacturing them. The two Bombe registers are currently on loan to the National Archives in Kew.[3]

Hut 7. The hut constructed in 1940 and used for punched card data processing as the Hollerith tabulating and records section. This was managed by Freddie Freeborn, an experienced manager from BTM in Letchworth, that company constructing the Bombe codebreaking machines. Information was collected, sorted and processed to support the analysis of enemy messages on a database using punched cards with Hollerith machines. There is relevance here to International Business Machines or IBM who provided the expertise and design input for the equipment including Hollerith machines, licensed for use in the British Empire via BTM. In November

1942, the Hollerith and Records section was relocated to Block C. Freeborn then set up a new processing section at Drayton Parslow, some miles from Bletchley Park, growing to a substantial operation using hundreds of women personnel. The relocation was necessary due to lack of space for the equipment and punched cards. Information relevant to Enigma messages and settings together with processed data would be sent back and forth from Drayton Parslow based upon requests from the Bletchley cryptographers and experts. From December 1942 Hut 7 became the cryptographic department of the Naval Section. It was later joined by the Japanese section in 1943. A battery room would be constructed in 1943. Wooden structures were demolished between 1948 and 1954, and the battery room modified in the 1950s. One woman, a Canadian who worked at Bletchley, including in Hut 7 and Block C during the war on Hollerith machines, was Doris Marshall, née Phillips. She worked very long hours alongside her female colleagues, and lived not far from the site. See *Freeborn*. See *Hollerith*. See *BTM*.

Hut 8. Tasked with working on cracking the Nazi *Kriegsmarine* (Naval) ciphers, Hut 8 would play a significant part in helping to protect British and Allied convoys across the Atlantic and elsewhere. Alan Turing would be in charge of the team at Hut 8 until Hugh Alexander took over from him in 1942. There was a strong link at Bletchley Park with Hut 4, which dealt with translations and analysis of the decrypted messages from Hut 8. A cold, and very basic wooden structure originally, there would later be a combination of people from the huts, including the personnel from Hut 8, relocating to a brick-built structure in February 1943 as Block 'D', with the Hut 8 name retained. The codebreakers in Hut 8 would have both successes and failures, with the latter particularly during a period of around ten months in 1942 when the additional fourth wheel rotor of the improved Naval Enigma machine defied decoding by those at Bletchley Park. This version of Enigma was referred to as Triton. The hut team would also break Luftwaffe ciphered messages as well as naval messages. The personnel codebreakers relied upon firstly the Y-stations, who intercepted and recorded the enciphered Morse code radio messages from the enemy, and the Wrens who operated all the Bombe codebreaking at the outstations, a small handful of machines being at Bletchley Park itself, mostly for training purposes and experimentation. The Americans were successful in intercepting the four-rotor-wheel Naval Enigmas, using their own improved version of the Bombe codebreaking machine built in Midwest America and moved to Washington for operation. Hut 8 at Bletchley Park is now formally listed Grade II as reference 1391796 by Heritage England.

Hut 9 and 9A. Constructed in autumn 1939 and housing military codebreaking and intelligence. The original Hut 3 was redesignated Hut 9, and a new hut, 9A was built as an extension to the north of Hut 9. It housed the diplomatic Yugoslavian and South American intelligence section and later ISOS. From 1942, both huts housed administration functions. It was extended in 1942 and demolished after the war. Hut 9 had blast walls protecting and surrounding the hut. The two huts were linked with covered ways when in existence, although it is unclear when they were constructed.

ORGANISATIONS

Hut 11. The hut containing several codebreaking Bombe machines for breaking the Enigma message settings. It would contain a small fraction of the overall quantity of Bombes housed at the five outstations in comparison. The hut was also used for training personnel on operational Bombe machines.

Hut 11A and 11B. This was part of the complex along with Hut 11 that formed part of GC&CS at Bletchley Park. Hut 11A was originally planned for use by the meteorological section, but that was put into Block A. Huts 11A and B were built between October 1941 and February 1942 and used for Bombe development, management of machines and maintenance. Historic England indicate seven Bombes were in these huts, but the author's research indicates a total of eight machines, based on the official Bombe registers. As new outstations for the Bombes were allocated elsewhere, the role of Hut 11A changed. It became a control and communications centre and linked Huts 6 and 8 with the outstations. These most probably incorporated teleprinter links. There was also Bombe training for personnel. Post-war, Huts 11 and 11A were used as carpenters' stores by the Ministry of Works. Hut 11A is a single-storey brick building with corrugated roof sheeting and steel roof trusses.

Hut 14. Communications section. Central Signals Register. Traffic and Records Section. Various teleprinters.

Hut 15. SIXTA. This was a collection of four huts.

Hut 16. Renumbered from Hut 6. Naval Section overflow.

Hut 18. Intelligence section, Oliver Strachey. Renumbered from Hut 8. Naval Section, Japanese Training School.

Hut 23. Renumbered from Hut 3. Photographic section, engineering, Bombe machine technical support.

The Mansion A substantial brick and stone two-storey building in the grounds of Bletchley Park overlooking the lake. It would be used for administrative purposes largely, with the mathematicians located around the site in huts, cottages, and a variety of single-storey buildings. The internal décor is rather ornate and grand, but the building had to be used during wartime in a practical way. Some of those working there were typists, mainly female, keeping records, filing, and acting as administrators. The mansion was listed Grade II by English Heritage in 1990 as it has important architectural features as well as having a place in British wartime history.[4] The mansion house combines Tudor, Gothic and Dutch Baroque architectural styles. The original house was enlarged and expanded by Sir H.S. Leon in the nineteenth century. One of the scenes in the bar of the film *The Imitation Game* was apparently filmed within the mansion. The building dominates the site and can form a reference point when wandering around the large estate, now an established museum.

Block B – Outstation Eastcote

While not strictly speaking an organisation, 'Block B' at the outstation was under the umbrella of HMS *Pembroke* V, the administrative naval term for 'Special X' duties operational work and personnel. It would be a series of linked finger blocks of single-storey huts on the north side of a public footpath, and they contained a large number of codebreaking Bombe machines operated by Wrens. The security of Block B included armed guards at entrances and exits, manned by the Royal Marines. All staff would have to show their security passes when passing through the gate, whether they were entering or leaving. Loss of a security pass was a serious issue for a Wren. The presence of a public footpath between Blocks A and B would be somewhat of a security concern. That footpath still exists to this day. A total of 103 Bombes were situated at Eastcote at the end of the war, based on the official Bombe archive records. However, the commemorative plaque outside the residential development on site that replaced the outstation indicates 110 Bombes. The difference between the two figures is considered to be marginal.

British Army

The British Army fought in North Africa, Sicily, Italy, Greece, France, Belgium, the Netherlands, Germany, the Philippines, Singapore, Borneo, and elsewhere during the war. It relied on military intelligence via a number of different sources. From spotter planes, observers, aerial photography, use of agents, resistance fighters, and also intercepted messages that may have found their way to Bletchley Park via Y-stations. The key here was for the messages to be decoded and communicated in good time to assist the Allied commanders and generals who were involved in planning operations, and this would not always be the case. Also, some of the British radio messages would be intercepted by the enemy. Effective communications would be essential to be one step ahead of the enemy, and to communicate with allies, which included the United States and Russia. The entry of the United States into the war after Pearl Harbor was a boost to the British Army as it virtually guaranteed the supply of valuable military resources, which were being stretched beforehand.

The British Empire

At the start of the Second World War Britain was relatively powerful as regards world influence, having established the British Empire through a combination of trade, wars, and occupation/colonisation. Countries within the Empire included Canada, Australia, India, several Caribbean islands, some African countries, and many others. Adolf Hitler was impressed with Britain and its world powers via the

Empire. He wanted the equivalent across the world, but for Germany. When war progressed against the Axis powers, many countries within the Empire provided soldiers, sailors, and airmen to support Britain and its resistance against the enemy. Many would lose their lives or become injured both in battle and in air raids. Some would contribute to codebreaking and intelligence-gathering abroad. But all was not well with the Empire. It had succumbed to occupational overstretch in terms of governing so many faraway places across the globe. The fall of Singapore during the war when invaded by the Japanese was of great concern to Churchill, who was fighting to protect not just the UK, but the Empire as well. By the time the war ended, the Empire was considerably weaker as regards British control and influence than before, and would never regain the power base that it once had. The analogy was the Royal Navy, which at one time ruled the seas with a considerable force of battleships and military vessels, but which significantly reduced in size over time. It has now become more of a support force under NATO than a power machine with great influence across the world. The Empire as such no longer exists, but several countries within the original 'club' retained strong links with Britain post-war. The influence of the Empire in the war helped Britain recruit and assemble manpower, resources and equipment to help defeat Hitler, Mussolini, and the Japanese. Hitler wanted his own version of the British Empire, but with a much more aggressive approach, and planned extermination of parts of the population, which was part of his strategy for domination of Europe, Africa and other continents. While there clearly were issues of human rights with the British Empire, Britain was poles apart from Hitler and the Nazis in terms of ideology.[5] Furthermore, Churchill was a leader but not a dictator, which Hitler certainly was.

The British Government and Cabinet

During wartime the British Government was led by Churchill as Prime Minister with his wartime Cabinet. It would be Churchill who would put so much emphasis on seeking out intelligence via Bletchley Park, the outstations and listening stations, as well as use of agents and double agents via the security services. He was aware that without knowing what the enemy intended and planned, Britain was in a relatively weak position strategically. Churchill worked closely with President Roosevelt and later President Truman after the USA entered the war. Secret communication links would be established to enable confidential conversations across the Atlantic between the allied nations. Sharing of intelligence would be crucial to enable the Allies to work more effectively against the enemy. A balance would also be needed to provide supplies, equipment, and intelligence to Russia, which was an unknown at the time but shared the hatred of the Nazis and all they stood for. Churchill was fighting not just for the UK against fascism and Hitler, but also for the British Empire, and the British aristocracy and in maintaining their way of life. He would be disappointed post-war at the elections when he would be out of office and a Labour government would sweep into power, making changes to society in welfare, health and improving living conditions for the British people. Churchill would be most remembered for his quality of leadership and his rousing speeches during the war, heading a Cabinet that brought the country together at a difficult time of immense challenges. Churchill understood that if the British negotiated peace with Hitler and the Nazis, they would become a puppet country without any powers, and would probably be invaded in later years. The British way of life would have been changed forever, and Churchill was not prepared to accept that gamble. Fortunately, most of the British people were behind Churchill, and trusted in his leadership. Britain, by its actions, had bought a little time for the Allies prior to America entering the war. Probably the darkest time was the defeat at Dunkirk, and the evacuation of most of the British Army to England. There would be much pressure from Foreign Minister Viscount Halifax to appease Hitler and use Mussolini as a negotiating tool. Churchill resisted this, and Halifax was eventually sent out of the way to Washington to a new post of British Ambassador. However, he was useful as he was in a country that would soon be brought into the war with Britain as a key ally. The War Cabinet met frequently in the Cabinet War Rooms in Westminster, and debates, discussions and heated arguments would rebound on the walls of the room to come together as a strategy. Churchill would seek opinion from others but would not entertain appeasement with Hitler. Chamberlain, Halifax, Caldecote, Cooper, Anderson and the Chiefs of Staff would attend these sessions with Churchill at the helm in the most challenging times. The threat of a Nazi invasion of Britain was a chilling consideration at a time when the British Army had been defeated in France, with most of its heavy equipment left behind on French soil. The War Cabinet knew and understood the German army and air force worked exceptionally well together in their *Blitzkrieg* movements across France, Belgium and the Netherlands. Their equipment was far superior to anything the British had. The only saving grace for the UK was the Channel separating France and England, which bought the British some time.

BTM

The British Tabulating Machine Company, or BTM, was a specialist engineering firm with a headquarters in London and factory in Letchworth, Hertfordshire. BTM built 211 Bombe codebreaking machines for Bletchley Park. Their chief engineer would be Harold Keen and he established a sophisticated production line to build the Bombes in a semi-modular form, taking components assembled from other nearby factories, many of them using female workers. The factory would allocate between one quarter and one third of its production area to making and assembling Bombe codebreaking machines. One of the problems was the increased demand for such machines by Bletchley Park as the war progressed. BTM would utilise other factories such as Spirella and other locations around the city of Letchworth to help manufacture wiring loom modules and components for the Bombe. The background to BTM was to provide equipment and systems to enable processing of data for census operations for various countries. This would be aided using Hollerith tabulating machines from America. The Hollerith machines would eventually be utilised on a large scale by Bletchley Park for data storage and

ORGANISATIONS

retrieval using punched cards. The Bombe codebreaking machines constructed in the Letchworth factory in Hertfordshire would be transported by road, under a tarpaulin for secrecy. BTM would have links with IBM in America and would develop via various company mergers post-war into International Computers Limited or ICL, between 1968 and 2002. It would eventually be acquired by the Fujitsu Company. (See references to BTM under 'Events' chapter.)

CESD

Communications Electronic Security Group.

CESG

Communications Electronic Security Department. This developed from CESD, which was absorbed into GCHQ in late 1969.

COMINT

Communications Intelligence. SIGINT, or Signals Intelligence, and COMINT would become synonymous with each other, and formed a framework for cryptographic work at Bletchley Park and elsewhere during the war. The work started prior to the war, and was improved, fine-tuning systems and modifying the approach to intelligence gathering and analysis to make it more efficient over time.

CSO

Composite Signals Organisation. Responsible for gathering information for GCHQ.

CSDIC

Combined Service Detailed Interrogation Unit. This was used to interrogate suspects, prisoners of war and those seen as a threat from Russia, Germany and Japan. Post-war, the threat was Russian agents and resources were allocated to expose them. This occurred between 1942 and approximately 1947, and had units across Belgium, Germany, the Middle East, Italy, the United Kingdom, and elsewhere. They worked with the British Army, MI5, and intelligence agencies. The unit closed down in 1947.

ELINT

Electronic intelligence, being a subset of SIGINT. Electronic pulses and signals from equipment. There are three separate aspects of ELINT: Tech ELINT; Op ELINT; Tel ELINT.

GC&CS

The Government Code and Cipher School would be established at Bletchley Park as the headquarters of codebreaking and security intelligence from 1939. The origins of GC&CS would go far back to Room 40 at the Admiralty in London, well before the war. It would emerge on 1 November 1919, and would be principally under Foreign Office control from 1922. Investigation of foreign powers and diplomatic communication were high priorities. From around fifty staff at the beginning, it would reach 200 personnel at the start of the Second World War. It would develop from GC&CS later into the Government Communications Headquarters, or GCHQ, via a metamorphosis of systems and personnel in the areas of intelligence and codebreaking. The war years would introduce machinery to assist in decoding enemy ciphers, alongside manual codebreaking methods. GC&CS was, indeed, a type of school or university where the mathematicians and codebreakers learned their specialist craft on the job. They researched new methods of decoding enemy ciphers, about their construction, cribs or clues, and the wiring of the rotor wheels on Enigma. Those at Bletchley in the codebreaking huts had to understand the links between enemy code books, changes in cipher keys, and the modifications to Enigma over time. It would be a constantly changing situation. New blood at Bletchley would help to a degree, and the diverse background of codebreaking personnel and support staff would be of great benefit in problem solving of complex ciphers. Mathematicians were sought after, of course, but so were those who could apply logic to a problem, including classicists, linguists, and others. The development of GC&CS in practical terms took time at Bletchley Park, but worked as efficiently as was practically possible with the separation of key tasks and communicating between the various huts and sections. There were around 10,000 staff at GC&CS at the end of the war, soon to be reduced to a fraction in the post-war years. However, this was a journey to develop GCHQ, which would have arguably even greater challenges in peacetime.

GCHQ

The Government Communications Headquarters was developed from a combination of intelligence personnel in the Admiralty and War Office, which developed eventually into GC&CS, and Bletchley Park in Buckinghamshire. A plaque at Watergate House in The Strand, London, commemorates 100 years of the GCHQ up to 2019, when the plaque was unveiled by HM Queen Elizabeth II. The modern GCHQ monitors and advises the British Government on matters of terrorism, cyber-crime and technical issues that affect national security. It is based in Cheltenham. Prior to being established there, it was at Eastcote in Middlesex until the early 1950s. By 1954 the transfer to Cheltenham was largely in place. There are a number of support sites around the country that assist GCHQ in their operations, and some of these are not generally known

ORGANISATIONS

about by the British public. The rise in cyber-crime in recent years has expanded that counter-intelligence section, particularly as foreign powers are allegedly using cyber-crime and hacking to disrupt economic and telecommunication infrastructure as part of espionage and attack on other nations. Being one step ahead of the enemy in understanding the imminent threats, the priorities, and the consequences of a successful attack by foreign powers is essential in a modern world. GCHQ liaises with security organisations such as the NSA in the USA and other equivalents across the world, sharing certain information on counter-terrorism and threats to society. The war in Europe has made such intelligence even more important than previously. The National Cyber Security Centre was opened in London in 2016.

A listing of some relevant GCHQ sites:[6]

GCHQ Cheltenham
GCHQ Ascension Island
GCHQ Bude, Cornwall
GCHQ Cyprus
GCHQ Scarborough, N. Yorkshire
GCHQ Joint Service Signal Unit (Digby), Lincolnshire
GCHQ London. (NCSC)
GCHQ Manchester
RAF Menwith Hill, N. Yorkshire

Former stations:

GCHQ Brora, Sutherland
GCHQ Cheadle, Staffordshire
GCHQ Culmhead, Somerset
GCHQ Hawklaw, Fife
GCHQ Hong Kong

Relevant organisations to GCHQ and its predecessors:

Room 40 Admiralty NID25&MI 1b (Pre-1919)
GC&CS[7] 1919–46
GCHQ[8] 1946–
LCSA 1952–65
JTLS Title adopted 1955
CESD 1965–1969
CESG 1969–

Full text of the last section can be found in the National Archives document 'Operational Selection Policy OSP 28 – Government Communications Headquarters & Its Predecessors'.

GRU

The Soviet Main Intelligence Directorate, Russian Federation. Established in February 1942 by Josef Stalin, in spring 1943 it gathered intelligence from countries and sources outside the Russian federation. It was run on behalf of the General Staff of the Armed Forces of Russia, and would become extremely busy after the Nazis invaded Russia. It would also make significant progress in the Cold War era in the 1960s against the West as regards intelligence.

Hollerith

An American organisation formed by an inventor of a tabulating machine, Herman Hollerith, an American-German statistician, which became highly successful as a production company both in America and abroad. Hollerith used his machines for census statistics and grew from strength to strength doing so, writing papers on the subject. The company was initially known as the Tabulating Machine Company at the end of the nineteenth century. Later, it became the Computing Tabulating Recording Company, but changed its name again in 1924. In the 1930s, the British Tabulating Machine Company in England (BTM) obtained the rights to market, hire, and sell Hollerith machines across Europe and the British Empire, paying royalties to the inventor. The significance of this was twofold: Firstly, BTM, through their use, application and expertise with these machines, went on to win the contract from the British Government to engineer and build Bombe codebreaking machines for Bletchley Park. Also, they would be experts in the use of the Hollerith machines to assist Bletchley codebreakers in collecting and filtering data from the enemy that had been decoded through interception of messages sent via the Nazi Enigma machines. Different versions of Hollerith machines would be provided, some known as pin-box tabulators. These were noisy machines, sorting information on punched cards en masse, in huge quantities, via electro-mechanical operation. BTM had used the machines for census operations for countries as far away as Africa, and understood their potential. The Hollerith organisation would be the first stage in the creation and development of International Business Machines, or IBM, from 1924, which would eventually dominate the business computing market, post-war. (See References to Hollerith under BTM and 'Events' chapter)

JSRU – Joint Speech Research Unit

This unit researched speech synthesis, analysing recordings, writing papers, and was set up at Eastcote in 1956. It eventually relocated to Benhall, in Cheltenham, in 1978. That is the site of GCHQ, the 'doughnut' building. In 1986 JSRU became the Speech Research Unit. There would be experiments carried out on magnetic tape, comparing physical conditions such as ambient temperature, humidity, barometric pressure, etc.[9] JSRU was overseen by Dr John Swaffield, a Post Office engineer, and with the development of a vocoder device. They would become involved with experimentation with vocoders since the 1940s. This was for more efficient use of submarine cables and audio communications. A vocoder is a speech synthesis device, and it became popular in the 1970s with some modern musical artists to distort speech in various ways.

JTLS – Joint Technical Language Service

This is a British technical translation service that provides technical support on language translation and interpretation across Government departments. While now within GCHQ, it started at Eastcote, in Middlesex.

Kriegsmarine

The German Navy, with Admiral Dönitz as senior commander. Dönitz moved from this role as the war progressed, and worked to support Hitler even more closely than previously as the Third Reich began to crumble under Allied pressure. Dönitz had considerable success with his U-boat wolfpack strategy, particularly in the North Atlantic, sinking numerous Allied convoys that were supplying Britain and America with resources. It was the naval part of the German Armed Services that would introduce a four-rotor-wheel Enigma for communication, and increase the permutations of the message settings considerably. Eventually, the Americans would design and build their own codebreaking machine to challenge the four-wheel Enigma.

LCSA – London Communication Security Agency

This came into being around March 1954. In 1958, the word 'Electronics' was added to its title, so it became the London Communication Electronics Security Agency, or LCESA.

LSIC

London Signals Intelligence Centre.

Luftwaffe

The German air force, headed by Hermann Goering. The Luftwaffe would communicate via Enigma, at least for part of their operations, and to request supplies and fuel. Goering was frustrated in not overcoming the RAF and air superiority prior to an invasion of Britain. The invasion, Operation Sealion, was postponed, and never occurred. Goering fell out of favour with Hitler for his failure, and never recovered his status in the hierarchy of the Führer's trusted generals and field marshals.

OP-20-G

This stood for Office of Chief Naval Operations, abbreviated as OPNAV. It was the 20th Division of naval communications, being the signals intelligence division of the US Navy. With around 150 personnel in 1940, they would set up a network of radio-telegraph listening stations. While military intelligence was its principal core work, it also collected foreign diplomatic intelligence for analysis. The four-wheel US Navy Bombe would be built under the umbrella of this organisation for cracking the four-wheel Enigma encoding machine. The machines would be built with the help of skilled women workers, WAVES, and civilians.

OP-20-M

A sub-section of OP-20-G, being tasked to research the feasibility of designing and building a codebreaking machine based on the British Bombe, but a more efficient version. It would need to tackle Enigmas with four rotor wheels as used by the Nazi *Kriegsmarine* in the Atlantic war with U-boats. The outcome of the research was the eventual commissioning of NCR in Dayton, Ohio, under Desch, chief electrical engineer, to build the Naval US Bombe codebreaking machines.

MI5

MI5 was the principal British security service during wartime and post-war, with an interest in maintaining and monitoring national security. It still exists but with modern technology and systems supporting it. Security was breached during wartime, and particularly during the post-war period by several British agents who defected to the East and Russia, and who provided secrets to the enemy. Most of these men were never caught. Some even boasted about how easy it was to steal British state secrets and hand them over to the Russians. The 'Cambridge Five' will go down in history as university-educated men who caused much damage to Britain in giving national secrets away, some over long periods of time. It was a wake-up call for the UK and its security services, who had allowed agents to infiltrate the organisation with some ease.

MI6

The international version of MI5, MI6 worked closely together with MI5 on certain joint operations, such as bugging prisoners of war during wartime at a senior officer level, and gathering intelligence. It now works alongside GCHQ and the UK Armed forces as a secret intelligence service with an interest in foreign powers and states, and identifying potential threats to the UK.

NKVD

People's Commissariat for Internal Affairs, Interior Ministry of the Soviet Union. A feared department of Soviet investigation and oppression from a political viewpoint, which would, arguably, develop later into the KGB. Its purpose was principally to protect Soviet state security at all costs, using whatever methods it deemed necessary. It would include the Russian Secret Police, which was feared by most when they arrived outside a house or business. It would operate from 1934 to 1946. During the early part of the Second World War, NKVD officers would execute thousands of Polish prisoners for political reasons.

OKH

German Army high command.

OKH-GdNA

Signals intelligence agency of the German army.

OKW

The high command of the German forces (Wehrmacht).

OKW-Chi

Decryption section of the German high command. This would monitor and intercept transmissions from enemy states, also from neutral countries. Additionally, it would control the security of the Enigma machine and systems, such as keys, and communicate information to authorised parties.

The Nazi Party

The political party officially known as the National Socialist German Workers' Party that took over Germany in the mid-1930s and whose aggressive policies towards neighbouring countries led to the Second World War. The party was active between 1919 and 1945, before being closed down following defeat by the Allies in the Second World War. The party would be structured with numerous sections and divisions across both political and military organisations. This helped form a national socialist fascist state for Germany, and later, Austria. Hitler was obsessed with recovering lost territory from Poland and adjoining countries. The alliances made with countries such as Russia soon disintegrated as the war developed. The invasion of Poland in September 1939 was the start of what would become almost six years of bloodshed and massive losses of men and women, until Hitler was eventually defeated by the Allies, leaving the Japanese remaining to be targeted. Racial segregation and forming an Aryan society of pure Germans by birth was a focal point policy of the party. Extermination of Jewish people and other minority groups such as Roma people would play a significant part in Hitler's strategy. His closest Nazi colleagues were constantly vying for position with Hitler to be seen as the one who stood out most, yet many of them despised their fellow colleagues, even to the extent of wanting to depose them from their hierarchical position. Goebbels, Speer, Goering, Himmler, and others would carve out their own niche to satisfy Hitler's demands. Some would be more successful than others. The Nazi Party is now banned in Germany as an organisation, and in many other countries across the world.

Pembroke V

A specific designation of specialist service within the Royal Navy, and relevant to the WRNS, who set up and operated codebreaking machines at bases termed Pembroke V or HMS *Pembroke* V. The name was an administrative term and was applied to codebreaking outstations and to part of Bletchley Park where Wrens operated Bombe machines.

Pers-Z

Department Z of the German Foreign Service.

Polish Cipher Bureau

This was also known as *Biuro Szyfrów*. It would be relevant between the First and Second World Wars, involved in signals intelligence and cryptography, with a track record in breaking early Enigma keys in the 1930s. Not only was the bureau targeting German and Nazi encoding machines, but Russian intercepts too.

Post Office Research Engineering Station

Abbreviated as PORES, the Research Station was based in Dollis Hill, north-west London, near Willesden. It would be the research engineering arm of the Post Office. The modern equivalent would be BT or British Telecom. The base would support Bletchley Park with engineered solutions for codebreaking machines, and would design and build the Colossus codebreaking computer to help crack the advanced Nazi secret writer non-Morse encoding machines. Tommy Flowers, one of the senior engineers, would be a pioneer in using valve-based technology as digital switches, but using many hundreds, if not thousands, of valves. Max Newman of Bletchley Park would work with Flowers to provide the technical brief for the machine. This was before the age of modern transistors and solid-state technology.

RAF

The RAF relied upon accurate intelligence in terms of everything from weather reports to flak to be expected on a raid, to the size and type of enemy resistance likely to be encountered. While the control centres of Bentley Priory and the Battle of Britain Bunker in Uxbridge helped to control Britain's aircraft defences and reaction times, the radar installations in England and Scotland combined with the Observer Corps were also key to the efficiency of repelling the enemy when they were approaching Britain's shores. There would be attacks on radar installations by the Luftwaffe, but over time they reduced as Britain and its allies commanded the skies over England and the Channel. TRE, the radar research experts in Malvern, had carried out extensive work to design systems to bend enemy tracking radio beams, and to provide aircraft with technology to their advantage.[10] At the time of the Second World War, TRE would be the largest research and production engineering factory in Europe, and would be visited by HM the King, but the location was kept secret. Bletchley Park had its part to play in continuing to crack Enigma message keys and decode enemy messages via Morse code intercepts using Y-stations around the country and abroad. It was up to the commanders in chief if they thought a particular type of intercepted message and detailed text was of sufficient interest to their subordinate officers. The Battle of Britain was not won by the British cracking Enigma, but more likely due to a comprehensive response and communication system in place to resist and counter enemy attack, together with highly skilled and brave pilots going back up again and again. Radar, the Observer Corps, and listening stations all played their part. The Commander in Chief, Air Chief Marshal Sir Hugh Dowding, was an exceptional leader, and knew how critical the situation was. When asked about reserve fighters, his response came back as 'no reserves, everything is up'. The cancellation or postponement of Hitler's Operation Sealion due to the failure of Goering to destroy the RAF gave Britain valuable time.

RAF Eastcote

The transition name for Outstation Eastcote and GCHQ, following their departure post-war. The base was used for a wide range of diverse duties and activities, and was then combined with US personnel. The US Navy were stationed there between 1981 and 1986 with Human Resources Management Centre, HRMC Code 016 London as part of CIRCUSNAVEUR London UK. Other USN commands included Military Sealift Command, Naval Investigative Service, COMNAVACTS, London Security Dept, US Civil Service Personnel Detachment, NAVComm Unit London Detachment. From 1986 it 1993 would have US civil servants occupying part of the site. The civil servants were then in charge of staffing, benefits, and human resources for American schools on military bases, and one such school was based at Eastcote on site. They were known as Department of Defense Dependents' Schools for the Atlantic Region. Marines would train on site and in Ruislip Woods not far distance from the base. The site would incorporate a morgue, a veterinary office, administrative offices, the Government's Property Services Agency, Post Office engineers, and many others. Block 4 was apparently occupied by the US Navy and Blocks 1 and 3 by the Ministry of Defence at various times.[11] An environmental impact report seen by the author prior to redevelopment of the site indicated there were plans of refurbished huts and blocks, so some physical improvements had been made over the years.[12] One woman who lived close by to the site at the time told the author there was a rifle range in the north-west part of the complex, but this has not been verified.

Royal Navy

The Senior Service built upon hundreds of years of Britain being a seafaring nation. The principal relevance to codebreaking and intelligence were the Wrens who carried out Special X duties and under HMS *Pembroke* V worked on the Bombe machines, later on Robinson and Colossus advanced machines. Also, the intelligence decoded by Bletchley Park and its outstations as to the location of enemy vessels, including U-boats, would be extremely valuable when fed back to Royal Navy commanders. The strong link to gathering intelligence and codebreaking is assisted by the forerunner to GC&CS being formed at the Admiralty and Room 40 in London many years ago. Later as the war progressed, Allied naval services would benefit from intercepted intelligence from the Japanese in the east, helping them to plan naval strategy. The coordination of Royal Navy shipping vessels and personnel during D-Day and its build-up was crucial to its success. Areas had to be swept and cleared of mines in the English Channel, and safe routes agreed for shipping crossing to Normandy.

RSS

The Radio Security Services were created by Vernon Kell, head of MI5, as a secret and instrumental part of gathering intelligence via radio and Morse code transmissions during the war. It was originally housed in cells in Wormwood Scrubs prison. Later it was relocated to Arkley View, north London. The cover reference was given as MI8c, for security reasons. Intercepts of interest were passed on to GC&CS at Bletchley Park. Some of the sources were logged and assisted by the Post Office, which monitored certain unlicensed transmissions. There may have been a degree of rivalry between Bletchley management and RSS, but it transpired that German Abwehr traffic was successfully intercepted by them, along with shipping intelligence among others. Through the RSS, some 1,500 radio amateurs were recruited to support the listening and monitoring services, the radio amateurs being Voluntary Interceptors or VIs and members of the Radio Society of Great Britain, or RSGB. The advantage of using experienced radio amateurs is that they were competent at listening into very weak signals. The atmospherics would vary from day to day and weak signals would come and go. A detailed TV documentary was made for the BBC some years ago by the RSGB via Paul Cort-Wright. Clearance from the security services to make the programme apparently took a couple of years. It is important to recognise that the listening services during the war were comprised of a number of organisations, including formally vetted radio amateurs under the umbrella of the Radio Security Services, and not just formal Y-stations.[13]

SCAG

Special Cryptologic Advisory Group. This was established by the Armed Forces Security Agency, and comprised academics, engineers and industrial mathematicians.

SCDU

Services Communications Development Unit.

SIGINT

Intelligence-gathering methodology that involves the interception and analysis of signals emitted by enemy communications systems, radar, and weapons. See also COMINT.

SIM

The Italian Army intelligence agency.

SIS

Secret Intelligence Service of the UK. Also known as MI6.

SIXTA

The traffic analysis section that moved to Bletchley Park on 5 May 1942, although not officially under the name of SIXTA, which was to come later. New huts were constructed for this purpose. This would be specifically radio traffic, incorporating everything about the intercepted messages, including frequencies, call signs, identification of transmitting units, time of transmissions, and supplementary information. It was a separate process to the cryptographic process of decoding messages. It would occur before the decoding, or in the early stages of the decoding. An example was the tracking of *Bismark*, where direction finding and other means were useful in locating the German warship. Bletchley Park combined the processes of SIXTA and cryptographic work. Caxton Street in London was also an important location for intelligence gathering and analysis. Call signs of the enemy were particularly of interest, and discovering networks and keys of the enemy communications. Log readers read message logs and compared messages with message data. A few log readers in the early years would initially be trusted with knowing about the Enigma encoding machine being broken. Gordon Welchman, codebreaker at Bletchley, was keen on keeping people informed about the work they were doing. This would improve morale and probably the output too. Card indexes and Hollerith machines were used as a sort of database of detailed information from the messages intercepted. Connecting network diagrams with lines, arrows, text and markers would be produced on a large scale to mark the communications links of the enemy, based upon the traffic analysis carried out. This was a visual prompt for the Allies to follow, and to learn about how the enemy was communicating and operating. SIXTA was really a combination of different sections and on 5 February 1944, it became officially known by that name. The abbreviation or name may have been based on the sections that came together, with TA standing for traffic analysis. Hut 6 was also relevant for intelligence reports and could have been the trigger for the new name. This combined service was set up several months before D-Day.[14]

SLU – Special Liaison Unit

Formed in 1940, and part of MI6 intelligence agency, it provided Ultra intelligence to British and later American commanders, and military senior officers.

SOE

The Special Operations Executive was formed to carry out special operations abroad, often in occupied enemy territory. It was a volunteer force formally established in July 1940. There were different branches of SOE, such as the Norwegian branch, which was based in Baker Street, London, where operations were planned to disrupt enemy strategies.[15] This location would also be the base for other SOE sections. The operations were a combination of sabotage and espionage. Most SOE operations were carried out in Europe, or part of occupied Asia, and involved both men and women, who put their lives at risk. Subsections of SOE would include propaganda, operations, and research.

Spirella

An American company originally, it would make foundation wear and women's corsets in Letchworth in Hertfordshire. Its workforce would make parachutes during the war for Irvin's, based down the road. The engineering factory BTM in Letchworth needed more space and workers to build the Bombe codebreaking machines, and negotiated with Spirella to allow it to use a large part of the factory for assembly of components with women workers. The corset production would move temporarily to London while this occurred. The components assembled on long tables by women would be transferred back to the BTM factory and incorporated into the Bombe machines. The workers would not be told what purpose their assembled components would be used for, as it was considered top secret. In utilising Spirella, BTM were able to keep up Bombe production to serve Bletchley Park and its outstations. Spirella concentrated on wiring and drum components, which would be delivered to the main factory as sub-assemblies for incorporation within the Bombe machines. A photograph exists of workers at the table assembling components and is termed 'Wizards with Wires'.[16] Spirella was a company with philanthropic leadership, and hospital beds would be set aside and paid for in the local hospital to ensure Spirella employees would receive good care without delay if they fell ill. The Spirella site would later be refurbished at great cost, and is now used by businesses. (See references against BTM under 'Events' chapter).

Y-Stations in Great Britain and support

Y-stations, or wireless listening stations were not a specific organisation. However, they were established by and managed by a different number of separate organisations. These included the Foreign Office, the Army, the RAF, and the Post Office. There was also FORDE, or the Foreign Office Research and Development Establishment, a section of the Foreign Office. The listening stations would be situated in both Britain and abroad, listening out for enemy radio transmissions, often in Morse code, and encoded via Enigma or a similar encoding machine. Some of these transmissions would be from Britain's allies, such as Russia, or neutral countries such as Switzerland. Switzerland was particularly vulnerable, however, due to their neutrality and interest in them by the Nazis, to the monitoring of transmissions and transactions in their financial sector. Without the Y-stations, the vast majority of radio traffic would not be intercepted and the intelligence decoded. Overseas listening stations in Allied countries such as Ceylon and elsewhere became important bases in helping with the collection of intelligence and radio transmissions, particularly across the Mediterranean and Far East. A vast network of Y-stations was resourced with skilled personnel from the ATS, RAF, Voluntary Interceptors, and others, to pass details of intercepts to Bletchley Park and traffic analysis experts, so they could filter out information that may be of use to the Allies. The radio equipment, aerials and equipment had to be maintained and replaced from time to time, and the Lend-Lease initiative by the Americans helped significantly in this respect in supplying American radios for some stations. Receivers used included the AR88 Military Receiver (RCA) and the National Receiver Company R106 HRO, which was also used widely in India, Hong Kong, Ceylon and elsewhere. Morse training sets and keys would be used for training personnel, such as the US signals Morse key. There would also be specialist spy receiver sets, such as the B2 Type 3 Mk2 spy set, used around 1942, and later a Mark 3 version. With the large aerials that were 60ft high, one might achieve reception of a range of 1,000 miles, subject to favourable atmospherics.

The National Archives

Based in Kew, Surrey, this records office and database of historical documents is the principal starting place for historians, researchers, and those wishing to study history. The two volumes of the wartime Bombe codebreaking machines are on loan, at the time of writing, to the National Archives.

TICOM – Target Intelligence Committee

The objective of TICOM would be for the British and their American allies to obtain secrets of the German codebreaking systems, signals intelligence, and to penetrate them. This was additionally relevant to the latter stages of the war, when there was a race between the Russians and the Allies to seek out secret technology, documents and cryptological system information from the Nazis, who would be retreating and trying to dispose of confidential military documents. The Russians had the advantage in the east and the other Allies in the west. Russia also had the intention to capture and occupy large areas of Poland and other countries during their advance on Germany.

TRE

TRE stood for Telecommunications Research Establishment, a secret radar research base. It was originally based in Dorset and then relocated during the war to Malvern in Worcestershire. It would develop complex technical solutions using radar, radio waves, and similar for aircraft, but also contribute to some of the codebreaking machines. It would occupy the site of Malvern College for the war's duration, and expand the site to employ several thousand people, from scientists to engineers. TRE would study and record the radar signature of the V1 flying bomb as part of its work. TRE would have links with Bletchley Park and the Post Office Research Engineering Station in Dollis Hill, and provide technical support when needed. One of the physicists was Wynn-Williams, who contributed to the Robinson advanced codebreaking machine. Several of the physicists and scientists would go on to greater achievements post-war, such as Sir Bernard Lovell, who was the director of Jodrell Bank Radio Telescope. The development of Window, or chaff, was achieved at TRE during wartime, and it is still used today by air forces around the world to confuse enemy radar when missiles are being targeted at planes. It consists of numerous aluminium or metal foil strips of lengths calculated to interfere with enemy radar frequencies. TRE was able to identify the radar signature of the V1 and V2 rockets, although the latter was less relevant due to the speed at which the missile flew that made it impossible to shoot down once it had been launched.

The modern equivalents of TRE are Qinetiq, which was a company and organisation formed in 2001, established from a reorganisation of the Ministry of Defence and DERA (Defence Evaluation and Research Agency). Qinetiq was originally wholly owned by the British Government.[17] It carries out specialist research to benefit the UK defence systems, and has contractual links with allies in America, Canada, Australia, and elsewhere. Some of its key sites are in Farnborough, Hampshire; Boscombe Down, Wiltshire; and Malvern,

Worcestershire, England. The last, Malvern, is the original geographical location of TRE. Qinetiq works in fields such as air defence, cyber training, simulation and training, electronic warfare, space technology, maritime systems, security and science and technology. New technology and research forms a substantial part of the organisation. Nations that lack such organisations are at a potential disadvantage in modern times, in terms of military and technical equipment and systems, and have to rely on those allies with the appropriate resources. Training is a large part of such organisations and is offered to other countries and nations with an interest in NATO.

US Signals Engineers

These were involved in intelligence and codebreaking support during WW2, with three sections sent across to England to assist with codebreaking activities, namely 6811th, 6812th, and 6813th US signals via the ETOUSA initiative.

Voluntary Interceptors

Voluntary Interceptors, or VIs, would initially be amateur radio enthusiasts who would be used to listen out for enemy Morse code transmissions on a part-time basis. They would be organised via the British Government, part of MI5 and the Foreign Office. Effectively, a secret organisation within another organisation. Feedback from the VIs would be recorded on log sheets and sent to PO Box 25 in Barnet, awaiting instructions. When VI radio operators were called up for military service, many would be offered the opportunity of continuing their radio work in a more formal support organisation, at Hanslope House or similar. This would develop into an important wartime network to gather intelligence alongside the numerous Y-stations, often targeting specialist enemy objectives. The Radio Society of Great Britain (RSGB) has detailed information on VIs and their equipment, which varied from enthusiasts' home-built receivers to American-supplied radios under the Lend-Lease facility. Providing one had one's amateur radio licence, there was no barrier to a government agent approaching you to recruit you as a Voluntary Interceptor. Specific radio frequencies would be allocated to the amateur, and then Morse code transmissions would be recorded on a log sheet giving the frequency, date and time. Communication would then be forwarded to Barnet, awaiting further instructions. Although the majority of VIs would be male, some female amateur radio enthusiasts were also recruited for this specialist work. The VIs would come under the umbrella of the Radio Security Service or RSS.

WAVES

Women Accepted for Volunteer Emergency Service was established by the US Government on 30 July 1942. This was part of the Navy Women's Reserve Act formally signed by Roosevelt. They would be women recruited between the ages of 18 and 36, and officers between 20 and 50, for US naval support on a variety of naval duties and tasks. A proportion of WAVES would work alongside OP-20-G, the communications and signals intelligence service. They would help build the US naval four-wheel Bombe codebreaking machines and then operate them. The Bombes would be built in the Midwest and then transported across to Washington to be used against Nazi U-boat intelligence. Mildred McAfee was sworn in during August 1942 as the first Naval Reserve Officer in charge of the WAVES. She would also be the US Navy's first female officer. Relatively few WAVES personnel would be on the four-wheel-Bombe production. Many of the WAVES were stationed at naval air bases and worked on aircraft, and aircraft systems maintenance, releasing men to go to sea and fight. The organisation was extremely successful overall in providing a valuable resource to the American war effort.

WRNS

The Women's Royal Naval Service, abbreviated as WRNS, or 'Wrens' was created during the First World War. Part of the Royal Navy, the WRNS was officially established on 23 November, 1917 and the director was Dame Katherine Furse. HM King George V granted Royal Assent for the establishment of the WRNS a week later, on 28 November. The headquarters were in Westminster. Initially, 10,000 women were targeted to be recruited to the new service, many of them officers. Officers would have to be mobile, but ratings could be either mobile or immobile and work at a nearby base. The first initial training course was established for officers on 26 January 1918. The first Wren to lose her life at sea was via a U-boat torpedo outside Dublin Bay on 10 October 1918. The WRNS was disbanded after the war, but then resurrected for the Second World War. Most of the bases for the WRNS were shore-based naval stations, some inland. During the First World War the female personnel amounted to 438 officers and 5,054 ratings.

Vera Laughton Matthews was appointed director of the WRNS in April 1939. Recruitment was widened to allow more ratings into the service, and there would be fewer upper-class or aristocratic women as officers as compared with the First World War. Ratings now came from all walks of life. There would be 74,000 Wrens in total across a wide range of jobs including administration, radio mechanics, air mechanics, air radio officers, dispatch riders, cooks, depth charge technicians, torpedo technicians and equipment support duties, radio work for the Navy, and 'Special X' codebreaking. Only a relatively small percentage of the whole would be in this latter category. Some would be trained at Mill Hill, north London, others at Wimbledon or in Scotland. Basic training lasted around two to three weeks. When appointed to specialist 'Special X' work, they would attend Bletchley Park or one of the five outstations to work there, usually on a shift basis. They would then be taught about the secret machines for codebreaking and had to sign the Official Secrets Act before starting specialist training. They would set up the Bombe machines, make connections, record output, and operate auxiliary equipment, as well as communicating back to HQ with output information. Some WRNS personnel would work at 'Signal City' in Greenock, Scotland. Many were later sent abroad to work in Ceylon against the Japanese. Several hundred Wrens worked at tropical Y-stations, listening stations using radio equipment. Both Wrens and WAAFS worked on Combined Headquarters operations at Portsmouth on the coordination of D-Day landings. More than 5,000 radio signals were sent out from there on D-Day, 6 June, 1944. What is less well known is that Wren officers worked as official Government censors at the English ports to maintain secrecy and avoid key information being passed to the enemy from soldiers' and sailors' letters. The WRNS was dissolved in the 1990s but all posts are now open to both men and women in the Royal Navy. There is an Association of Wrens for those who worked in the Wrens. Many Wrens also appear on the Bletchley Park Roll of Honour to mark their involvement in codebreaking duties during the war. Those on the Roll are entitled to a certificate and a GCHQ medal. The National Arboretum has a memorial to a group of young Wrens who were killed and torpedoed during the war on SS *Aguila* in a convoy on their way to serve in Gibraltar as cipher clerks.

Commentary on Organisations

The organisations listed are many and varied. Indeed, one could have almost doubled the chapter with many other, mostly rather obscure organisations, but the purpose of this glossary is to give the reader a flavour of the subject matter. Bletchley Park was a type of pseudo-organisation, i.e., an organisation within a larger one, i.e. the British Government. Due to its importance and relevance, more time had to be spent in giving it space here. When one considers the codebreaking outstations, the relationship to their controlling organisations was rather peculiar. They provided work for Bletchley Park, and that was the reason for their existence. However, they were not, strictly speaking, part of Bletchley Park. They were support to GC&CS, housing more than two hundred Bombe machines. The personnel running the outstations were a mix of RAF engineers, and rather a lot of Wrens from the Royal Navy, operating and managing the codebreaking machines. Mention the Royal Navy to anyone and one automatically thinks of large warships, sailors in uniform, and the sea. However, none of the Wrens at the outstations were at sea, on ships or anywhere near the sea, so that was a strange situation. Some cipher officers transported from Liverpool to Gibraltar on merchant ships were torpedoed by U-boats, and sadly lost their lives. The sea was a very dangerous and hazardous environment in wartime. The interesting aspect of organisations in wartime to the author is the diversity of them. From the Wrens in the Royal Navy, to PORES, being a Post Office engineering arm, to BTM, a commercial factory and company, to Spirella, a company largely taken over for Bombe part production by BTM, to SIXTA, an intelligence section that developed over some years to aid codebreaking. The communication had to be via letter, typed memoranda, telephones, or personal meetings. There were no computers, smartphones, tablets or laptops, and no hard drives to store information or data, only punched cards and punched paper tape. This meant lots of indexes to be catalogued and managed to store and retrieve data. Movement from one organisation to another was sometimes straightforward and sometimes not. If you were in the Royal Navy and the WRNS, you had no choice if you were redeployed up in Scotland or sent to Outstation Stanmore or to Eastcote for duties. You were often trained on the job, and on a 'need to know' basis. But it was not usually possible to move from the Wrens to say, a factory or a commercial organisation, as your role in the services would be both prescriptive and formally contracted to the Royal Navy, and therefore limited. As a comparison, US Army signals engineers came to Britain from America to work on operating and maintaining special encoding/decoding machines such as SIGSALY, 60ft or so below ground level in the basement of a Selfridges annex in London, but that temporary redeployment was purely to assist the war effort in maintaining secure communications across the Atlantic between allied world leaders. They would return to the US after the war and dismantle their equipment to take it with them. Those within Bletchley Park could sometimes develop a niche for themselves and sections would develop and improve over time, such as SIXTA. Those with a good knowledge of German, Japanese or Italian languages would be promptly identified and tasked with using their language skills in translating foreign messages.

The metamorphosis of Bletchley Park in wartime is a subject by itself, with huts being modified, relocated, merged, demolished, and rebuilt as the need for the sections and experts developed. Add to this the moving about of skilled personnel, establishing various teams of people to perform important tasks, in order to feed decoded intelligence to the commanders, generals and sometimes to Churchill.

The 'mix' of organisations in wartime

Even Churchill, as Prime Minister, would have struggled with the vast range of different organisations working together in the war effort. Some would have been more familiar than others, and be referred to in memos, reports, and top-secret documents. Churchill relied on others to put him straight on who did what and their relevance; after all he was mainly concerned with the big picture of things, and not the trivia. But he was able to step in and make a speedy decision when four codebreakers at Bletchley Park wrote to him because they were concerned about a lack of resources. The interaction between several different organisations can be appreciated to a degree by studying this glossary. However, due to the vast number of them, many across different countries and continents, much detailed research may be required to truly understand the influence of an organisation or those within it on the Second World War and beyond.

Several countries would have their own intelligence and cryptologic base and organisation, developing further over time. The Poles are an example of this, utilising their knowledge and skills before the invasion of Poland, and then establishing a different location outside their country to continue their work, such as at Uzès in southern France, and later in England. Luck also played a part in the story as well, such as the German traitor who fed Enigma secrets and documents to the French, which were later shared between the Poles and British and gave the Allies an advantage, at least for a time. If that traitor had not come forward at the time, looking for financial gain in return for selling state secrets, the journey to crack Enigma may have taken longer and perhaps could have changed history.

The development of organisations into the modern twenty-first century can be tracked, such as the Russian state bodies GRU, NKVD, KGB, FSB, and so on. The same is true to a degree in Britain, the United States, and elsewhere. Cyber-crime is now a potential threat to the security of a country or state and has to be taken extremely seriously, sometimes even using 'turned' criminals to work for the state, utilising their knowledge and expertise to identify weaknesses and plug the holes in security systems. Cyber-crime is a relatively modern trend, but realistically it is largely about deception and deceiving people. That is what the Allies were trying to do with the enemy in the Second World War. The methods to deceive the enemy were many and varied, and involved large quantities of people across different organisations, who identified both tactical and strategic options of deception. D-Day may have been the greatest prize in that respect, accepting that it is rather difficult to conceal thousands of ships and craft moving from England across to France. The deception tactics used by many organisations and filtering down to individuals such as double agents appeared to have made an important difference to success in Normandy, buying crucial time for the Allies.

Communications

Keeping communication lines open between organisations was, of course, essential, and necessary in wartime, and that included comms between different nations, e.g. the Canadians, Americans, British, Commonwealth countries, those in the Pacific, etc. Timing of assaults and battles became critical to have the greatest impact on the enemy, whether that be arranging a barrage of shells from tanks and field guns, or a coordinated attack on an enemy airfield or bridge. Feedback from the enemy intercepts would be valuable to the Allies and some of that would come via Y-stations and Bletchley Park, but not all. Local intercepts of the enemy on the battlefield and across the countryside would also be of interest. Captured prisoners of war would sometimes be helpful in identifying units, unit strength, Panzer divisions, fuel resources, or call signs of units. SIXTA back at Bletchley would be pulling together network diagrams of the traffic analysis as fast as they could. There are some reports that indicate as the war progressed SIXTA had identified a more comprehensive picture of German communications and units than even the enemy understood themselves. It took a great deal of work to achieve this level of detail, and clarity of the roles of skilled personnel. Codebreaker Gordon Welchman was very keen on informing log readers of the existence of Enigma, and in what they were trying to achieve, but had to obtain clearance before they could be brought within the security loop. He was supported by management and that may have boosted morale at Bletchley.

Post Office engineering

The Post Office and PORES are interesting as regards organisations. The GPO encompassed not only the postal services for the country, but additionally the telecommunications network, such as telephone exchanges, telephone boxes, cabinets with relays, and more. PORES was the research arm based in Dollis Hill, north London. It would take many years after the war for the British Government to recognise that the technical communications part was very different to the postal service, and it was then eventually sold off as British Telecom or BT, with members of the general public able to acquire and buy limited quantities of shares. During wartime, there was a drive to modernise the network as far as practically possible, subject to available materials and resources. The research station assisted with testing and building equipment for the telephone service. We need to reflect that in those times, the average member of the public did not have a telephone, and that even if you applied for one there would be a waiting list. This continued even post-war, until the network was expanded. Businesses and Government would get priority for telephone lines. To see the development of equipment and systems the reader is referred to UK telephone history online, which is based on the BT archives. Although top secret at the time, the public would have been amazed to learn that the Post Office Research Engineering Station was designing and building equipment to help decode and attack Nazi enemy encoded Lorenz teleprinter transmissions in conjunction with Bletchley Park. The public did not know of Bletchley at the time. Most had never heard of PORES either, and even if they did they might believe that it was really all to do with telephones and exchanges. In effect, this was a useful cover for those who ventured into codebreaking machines and systems. Only if you happened to work there would you know the location and certain activities, but secrecy and security was high on the agenda. Depending upon your job, you may have had to sign the Official Secrets Act.

Dollis Hill also had a track record in the 1950s, with its specialist telephone engineers successfully helping the Americans to tap into several Russian telephone lines in East Berlin from within an excavated tunnel penetrating the East German sector. George Blake, a Russian spy who worked for MI5 in the United Kingdom, exposed the existence of the tunnel after thousands of hours of recordings of Soviet telephone conversations had been recorded on to tape.[1]

BTM opportunities

The British Tabulating Machine Company Limited made a number of changes to its organisation before the war during wartime and later post-war. There was a London base for the business, but much of it relocated to Letchworth in Hertfordshire, and it was extremely successful at helping to manage census statistics for the UK and many countries abroad. It was, perhaps, this background that made certain senior officials in the British Government and possibly some senior civil servants look at BTM as a potential asset in helping to build decoding machines, the Bombes. It would be a gamble of course, as no one had designed or built such a machine, unless you count the Poles, with their far less complex 'Bomba'. But BTM had a good, robust track record, with strong contractual links to the United States in terms of licensing of Hollerith machines for calculation, and in sorting punched cards for data management. One wonders who else might have been approached in BTM's absence? There would be very few companies and organisations within this very specialist field in the early 1940s. One needed factories away from the big cities, so as not to arouse suspicion. Also, a resource of competent engineers, and space in the factories for the production of Bombes. With conscription in full force in wartime, some of the engineers may have received call-up papers to join the armed forces. However, strings may have been pulled to exempt some personnel as the work they were involved with might be of national interest to the state. BTM would have to involve other organisations to make it work as the need for more machines was identified by Bletchley Park. Spirella, down the road in Letchworth, would give up considerable space in their factory for BTM, and a production line of making and assembling components for Bombe machines would involve numerous women sitting at long benches, some who would have previously been making women's corsets and foundation wear. These would have been skilled and semi-skilled workers, with quality control high on the agenda. The final assembly would be back in the main BTM factory, on a big metal framework, where the Bombes were assembled. Post-war, BTM would become involved in mergers and acquisitions, and team up with competitor Powers-Samas. There would be links to IBM in America, and organisational transitions to both ICL and ICT in the UK. Bombe codebreaking machine production would have been useful to have on your CV when bidding for contracts, but it was only permitted after the mid-1970s when it was then declassified by the British Government, some thirty years after the war. The BTM managing director, Philpotts, was knighted for his wartime services, and several senior staff were awarded medals to acknowledge their contribution. The equivalent wartime organisation (in a loose sense) in the United States was perhaps the National Cash Register Company (NCR), which designed and built four-wheel Enigma Bombes for Washington using WAVES personnel to assist them.

German engineering and technology

German companies and organisations were generally very successful, and had expertise in engineering, specialist optics, cameras, aircraft, tanks, and, of course, encoding machines. Their cameras, such as Leica, Rolleiflex, Contax, and other specialist optical equipment were considered as probably the best in the world at the time, and this was certainly well before the Japanese were able to compete with them on quality. Many of the factories had to diversify in wartime to make armaments, munitions or similar. Siemens was one of those firms, and is today a blue chip company with a worldwide, international track record. Yet it would use forced labour during the war, partly due to a lack of men as they were fighting the Allies. The long hours of work and conditions would affect the physical and mental health of workers, but the alternative may have been deportation to a concentration camp and mass starvation. As far as we can ascertain, no forced labour was used by the British in the war, and prisoners of war were generally treated in accordance with the Geneva Convention.

Names and titles of organisations

The reader may have become aware that in reading the glossary various organisations and sections changed their names over time as they developed, merged, or transitioned into more modern versions of the original. The key example is probably GC&CS, which transformed into GCHQ, but is by no means the only example. GC&CS ended and GCHQ officially started in April 1946, yet GCHQ as a name was used some years before on occasions at Bletchley Park. CESD morphed into CESG, and originally did not have the word 'electronic' in the name, but is probably a reflection of organisations moving into modern technology over time. This can sometimes make the history and events of some organisations more challenging to track and follow. While GCHQ now has many 'arms' and branches, it is likely to stick with that same title for the foreseeable future, but cyber-tracking and monitoring with the help of artificial intelligence is likely to dominate its activities in a rapidly changing world.

Deception

Numerous organisations would play their part during the war in organising deception against the enemy. While this would include codebreaking activities, other specialist work, such as the use of the *Aspidistra* high-powered transmitter in England, would also make an impact, cause confusion, spread propaganda, and build a picture of uncertainty, using deception. Spies and double agents were waiting to act against Hitler and the Axis powers. Codebreaking assisted in achieving their objective.

Questions and Answers

A brief Q&A section is provided that may be of interest.

Q. *Did the codebreaking outstations communicate with one another or not?*

A. The codebreaking outstations were supporting Bletchley Park, so acted more or less independently, apart from the management of resources, supplies, food, and administrative supplies. The outstations were naval administrative shore-based stations, and naval discipline did impact on the outstations, which were run like ships with naval terminology. However, from reports, there was a bit more leeway for the Wrens at the country house outstations, as they were smaller than Stanmore or Eastcote. Personnel did transfer to and from bases from time to time across different outstations, so could then compare the facilities. Some may have met up with other staff they had previously worked with, or had dealings with some months before. The discussions would generally be rather mundane, on food quality, comparison of the berths or accommodation, of managing their free time with possible travel to London to see a show, and so on. It was generally discouraged to discuss technical aspects of other bases and outstations for reasons of security. One learned and became familiar with codebreaking machines and specific processes and procedures over time, and could then apply this knowledge effectively at other outstation sites, or at HQ, Bletchley Park.

Q. *To what degree did agents and double agents influence intelligence gathering for the Allies in the Second World War?*

A. Possibly quite a lot, but the most significant double agent was Garbo or Pujol, who appeared to have fooled the Germans in the build-up to D-Day, sending them false information with small elements of factual information to make it sound plausible. MI5 would be monitoring the messages and letters that Garbo would send his Nazi handler in Portugal and Spain, to ensure they were on top of things and there were no surprises, or opportunities for top-secret information being passed across. This was possibly the greatest deception act by the Allies during the war.

Q. *Was there a sort of rivalry and competitive element between the American codebreakers and the British at Bletchley Park?*

A. It would seem so, yes. On one hand the British had to share information and intelligence with the Americans, but that did not mean they considered the British approach to the design of codebreaking machines as perfect. They would build their own version of the Bombe and use it in Washington. When one considers there were exchanges of military personnel, (ETOUSA), and the 6812th US Signals coming to Outstation Eastcote to learn how to use the Bombe machines, there had to be a degree of trust and cooperation. On the whole, it worked well but the Americans may have become frustrated with Bletchley Park in terms of the methods of tackling the Nazi four-wheel Enigmas, and maybe that is why they designed and built their own version, using WAVES personnel.

Q. *Was the move to establish GCHQ at Eastcote a wise one if it was later relocated to Cheltenham?*

A. It may have been considered as a temporary measure at the time but we are not clear on this. Considering that Bletchley Park closed after the war, and personnel and equipment had to be transferred somewhere, Eastcote was as good a place as any. It was a time for restructuring the organisation, to regroup, identify new priorities in what had become the start of the Cold War period with the Russians and Chinese. Outstation Stanmore was considered as a location for GCHQ, but it was abandoned as too small to accommodate all the sections and departments necessary. The Americans were also at Eastcote and would expand considerably, and there was already a track record of working with them at Eastcote on things like the Bombe codebreaking machines. GCHQ Eastcote was a victim of its own success, in outgrowing the base that then needed further expansion, and there simply was not the room nor physical space available, whereas Cheltenham had the land to expand over time.

Q. *With so many codebreaking machines and systems during the Second World War and a range of decoding machines, was there confusion as to which to prioritise at a given time?*

A. A good question, and one that could even be asked of TNMOC at Bletchley, or the Bletchley Park Museum, which may have a more detailed understanding of the prioritising of machines and systems. It is important to appreciate that there were parallel systems of encoding and decoding machines during a significant part of the Second World War, and neither could be neglected. Even though Lorenz and the advanced encoding machines were of great interest, there were many more Enigma machines made and many more Enigma-transmitted messages. Both were of interest to the Allies, but the equipment to decipher them was quite different and specialist. It would have been a mistake to ignore Enigma when the advanced enemy encoding machines came in. The challenge for the Allies was very much how to allocate and distribute their limited resources. Traffic analysis became crucial as the war advanced.

Q. *How important was codebreaking during the Second World War for the Allies and their eventual defeat of the Axis powers?*

A. We can say that without it the Allies would have been far more exposed both strategically and militarily. Having said that, the war was won by brave men and women who either worked in manufacturing of armaments and equipment or who fought on the battlefields, sometimes making slow progress to gain ground. The military commanders valued the intelligence from Bletchley Park as it gave them another string to their bow in driving out the enemy. It helped them prioritise certain actions at times. Knowing your enemy and their resources available can be a bonus in helping to defeat them, or to encircle them. Decoded messages would sometimes confirm whether the enemy had fallen for a trap, or were mobilising in a particular direction or particular time, or perhaps building up strength in preparation for a counter-attack. Of course, the Nazis also played this dangerous game, and listened to Allied broadcasts of some military communications. The biggest challenge was tracking the Nazis' changes and modifications to encoding equipment, code books, cipher keys, and that was not always straightforward or successful.

Q. *Why did the Nazis not discover Bletchley Park or the outstations during the war?*
A. It was perhaps one of the best kept secrets in wartime, and was very sensitive information. People were scared off by the Official Secrets Act and the threat of jail for those who gave anything away. The German agents had been rounded up one by one in Britain, so feedback on Allied installations to Berlin would have been very limited. The Nazis had many maps of the UK and had collected photos and documents from their agents well before the war had started, as preparation. It is not understood how the Luftwaffe did not pick up reconnaissance photos of places like Knockholt, with large aerial arrays in Kent, or the movement of thousands of people around Bletchley Park and the surrounding area. The Germans were rather complacent in that they were convinced their encoding machines were unbreakable, and later on assumed that even if the British had cracked the odd Enigma message, they could not possibly cope with the vast volume of communication being sent and received in Europe. How wrong they were. It is a bit like the security passwords and security systems on your smartphone, or computer. Be aware, that while they may buy you some time in preventing hacking by others for a while, there is no completely secure security system out there. That is not appreciated generally, and there is now an industry of twenty-first century criminals out there, and many rogue states, who are targeting organisations and individuals to penetrate their firewalls.

Q. *Did Winston Churchill ever visit the codebreaking outstations during wartime?*
A. As far as we can tell, Churchill only visited Bletchley Park and not the outstations. However, he was well aware of the outstations and reports would be summarised of progress to him. In 1908, the year of Churchill's marriage and honeymoon, he was only a few yards away from the site that would later become Outstation Eastcote in 1943.

QUESTIONS AND ANSWERS

Q. *Did the Robinson or Colossus codebreaking machines exist at the outstations?*

A. The Robinson and Colossus machines were principally at Bletchley Park, and built for them by the Post Office Engineering Establishment, and partly by TRE as regards the former machine. There were two Colossi that did go to Eastcote, but only after the war ended and Bletchley Park had closed down.

Q. *Did Alan Turing consider the Bombe machine to be a computer?*

A. Although not a true computer, the Bombe was an electro-mechanical machine using relays to operate it. It was, however, a device that mechanically assisted to reduce manpower in determining the elimination of millions of permutations of message settings, and arriving at the appropriate correct message settings so that Enigma could be broken for a particular key and day. This degree of automation may have convinced Turing that it was a computer, but in modern-day terms it lacked a storage memory, and other features that we consider are necessary to be a computer. The Colossus was a semi-programmable computer, albeit a specialist one. Other functions could be applied to it by simple programming, as well as the codebreaking. It also used digital switches using valves. It is possible that Turing considered the Bombe to be a computer, but he had nothing else to compare it to at the time.

Q. *How many Enigma keys did the Americans at Eastcote break during their work on the ten codebreaking Bombe machines?*

A. The 6812th US Signals cracked or broke 425 Enigma keys during their time at Outstation Eastcote.

Q. *Are there any lessons we can learn and apply from the wartime codebreaking and intelligence activities to the twenty-first century?*

A. There may be a number of lessons to be learned. Firstly, do not assume that your friend and ally one moment will always remain so. History shows that loyalties can change over time, and countries can change their allegiances. Then, do not assume any encoding system is perfect. Most have flaws and weaknesses, and the trick is to keep plugging those weaknesses, and to continue to confuse the enemy. One should use a variety of techniques and systems to collect and process intelligence information, not just one type. That is, one should use encoding machines, agents, drones, listening devices, bribery of foreign people with access to information, and to try to create a map of the enemy's communication systems. Teamwork is essential by intelligence agencies in peacetime and in war. Identifying and agreeing what to share as regards intelligence and what information to keep for yourself is a key factor. But a balance must be struck with your allies, and you must accept that there will be risks taken, with consequences of those risks where something sometimes goes askew, exposing weaknesses. Finally, have a robust security system and checks in place that prevent your systems being hacked or compromised.

Q. *Did the United States cope better or worse with signals intelligence than the British during the Second World War, as regards successes?*

A. The answer to that question lies deep within *A Documentary History of the US Signals Intelligence in World War 2,* which was published in 1993 via the Center of Military History in Washington DC. It is a highly complex subject, and there were successes and failures on both sides of the Atlantic. Readers are directed specifically to Chapter IX, Tactical COMINT, which sets out the operational history of the Signal Security Agency and associated Signals intelligence divisions and detachments. The history is both fascinating and highly detailed. There is acknowledgement of the importance and differences between tactical intelligence, and strategic intelligence. It is not easily summarised due to the complexity, but essentially, both the British and the Americans played their important and crucial roles in collecting and processing signals intelligence during the war.

Q. *Were the Wrens at codebreaking outstations early computer programmers?*

A. That all depends upon whether you consider the Bombe codebreaking machines to be computers or not. The general consensus of opinion is that the Bombes were electro-mechanical machines, and were not structured as computers would be, as there was no memory bank, no central processor, and no formal operating system. The Wrens were principally data-processors on the *Bombes*. But with the more advanced machines, such as Colossus, which was the world's first semi-programmable computer and codebreaking machine based at Bletchley Park, the Wrens who operated those could be considered as early computer programmers. The encoded data was read by a magic eye sensor, and the programming was via setting multiple switches based on instructions from Bletchley Park. Colossus could also be 'programmed' to do other things such as calculations, whereas the Bombe could not.

Q. *How significant were the Poles in codebreaking during the war?*

A. As Polish mathematicians and codebreakers were heavily involved in cryptographic work even before the war commenced, they had a head start on the British and other nations. They built the first codebreaking machine to tackle Enigma, and would later share technical information with the French and the British on the German encoding machine. Their work in Poland, Vichy France, Algiers, and the United Kingdom gave the Allies a boost in terms of cracking Enigma and problem solving on ciphers. They saved the Allies valuable time with their work and their expertise.

Abbreviations

ACSWSA	Admiralty Civilian Shore Wireless Service
AFHQ	Armed Forces Head Quarters
AFSA	Armed Forces Security Agency
AI	Artificial Intelligence
APO	Army Post Office
ASDIC	Anti-submarine detection investigation committee (Sonar)
ATS	Auxiliary Territorial Service
BP	Bletchley Park
BTM	British Tabulating Machine Company
CESD	Communications Electronic Security Department
CESG	Communications Electronic Security Group
COMINT	Communications Intelligence
CPC	Communist Party of China
CSDIC	Combined Services Detail Interrogation Centre
CSO	Composite Signals Organisation
D/F	Direction finding
EDSAC	Electronic Delay Storage Automatic Calculator
ELINT	Electronic Intelligence
ETOUSA	European Theatre of Operations United States Army
FECB	Far East Combined Bureau
FID	Field Intelligence Division
FRUEF	Fleet Radio Unit Eastern Fleet
FUSAG	First US Army Group
GC & CS	Government Code and Cipher School
GCHQ	Government Communications Headquarters
GPO	General Post Office
HSK	High-speed Keen
HUMINT	Human Intelligence
ISK	Intelligence Services Knox
JDU	Joint Discrimination Unit
JISD	Japanese Intelligence Signals Digest
JSRU	Joint Speech Research Unit
JSSU	Joint Service Signal Unit
JTLS	Joint Technical Language Service
LCSA	London Communication Security Agency

LEO	Lyons Electrical Office
LSIC	London Signals Intelligence Centre
MCIC	Maritime Cryptologic Integration Center
MI 1(b)	War office/British Army intelligence in Whitehall, London
NASD	Naval Air Signals Intelligence Digest
NATO	North Atlantic Treaty Organization
NCSC	National Cyber Security Centre
NSA	National Security Agency (USA)
OKW	Oberkommando der Wehrmacht. (High Command of German Armed Forces)
OKW-Chi	OKW-Chiffrierabteilung. Decryption department of the German high command
OP-20-G	Office for Chief Naval Operations (US Navy)
OSA	Outstation Adstock
OSE	Outstation Eastcote
OSG	Outstation Gayhurst
OSS	Outstation Stanmore
OSS	Office of Strategic Services (USA)
OSP	Outstation (Bletchley) Park
OSW	Outstation Wavendon
PLUTO	Pipeline Under the Ocean
PORE	Post Office Research Establishment
PORES	Post Office Engineering Research Station
RAF	Royal Air Force
RN	Royal Navy
RNELH	Ruislip Northwood Eastcote Local History Society
RSRE	Royal Signals & Radar Establishment
SCU	Special Communications Unit
SIGSALY	Signal voice encoding/decoding US-built machine
SIS	Signals Intelligence Unit
SCAG	Special Cryptologic Advisory Unit
SCDU	Services Communication Development Unit
SHAEF	Supreme Headquarters Allied Expeditionary Force
SIGINT	Signals Intelligence
SLU	Special Liaison Unit
SOE	Special Operations Executive
TA	Traffic Analysis
TICOM	Target Intelligence Committee
TNMOC	The National Museum of Computing
TRE	Telecommunications Research Establishment
WAAF	Women's Auxiliary Air Force
WATU	Western Approaches Tactical Unit
WAVES	Women Accepted for Volunteer Emergency Service
WEC	Wireless Experimental Centre
WRNS	Women's Royal Naval Service

Terms and Names

Abwehr The German Secret Service during the Second World War.

Aspidistra A joint Anglo-American transmission system used to fool the Germans during the war, principally developed by RCA in America and installed in Crowborough, East Sussex.

Banburismus A system devised by Alan Turing to improve the efficiency of codebreaking when attacking enemy messages to establish Enigma settings.

Baudot International teleprinter code invented by Emile Baudot. A version of special binary digital code applied to punched paper tape using the alphabet, and some additional characters and commands.

Bodyguard The code name for the Allied deception operation in 1944 comprising Fortitude North and Fortitude South.

Bureau B A name given to conceal the identity of Bletchley Park and used by BTM in Letchworth.

Cadix The code name for the intelligence centre used by the Poles in southern France at Uzès, under the control of Vichy France before German occupation of the area.

Cambridge Five A group of five British individuals educated at Cambridge University in England, in positions of trust, such as within MI5, who passed secrets to the Soviet Union, and acted as spies either during the Second World War, post-war, or both. They were Anthony Blunt, Guy Burgess, John Cairncross, Donald Maclean and Kim Philby.

Cantab The name given to the project for design and construction of codebreaking Bombe machines at BTM in Letchworth.

Cipher A term often synonymous with code. It is a process for encoding or decoding a message or similar. One may speak of cipher 'keys', and this is a type of cipher that can be deciphered with knowledge of the key settings. Enigma was one encoding/decoding machine that relied on the settings of a key, and the Allies were tasked to crack as many keys as possible to read enemy messages.

Cobra A separate and specialist piece of codebreaking equipment that would be attached to Bombe machines with a long thick cable, so as to improve the performance.

Code Synonymous with the term cipher or cypher, a code is a set of rules applied, usually in secret, to enable communication with others who can access those rules. It can be based upon a system of letters of the alphabet, numbers, hieroglyphics or images applied in a particular sequence, or via a specific set of rules. The object is to maintain secrecy and to have control over who can access the message or data being encoded. One encodes messages or data, and then another decodes them, using the relevant rules.

Code book A book or document that contains the rules applicable to a particular cipher or code, to enable consistency of approach by those who wish to encode messages or data. Distribution of such code books must be controlled to maintain secrecy and confidentiality. There would be various versions of code books used by the enemy.

Colossus The world's first semi-programmable computer designed and built by the engineering part of the Post Office for Bletchley Park. It was designed utilising 1,500 valves, and used to attack the German Lorenz and advanced teleprinter-based encoding machines used by the German high command. A Mark 2 version was produced near the start of D-Day in 1944, which was several times faster than the original.

Crib Clue.

Cryptanalysis A method of codebreaking using a mathematical or statistical approach.

Cryptography Writing of hidden messages, also known as encrypting.

Cryptology A codebreaking method that uses a more linguistic approach.

De-Chi Part of the Colossus decode element of advanced teleprinted non-morse messages, which was stripped away using the Colossus and Robinson codebreaking machines. This is discussed in some detail in Captain Jerry Roberts' book *Lorenz*.

Divisions The naval term for 'parade', used by the WRNS or Wrens.

Dolphin The name given to the Enigma cipher used by U-boats to attack Allied shipping in the Atlantic.

Enigma A rotary-based encoding machine designed by Arthur Scherbius, and used by the Nazis and other enemy countries during the war. Enigma literally means riddle or puzzle. Different versions were made, some with three wheel rotors, others with four.

Fish Communication links across Europe used by Hitler and his generals for German high command communication. Around nineteen links were established. The routes would have names of Fish to identify them, such as 'Gurnard' or 'Bream'. Fish was a Bletchley Park code name for this traffic. Fish link messages were often 10,000 characters long, and needed special equipment and processes to analyse and decode.

TERMS AND NAMES

Some examples are given below:

Squid – To Army Group South
Octopus – To Army Group A and 7th Army
Trout – To German authorities in Memel
Bream – To Rome
Herring – North Africa
Gurnard – Berlin to Zagreb
Dolphin – U-Boats Atlantic (Heimisch)
Jellyfish – Berlin to Paris

Note Octopus was replaced by Stickleback

Fortitude The operation for deception of the Nazis, split into two parts, Fortitude North and Fortitude South.

Fortitude North The code name for the operation by the Allies to deceive the enemy, with activities and radio transmissions in Scotland, to tie up Nazi forces in Norway in 1944. Part of Operation Bodyguard in deception activities.

Fortitude South The code name for the operation by the Allies to deceive the enemy as regards where the main force in England would attack occupied France in 1944, and relevant to preparations for D-Day.

Freebornery A name given to the tabulating section under Freddie Freeborn from BTM that processed message data deciphered from codebreakers at Bletchley Park for a database using Hollerith punched card machines.

Geheimschreiber A Nazi 'secret writer' advanced encoding machine.

Ghost army An American specialist division that acted using deception techniques and operations to support main forces and Commando units during the war.

Green Hornet The nickname for the SIGSALY voice-encoding and decoding system designed by the Americans during the war.

Hagelin An American cipher machine.

Heath Robinson See Robinson.

HMS *Pembroke* See Pembroke.

Hydra A cipher key used by U-boats for Enigma communication.

Jellyfish The Berlin to Paris high command Nazi communication link, being one of several Fish communication links used by the enemy in the Second World War.

Job's Up Indication of a verbal statement by WRNS personnel in a Bombe machine room that the message settings had been calculated correctly and could be transferred to Bletchley Park for final processing via Typex machine.

Key Cipher letters and or numbers relating to an encoding machine.

Kriegsmarine German Navy.

Lorenz A German teleprinter-based attachment used by the Nazis during the last war to encode German high command messages. These would be in various models such as SZ40, SZ42a, and SZ42b. Relatively few were made compared to the mass-produced Nazi Enigma machines.

Luftwaffe German Air force.

Magic The Americans referred to wartime Japanese intelligence decoded via codebreaking staff and machines as Magic.

Medusa A cipher key used by OKW to command U-boats in the Mediterranean with Enigma.

Menu A set of instructions using letters and graphical connected lines provided by Bletchley Park codebreakers to set up the Bombe codebreaking machines, to tackle the message settings of the German Enigma encoding machine.

Morse code Communication system of dots and dashes transmitted electrically via an electro-mechanical key, sent either via wires or transmitted via radio telegraphy. Often encrypted during wartime.

Newmanry A specialist codebreaking section at Bletchley Park during the war involved with advanced codebreaking machines.

Non-Morse A type of system for communication of messages and data that was used extensively during the last war by the Nazis for high-speed, teleprinter-based communication. It was based on the Baudot code of dots and crosses to communicate the alphabet, plus certain punctuation marks. This was used to communicate messages from the German high command using teleprinter attachments, and machines such as Lorenz and more advanced German secret writers.

One-Time-Pad A method or tool used in encoding messages for encryption using random letters or numbers that makes them virtually impossible to duplicate by the enemy. One-time-pads are often used by modern organisations to send a code to a client or customer by text or telephone to be then inserted on a computer screen. A code that is re-sent to the customer will be completely different numbers or alphanumeric codes to aid security.

Overlord The code name for the D-Day invasion in June 1944.

Paddock The secret underground facility at Brook Road, Dollis Hill, London, for alternative Cabinet Rooms. Only used for a limited time period by Churchill.

Pembroke The first part of the naval term for administration and associated bases, which were 'Special Duties X' bases and often established as codebreaking outstations. Pembroke V was the most used term for codebreaking stations from an administrative viewpoint, but Pembroke III was previously used at some locations, if only for accounting purposes. Official naval onshore bases were termed HMS *Pembroke* and run as though they were ships.

TERMS AND NAMES

PV Royal Navy WRNS abbreviation for Pembroke V. This superseded the Station X designation.

The Pound A name sometimes used at Knockholt listening station in Kent for the base that occupied Ivy Farm.

Reflector Part of an Enigma encoding machine.

Robinson A codebreaking machine used at Bletchley Park to decipher message settings of the advanced German encoding machines. Also sometimes referred to as Heath Robinson, after the cartoonist, due to its haphazard wiring.

Rodding A system to assist decoding of enemy messages at Bletchley Park.

Room 40 British Naval intelligence HQ based in London and evolved from the First World War.

Rotors Wheel rotors used in the Enigma series of machines, and similar rotary-based encryption machines. These were installed using a code book with instructions and the sequence could vary. Rotors were increased to give more permutations of message settings and improve security. A series of rotors would be selected from a box and placed in a particular specific sequence in the Enigma machine, based upon a code book with instructions. The rotors would be identified with Roman numerals such as I, II, III, IV, V. The quantity of rotors would increase over time for some machines, increasing the permutations of message settings by a considerable degree.

Secret writer An advanced type of Nazi encoding machine.

Settings (Enigma) The configuration of the Enigma machine prior to either sending an encoded message or receiving an encoded message. The settings must match exactly on both the sending machine and receiving machine in order to be able to read and decode the message.

Siemens relay An electrical component originally made by the Siemens factory in Germany, and copied by British engineers to use in codebreaking machines as they were more efficient than our designs.

Shark Naval encoded German messages, often with U-boat positions, movements, and associated intelligence, transmitted over the airwaves using Morse code and enciphered via Enigma. It was the German Triton U-boat communication, given another name.

SIGABA An American encoding machine.

Special Duties X Another term for a top-secret base with intelligence processing and codebreaking. Many Wrens were allocated to such bases and specialist duties, although their administrative name for the onshore locations was Pembroke V, or HMS *Pembroke* V.

Station X Another name for Bletchley Park, headquarters of GC&CS in Buckinghamshire.

Steckerboard The plugboard on certain Enigma machines with connecting cables to increase the permutations and security.

Sturgeon The code name for the German T52 secret writer encoding machines and group of machines.

Teleprinter An electro-mechanical machine for communication of text from one site to another. Used at Bletchley Park, Y-stations and several codebreaking outstations during the war, and elsewhere.

Testery A specialist section at Bletchley Park during the war with a team of codebreakers and mathematicians working closely with the Newmanry on decoding advanced enemy encoded messages.

Torch Operation Torch was an amphibious landing on a large scale in North Africa in November 1942.

Triton This was a cipher used by U-boat HQ to communicate with operational Atlantic U-boats. Bletchley Park called Triton 'Shark'.

Tunny An advanced British designed and built machine to encode secret messages that used a teleprinter by the enemy, and which was prefixed SZ. Also, the range of enemy intelligence and Fish traffic from advanced encoding machines, such as Lorenz, which had to be intercepted by the Allies during wartime. It would also be the British nickname for the Lorenz SZ40 advanced teleprinter attachment used by the Nazis for encoding messages for the German high command.

Ultra The high-level intelligence encoded by the enemy during the last war, and largely or substantially decoded by personnel at Bletchley Park with the support and assistance of others.

Venona A post-war project to expose and examine foreign intelligence intrusion into the secrets of Western powers, which had used a number of different methods of espionage, including use of foreign agents to infiltrate their security services. Initial clues of espionage by the Russians were exposed as far away as Canberra, Australia, and the project lasted several years. GCHQ Eastcote was part of the Venona project, among others. The investigation was funded for many years before winding down in the 1980s.

Voluntary Interceptors Sometimes abbreviated as VIs, these were radio amateurs recruited by the Foreign Office to listen for intelligence on the radio, including for Morse code intercepts. They were recruited via membership of the Radio Society of Great Britain. The original idea of using amateurs can be accredited to Lord Sandhurst.

Wheel rotors Another way of describing Bombe machine wheels, which are needed to set up the codebreaking machine and to emulate the Enigma encoding machine. See *Rotors*.

TERMS AND NAMES

Woburn A country house estate with grounds use as a billet for WRNS personnel during the Second World War who needed access to Bletchley Park.

Women Accepted for Volunteer Emergency Services (WAVES) American female volunteer personnel, also used to construct the American naval version of the British codebreaking Bombe machine.

Wren Name associated with British WRNS female naval personnel. Wrens operated most of the codebreaking machines at Bletchley Park and the outstations during the war, at shore-based stations that were generally run as ships using naval terminology and protocols.

Wrennery Buildings near or attached to an operational base and usually being adjacent to an onshore naval base with accommodation for WRNS personnel or Wrens. Woburn Abbey was one such wrennery, during the war, although it was not a naval base, but a country house estate. The Wrens had accommodation there so as to have access to Bletchley Park nearby.

Acknowledgements

The Association of Wrens

Bentley Priory Museum, Stanmore

Bletchley Park Heritage Trust

Bletchley Park – David Kenyon, Research Historian

Bletchley Park – Guy Revell, Museum Archivist

British Telecom (BT) archives

The Channel Islands Military Museum, St Ouen, Jersey

The Churchill Rooms, London

Eastcote Residents' Association

GCHQ Archives and Museum, Cheltenham (particular thanks to Craig at the Museum of GCHQ for assistance in licensing various photographs)

NB all photos in this book that are copyright of GCHQ are licensed by kind permission of the Director of GCHQ

Hall Place, Bexley, Kent

Headstone Manor and Museum, LB Harrow

Heritage Foundation Letchworth Garden City

The Imperial War Museum, London

LB Hillingdon, Uxbridge Reference Library

Historic England

Historic England website and photo-reconnaissance photographs

Letchworth Tourist Information Office

Letchworth – Garden City Collection, www.gardencitycollection.com

The London Borough of Harrow

The London Borough of Hillingdon

ACKNOWLEDGEMENTS

The National Archives at Kew

The National Cryptologic Museum, Maryland, USA

The National Museum of Computing, Bletchley Park, Block H, Bletchley Park, Milton Keynes

Pembroke Park Estate and Public Footpath – LB Hillingdon

The Royal Navy

The Radio Society of Great Britain (RSGB)

Ruislip Northwood Eastcote Local History Society

The Science Museum, London

Wikipedia

WinstonChurchill.org

WRNS, *Wren History 1939–1945* online source

BBC WW2 People's War – online source

BBC and BBC News – online sources

Bibliography

Books, articles, and publications

Agar, John, *Turing and the Universal Machine* (London: Icon Books Ltd, 2001)
Agar, John, *The Government Machine – A Revolutionary History of the Computer* (Cambridge/London: MIT Press, 2003)
Aldrich Richard James. *GCHQ* (London: Harper Press, 2010)
Avarez, D., *Allied & Axis Signals & Intelligence in WW2* (London: Routledge, 1999)
Batey, Mavis, *Dilly – The Man who Broke Enigmas* (London: Biteback Publishing, 2017)
Brown, Louis, *A Radar History of World War II* (Bristol: IoP Publishing Ltd, 1999)
Buttar, Prit, *Between Giants – The Battle for the Baltics in World War II* (Oxford: Osprey Publishing, 2013)
Campbell-Kelly, Martin, *ICL – A Business and Technical History* (Oxford: Oxford University Press/Clarendon Press,1990)
Cawthorne, Nigel, *Alan Turing – The Enigma Man* (London: Arcturus Publishing Ltd, 2016)
Coghlan, Peter & Dr Thomas Cheetham, 'Knockout Punch', *Ultra*, Bletchley Park Magazine Issue 18, 2022
Copeland, B. Jack plus others, *Colossus – The Secrets of Bletchley Park's Codebreaking Computers* (New York USA: Oxford University Press, 2010)
Corera, Gordon, *Intercept The Secret History of Computers and Spies* (London: Weidenfeld and Nicolson/Orion, 2016)
Cox, Colleen A., *A Quiet and Secluded Spot-Ruislip, Northwood, and Eastcote* (London: Ruislip, Northwood, and Eastcote Local History Society, 1991)
Dunlop, Tessa, *The Bletchley Girls* (London: Hodder & Stoughton Ltd, 2015)
Erskine Ralph & Smith, Michael, *The Bletchley Park Codebreakers* (London: Biteback Publishing, 2011)
Ferris, John, *Behind the Enigma The Authorised History of GCHQ Britain's Secret Cyber-Intelligence Agency* (London: Bloomsbury Publishing, 2020)
Gannon, Paul, *Colossus – Bletchley Park's Greatest Secret* (London: Atlantic Books, 2006)
Gladwin, Lee A., *Alan Turing, Enigma, and the Breaking of German Ciphers in World War II* (article, Archives.gov., Fall 1997)
Greenberg, Joel, *Alastair Denniston* (Barnsley: Frontline Books, 2017)

BIBLIOGRAPHY

Greenberg, Joel, *Gordon Welchman* (London: Frontline Books, 2016)

Harper, Stephen, *Capturing Enigma* (Stroud: The History Press, reprinted 2016)

Hinsley, F.H. & Stripp, A., *Codebreakers – The Inside Story of Bletchley Park* (University of Oxford: Oxford University Press, 2001)

Jenkins, Roy, *Churchill* (London: Pan Books, 2001)

Jennings, Christian, *The Third Reich is Listening – Inside German Codebreaking 1939–45* (Oxford: Osprey Publishing, 2018)

Jones, R.V., *Most Secret War* (London: Hamish Hamilton, 1978)

Kasekamp, Andres, *A History of the Baltic States* (London: Red Globe Press, 2018)

Kenyon, David, *Bletchley Park and D-Day* (New Haven and London: Yale University Press: 2019)

Kerrigan, Michael, *ENIGMA – How Breaking The Code Helped Win World War II* (London, Amber Books, 2018)

Kippenhahn, Rudolf, *Codebreaking – A History and Exploration* (London: Constable, 1999)

Koorm, Ronald, *Backing Bletchley – The Codebreaking Outstations from Eastcote to GCHQ* (Stroud, Amberley Publishing, 2020)

Lamb, Christian, *Beyond The Sea – a Wren at War* (London: Mardle Books, 2021)

Large, Christine (Director at Bletchley Park), 'Some Human factors in codebreaking', from a paper published in 2002 given at RTO HFM Symposium

Levine Joshua, *Operation Fortitude* (London: Harper Collins Publishers, 2012)

Lopez, Aubin, Bernard, Guillerat, *World War II INFOGRAPHICS* (London: Thames & Hudson, 2019)

Macintyre, Ben, *Double Cross* (London: Bloomsbury Publishing, 2012)

Matthews, Peter, *SIGINT* (Stroud: The History Press, 2018)

McKay, Sinclair, *The Secret Life of Bletchley Park* (London: Aurum Press Ltd, 2011)

McKay, Sinclair, *The Secret Listeners* (London: Aurum Press Ltd, 2013)

McKay, Sinclair, *The Lost World of Bletchley Park* (London: Aurum Press Ltd, 2013)

McKay, Sinclair, *The Spies of Winter* (London: Aurum Press Ltd, 2016)

McKay, Sinclair, *100 People you never knew were at Bletchley Park* (London: Safe Haven Books Ltd, 2021)

McKay, Sinclair, *Secret Britain* (London: Headline Publishing Group, 2021)

Messenger, Charles, *The D-Day Atlas* (London: Thames & Hudson, 2014)

Miller, Russell *Codename Tricycle* (London: Pimlico, 2005)

Montefiore, Hugh Sebag, *ENIGMA – The Battle for the Code* (London: Weidenfeld and Nicolson/Orion, 2011)

Morris Moses & John Wade, *Spycamera – The Minox Story* (West Sussex: Hove Collectors Books, 1998)

Page, Gwendoline, *We Kept The Secret* (Norfolk. Geo. R. Reeve Ltd, 2008)

Patch, John, Commander John Patch US Navy (Retired), 'Fortuitous Endeavour – Intelligence and Deception in Operation Torch' (*Naval War College Review*, Vol. 61 No. 4 Autumn Article 9, 2008)

Paterson, Michael, *Voices of the Codebreakers* (Barnsley: Greenhill Books, 2018)
Pearson, Joss, *Bletchley Park's Secret Room* (Stroud, Amberley Publishing, 2015)
Philpott, Colin, *Secret Wartime Britain* (Yorkshire: Pen and Sword Books Ltd, 2018)
Ramon, Jose, Fuensantana, Francesco Javier Lopez-Brea Espian, Frode Weierud, *Spanish Enigma: A History of the Enigma in Spain* (2010) Taylor & Francis Group LLC (2010)
Ramsey G. Winston, *The War in the Channel Islands – Then and Now* (Poland: After the Battle Magazine Publications, 1981/2012)
Rich, Ben R. & Leo Janos, *Skunk Works* (New York: Back Bay Books, Little Brown and Company, 1994)
RNELHS, *The Home Front Ruislip, Northwood and Eastcote in Wartime* (London: Ruislip, Northwood and Eastcote Local History Society, 2007)
Roberts, Captain Jerry, *Lorenz* (Stroud: The History Press, 2018)
Singh, Simon, *The Code Book* (London: Fourth Estate Limited, 2000)
Smith, Michael, *Station X – The Codebreakers of Bletchley Park* (London: Pan Books, 2004)
Smith, Michael, *Bletchley Park – The Code-Breakers of Station X* (Oxford: Shire Publications, 2014)
Smith, Michael, *The Debs of Bletchley Park* (London, Aurum Press Ltd, 2015)
Storey, Neil R., *WRNS The Women's Royal Naval Service* (Oxford: Shire Books/ Osprey Publishing, 2017)
Summers, Julie, *Our Uninvited Guests* (London: Simon & Schuster, 2018)
Taylor, Neil, *Estonia – A Modern History* (London: Hurst & Company (Publishers, 2018)
The National Archives, *Operational Selection Policy OSP28 – Government Communication Headquarters & its Predecessors* (National Archives, revised January 2006)
Tidy, Josh, *Letchworth Garden City in old photographs* (Letchworth: Heritage Foundation Letchworth Garden City, 2016)
Tidy Josh, *Letchworth Garden City Through Time* (Stroud: Amberley Publishing Ltd, 2015)
Turing, Dermot, *XY & Z The Real Story of How Enigma was Broken* (Stroud: The History Press, 2018)
Turing, Dermot, *Prof – Alan Turing Decoded* (Stroud: The History Press, 2016)
Vogal, Steve, *Betrayal in Berlin* (London: John Murray, 2018)
Welchman, Gordon, *The Hut Six Story* (Kidderminster: M&M Baldwin, 2018)
Weller, A., *Secret Eastcote.* (London: Friends of Eastcote House Gardens Community Archive Publication, date unknown)

Articles and Papers

After the Battle, Issue 37 (Historical Society)
Atlas, Company historical information ICL and ICT

BIBLIOGRAPHY

Avery, Andrew J., *All The King's Men – British Codebreaking Operations 1938–43*, thesis, East Tennessee University (2015)

Bletchley Park – Outstations – A Brief History, mkheritage.org.uk

Boon, Rachel, PhD student University of Manchester. 2020 Thesis: *Research is the Door to Tomorrow – The Post Office Engineering Station Dollis Hill 1933–1958* (University of Manchester, Centre for History of Science, Technology and Medicine.

COBRA Paper by David Whitehead CEng MIEE (1994)

Ford, Steve, *RAF Eastcote High Road, Eastcote – Archaeological Desk-Based Assessment* for George Wimpey (West London) Ltd (March 2007)

Edited by J. Gilbert & J.P. Finnegan, *US Army Signals Intelligence in World War II – A Documentary History* (Center of Military History United States Army, Washington D.C. 1993)

Graces Guide to British Industrial History, Graces Guide, 2012 (Graces Guide Registered Charity) Information on BTM Co.

Hanyok, Robert J., *Eavesdropping on Hell – Historical Guide to Western Communications Intelligence and the Holocaust 1939–1945* Series IV Vol. 9 (Center for Cryptologic History, National Security Agency 2005, Second Edition, United States Cryptologic History/ADET)

Judkins, Dr Phil, *Enigma: On Cruise Missiles, Rockets and Superguns – First Time Around* (Chairman, Defence Electronic History Society: Paper presented 15 October 2013)

Large, Christine (Director at Bletchley Park), *Some Human factors in codebreaking*, from a paper published in 2002 given at RTO HFM Symposium

Local Paper article (2014), on unveiling of the commemorative plaque at Pembroke Park for Outstation Eastcote and GCHQ

Mowry, David P., *Cryptologic Aspects of German Intelligence Activities in South America in WW2*, Series IV, WW2, Vol. 2 (National Security Agency, Center for Cryptologic History, 2011)

Newton, Katherine, History of Government/Gov.Uk. *Aspidistra: The wartime breakthrough you've never heard of* (Blog August 2019)

Sale, Anthony, *The American 6813th Technical History 1945,* reformatted by Tony Sale, 2003

Signal City, Geoffrey Dykes, RN Communications Branch Museum/Library

The Independent, Article on Dorothy O'Grady (Date unknown)

The National Archives, *Operational Selection Policy OSP28 – Government Communications Headquarters and its Predecessors* (Revised January 2006)

Patch, Commander J., US Navy Retired – 'Fortuitous Endeavour'- Intelligence and Deception in Operation TORCH. Naval War College Review Vol. 61 No.4 Article 9. (2008)

The Rutherford Journal, The Turing Bombe (Online)

Toms, Susan (RN&E LHS), *The History Behind the Road Names for Pembroke Park, Eastcote*

Toms, Susan (RN&E LHS), Papers and articles from The Ruislip, Northwood, Eastcote Local History Society, *Codebreakers at Eastcote*

Toms, Susan (RN&E LHS), *Enigma and the Eastcote Connection – 2005*, The Ruislip, Northwood, Eastcote Local History Society
Tony Sale – Menus
Wilcox, Jennifer, *Solving The Enigma*, History of the Cryptanalytic Bombe, Reprinted 2015, Center for Cryptologic History, National Security Agency (NSA)

Websites

www.airmuseum.com/archives
www.bletchleypark.org.uk
www.Bombe.org.uk (Bombe types)
www.Britishtelephones.com (UK telephone history)
https://chris-intel-corner.blogspot.com/search?q=italian+cryptography (Italian cryptography)
www.codesandciphers.org.uk (The British Bombe, 6812th Signal Security Detachment (Prov) APO 413 US Army/pdf scan via Tony Sale)
www.commsmuseum.co.uk
www.Cryptomuseum.com (Netherlands)
www.Firstworldwar.com
www.goldbeach.org.uk
Hertsmemories.org.uk (BTM webpage)
www.HistoryNet
Online Podcast E80 by Bletchley Park, October 2019, on Outstation Eastcote
Online Podcast E145 Torch to Tunis – Bletchley Park
Online Podcast E128 by Bletchley Park, 'Whitehall 7947'
www.maproom.net
www.mullard.org
www.heritagegateway.org.uk/gateway, the search 'Drayton Parslow'
www.Prabook.com
www.theintercept.com
Radio Boulevard, Western Historic Radio Museum
Rusilip.co.uk, Ruislip Online, online source, including extracts from DTI staff articles relevant to Eastcote, post-war
Russia Beyond, www.rbth.com
www.theintercept.com
www.troodosmountain.org
War History online, www.warhistoryonline.com
The Wartime memories project, www.wartime memoriesproject.com
WATU, https://en.wikipedia.org/wiki/Western_Approaches_Tactical_Unit
Wikipedia.org/wiki/Typex
Wikipedia /Wikipeda.org/wiki/Y-station

Miscellaneous Sources

Bill Thompson USN (Ret).
Commanders of World War Two, Key Publishing Ltd.

BIBLIOGRAPHY

Correspondence and discussions with an ex-Wren, Eileen Lawrence (née Hughes), who worked at two codebreaking outstations during the war, and who later became an MI5 officer.

Discussions with managers of various military-based museums on wartime historical events.

Discussions, letters, and communication with certain ex-Wrens who worked on codebreaking machines and equipment during the war and who contacted the author's publishers after reading his book, *Backing Bletchley*, published in 2020.

My particular thanks to Damien Horn of Jersey, C.I., curator of the Channel Islands Military Museum at St Ouen, Jersey, to allow reproduction of certain photographs of wartime military equipment to be used within the glossary, from a private collection.

Discussions or emails with individuals who worked on the outstation base at Eastcote or had family members who had links with the base or Y-stations. This included some ex-Wrens.

Discussions with individuals who have had some knowledge of the Eastcote Outstation, and mainly post-war, several of them locals.

Discussions with Betty Hollingberry, ex-Wren, based at Eastcote during wartime as Betty Vowles.

Discussions with a Bletchley Park voluntary guide at Northwood Hills Library in 2018.

Discussions with a member of the National Museum of Computing at both Northwood Hills Library and at Ruislip Manor Libraries in 2018.

Discussion with a number of ex-British Telecom engineers who trained at Bletchley Park after the war.

Discussions with T. Voore, ex-BBC test engineer, on radio equipment and electronic equipment used in wartime. Additionally, discussions with him on the George Blake prison escape outside Wormwood Scrubs prison.

Emails and correspondence with members of the Association of Wrens over the last few years.

Researching wartime WRNS officer records online.

Research and investigation of various relevant maps, charts, diagrams, statistics relevant to the subject matter.

Examination of local maps of the Eastcote and surrounding areas sourced at Uxbridge Reference library and elsewhere.

Exhibition at The Science Museum in 2019 on GCHQ and codebreaking.

Extracts from Microsoft Powerpoint Presentation (R. Koorm FRICS) on Codebreaking Outstations – Eastcote to GCHQ (copyright 2018).

Extracts from Microsoft Powerpoint Presentation (R. Koorm FRICS) on Support Services to Intelligence Operations during WW2 (copyright 2019).

Extracts from Microsoft Powerpoint Presentation (R. Koorm FRICS) on D-Day and Codebreaking during WW2 (copyright 2019).

Extracts from Microsoft Powerpoint Presentation (R. Koorm FRICS) on Fake News or Deceiving the Enemy During WW2 (copyright 2020).

Investigation of various relevant maps, charts, diagrams, statistics relevant to the subject matter.

Investigation and study of the two volumes of the Bombe registers on loan to the National Archives at Kew (HW25/19 and HW25/20).

Maps, photographs, and information via the collections officer at the Garden City Collection, Letchworth, following detailed discussions with the collections officer.

Maproom.net. My thanks to this online organisation for their help and assistance in providing certain specific maps. Also, in their excellent communication and prompt response to the author's queries on maps of London.

Personal War diary entries of Corporal Edward Thomas William Pearce, Royal Engineers 238th Field Company, 1943 and 1944.

Radio Society of Great Britain (RSGB) Emails exchanged with the Radio Society of Great Britain (2021/2022) (RSGB).

Smithsonian Channel, various documentaries on the Second World War.

The Valve Museum and articles by Tony Sale on Colossus

Various Television documentaries on codebreaking and intelligence and the Second World War.

Various TICOM reports: TICOM Secret Intelligence in Nazi Germany – Fish and the Jellyfish Convoy.

Personal war diaries of Royal Engineer E. Pearce.

NB: A proportion of the above presentations were prepared by the author for museums, history societies, and similar. Some were given in person and some online. The presentations are the copyright of the author. Photographs within the presentations are credited to the source or sources where appropriate.

Some of the National Archives reference documents (reference codes) researched are listed as follows, but are not a complete list, only a snapshot of some that have relevance to the subject. Note that the endnotes also contain references in places to specific National Archive documents:

HW 25/19, HW 25/20 [Vols 1 and 2 Bombe Registers]

HW 14/9, HW 14/57, HW 14/48, HW 14/43, HW 14/56 (cover story for Stanmore and WRNS staff recruitment), HW 14/58, HW 14/123

HW 14/48, HW 64/63, HW 64/65, HW 14/51, HW 14/60, HW 34/17, HW 34/21, HW 47/1, HW 64/25, HW 50/6, HW 14/164

HW 15 (GC&CS Venona Project Records)

HW 64/63, HW 64/25, HW64/45, HW 64/68, HW 64/76, HW 14/164, HW 14/62

FO 366/2221 (Financial arrangements GC&CS Eastcote)

WO 208/5092 (Polish outstations), HW 4, HW 2 /69, HW 25/20, HW 25/22, HW 25/36, HW 41 /401, HW 50/72, HW 55/1, HW 64/28, HW 192/420, HO 391/12, HW 8/97, FO 366/2221

BIBLIOGRAPHY

Museums in the UK that may be of interest to the reader

The Imperial War Museum, Lambeth, London (www.iwm.org.uk)
Bletchley Park, Bucks. (bletchleypark.org.uk)
TNMOC, The National Museum of Computing, Bletchley Park, Bucks. (www.tnmoc.org)
Battle of Britain Bunker Museum, Uxbridge, Middlesex (battleofbritainbunker.co.uk)
Bentley Priory Museum, Stanmore, Middlesex (bentleypriorymuseum.org.uk)
Hall Place Museum, Bexley, Kent

Note on selected images and photographs

Those monochrome images provided by GCHQ and the Museum of GCHQ under licence are © Crown Copyright, by kind permission Director GCHQ.

We have tried to acknowledge all those contributors who provided photographs, diagrams, charts, maps, tables, or statistics within this glossary and the series of glossary volumes. Several of the diagrams provided are the author's sole copyright, and are annotated as such.

Author's Note

Writing these glossary volumes has been a challenge in terms of the time, research, and checking/verification process. Where occasional errors have crept in it is hoped these are relatively minor. The intention has been to provide the reader with a reasonably balanced view as to what went on years ago, in respect of codebreaking, support, deception, intelligence, incorporating people, activities and events on both sides of the war. Just as there is a difference of opinion as to how the war in Ukraine is being seen and reported between Russia and the West, there are bound to be differences as to who did what and when during the Second World War, the lead-up to the war, and the post-war era.

Most of the people involved are no longer around today, and we have to rely heavily on reports, books, diaries, memoranda, historical archived records, and the occasional memory of a surviving wartime veteran. I have been fortunate enough to have spoken to some of those veterans, who really knew what it was like to work at outstations, at Y-stations and other supporting establishments. This includes the intense drudgery and boredom at times, as well as the lighter moments. It is difficult for us today to appreciate the level of commitment from these specialists, at a time when there were no smartphones, iPads, or computers around. Maps were tangible, physical things, not on a screen with pixels on a phone. The teamwork between quite different groups of people, from very different social backgrounds, was extraordinary. Without that teamwork the Bombe, the Colossus, the Y-stations, outstations, Bletchley Park, Post Office Research Station, and BTM would have been largely ineffective. That so many workers from different backgrounds kept the secret of what they were doing in wartime and beyond, or what they were building in special factories in Letchworth and elsewhere, is a credit to them. I salute all of them, irrespective of which part they played years ago.

As I was finishing the draft of this volume of the glossary, I was informed of some sad news in 2023, the passing of ex-Wren Eileen Lawrence (née Hughes), who I had the pleasure of communicating and speaking with on several occasions. She reached the grand age of 97, and had many varied interests in life. Eileen had worked for MI5 after the war, and signed the Official Secrets Act twice in her career.

Finally, I was recently able to study some personal war diaries of my late father-in-law, Edward (Ted) Pearce, a born and bred Londoner, brought up in Holborn, and who fought during the Second World War, at Dunkirk, in Italy and in North

AUTHOR'S NOTE

Africa. He was in the Royal Engineers, and proud of that. While he was not in the codebreaking or intelligence sectors, it struck me when reading his diaries that he and his fellow soldiers and engineers relied very much on others in the background collecting military intelligence for them to do their job, i.e., those people at GC&CS/Bletchley Park, the outstations, the Y-stations, etc. Yet he and his fellow engineers would not have known anything about Enigma, Robinson, Lorenz, Colossus, or the complex structure of intelligence gathering and decoding of enemy signals intelligence.

After the war, he would have been no more enlightened on the subject due to the Official Secrets Act being in place. He was one of many hundreds of thousands of brave soldiers fighting to preserve freedom of our country and of Europe. Ted became extremely ill during the war with peritonitis, and only just managed to scrape through. After the war he even attended the odd Dunkirk reunion in France. He only rarely spoke of his wartime antics as a Royal Engineer. I consider that this book is as much for recognition of people like him as it is for those who worked on codebreaking and intelligence support duties.

When he passed away, in clearing out his things and personal possessions, we came across a wartime souvenir of his, which we had no idea was there: a Second World War hand grenade at the back of a cupboard! I personally took the grenade to the local police station in a plastic carrier bag one bright and sunny Saturday morning in June, and put it on the station counter. The horror on the face of the police sergeant when he took the object out of the bag had to be seen to be believed. Ted would have been looking down from above and laughing at the chaos he had caused with a little help from his son-in-law, and that there was no written procedure in the many police lever arch files on the shelves behind the counter as to dealing with a hand grenade handed in by a member of the public, and with the pin still intact. Was the grenade live or not? I had no idea. In the end I had to carry it alone, around the back and install it most carefully in one of their empty police dog kennels, and they then awaited the bomb squad to deal with it. I did wonder how the police dogs would react to finding a strange metal object in their kennels after returning from work that day? I was almost tempted to contact the RSPCA.

Well done, Ted!

List of Events

(in sequence as written)

- BTM awarded Hollerith licence
- Scarborough provides intelligence base and supporting GCHQ
- Deciphering the Zimmerman Telegram
- Scherbius patents the Enigma machine
- BTM established in Letchworth, Hertfordshire
- Enigma displayed to the public at an exhibition
- Enigma machines sold to general public initially
- Steckerboard added to Enigma
- Scherbius acquires Dutch codebreaking machine patents
- Poles discover an Enigma at a railway station
- Arthur Scherbius is killed in a tragic accident
- AVA Company start making copies of Enigma machines
- French obtain Enigma secrets from a German traitor
- The Poles crack the Enigma code
- Post Office Research Engineering Station opens
- Typex machines developed by the British
- Factories licensed to build the Enigma
- US passes the Neutrality Acts
- Enigma in the Spanish Civil War
- GPO introduces the scrambler telephone
- The Poles build the Bomba machine
- Enigma rotors increase in quantity
- Bletchley Park acquired and purchased
- Churchill addresses Parliament upon becoming Prime Minister
- Molotov–Ribbentrop Pact signed
- Denniston leads Bletchley Park
- Bletchley Park becomes GC&CS
- Alan Turing joins Bletchley Park
- Gordon Welchman joins Bletchley Park
- HMS *Flowerdown* established as a secret listening base
- Tiltman cracks Japanese codes
- Germany invades Poland
- Churchill agrees location of alternative War Cabinet rooms

LIST OF EVENTS

- Flowers researches valve tubes for use as digital switches
- Bletchley Park acquires an Enigma
- Keddleston Hall offered to the War Office for military purposes
- Enigma finds uses across a wide range of organisations
- Turing develops concept of the Bombe machine
- Welchman designs the diagonal board
- Capture of German trawler and Enigma keys
- Mill Hill base established for training Wrens
- Bletchley Wrens billeted at Woburn
- Churchill requires a summary of codebreaking intelligence and restricts access on Enigma information
- BTM awarded contract to build codebreaking Bombe machines
- Keen in charge of Bombe production at BTM factory
- BTM coordinates production of Bombes in Letchworth
- Cantab project established
- Bombe transfer system from BTM factory agreed
- Team established at Bletchley to help coordinate Bombes
- First codebreaking Bombe machine used at Bletchley Park
- Philip's valve technology relocated to England from the Netherlands
- Second Bombe installed at Bletchley Park
- Wrens operate Bombe codebreaking machines
- Capture of Enigma rotors and code books
- Radio intelligence passed to Russian HQ by communist partisans
- Swiss Enigma codes broken by Nazis
- WAAF expands and provides intelligence support
- U-boats dominate the Atlantic
- Hollerith processing commences at Bletchley Park
- Poles establish codebreaking base in southern France
- Knox pulls together his team of codebreakers
- The Germans discover part of a Typex machine on a beach in France
- Nazi Enigma machine version termed 'Shark' by British
- Discovery of non-Morse messages intercepted in England
- Photo reconnaissance established
- Delegation of US Army & Navy SIGINT personnel to Bletchley Park
- Four codebreakers write to Churchill about resources
- Y listening stations expended to support Bletchley Park
- Bombe Victory is modified
- Country house codebreaking outstations established
- Wren narrowly escapes electrocution at a codebreaking outstation
- Hitler convinced to have a separate and secure encoding system for German high command
- Nazi Lorenz senior military signatories identified
- Bombes transferred across codebreaking bases
- First recorded German Lorenz transmission

- Personnel shortages operating codebreaking machines
- Sinking of SS *Aguila*
- Cipher No. 3 is compromised
- Turing develops Banburismus
- Italian codes broken for Battle of Matapan
- Bletchley Park decodes intelligence from Berlin to Tokyo regarding Hitler's military intentions
- Operation Barbarossa commences
- A burglary in Rome at the embassy
- German Lorenz operators make error in transmission
- Japan communicates a coded message in fourteen parts
- Pearl Harbor
- US Senate allows Lend-Lease facility for European allies
- American signals services stations established and expanded
- Stowe School considered for outstation
- Turing visits America
- Tests in London arranged for potential new codebreakers
- Capture of enemy Enigma code books via HMS *Petard*
- Britain is exposed in the Atlantic via BAMS
- Photo reconnaissance of Peenemünde by Allies
- TRE relocates to Malvern, Worcestershire
- Ultra codeword adopted
- Introduction of four-wheel Enigma
- Midway in the Pacific
- ETOUSA established in London
- OSG, Outstation Gayhurst established
- US naval intelligence visits Bletchley Park
- WAVES established by US
- Traffic analysis at Beaumanor transferred to Bletchley Park
- Bletchley fails to crack U-boat codes for a specific period
- Bill Tutte cracks the Lorenz encoding machine
- Vernam-Baudot encoding becomes significant in wartime
- Royal Navy and WRNS abandon term 'Station X'
- Polish codebreaker Rozycki dies
- Codebreakers in America form new research team
- Production policy of Bombe machines affected by differences of opinion
- Fletcher writes a report on Bombe status and personnel
- OSS, Outstation Stanmore established
- Knockholt established
- Newmanry and Testery established
- British worried about Russian cipher vulnerability to enemy
- Ultra intelligence used for Torch landings in North Africa
- Double agent 'Garbo' works at a safe house in London
- Bombe No. 1 renamed and relocated for training

LIST OF EVENTS

- Eastcote site considered for a military hospital
- Britain regains confidence in its naval code books
- Rejewski and Zygalski relocate to England
- BTM approaches Spirella for production and manufacturing support
- Concept of high-speed Bombes developed
- Siemens relays copied by the British
- Siemens uses forced labour in its factories during wartime
- Outstation Stanmore receives high-speed machines
- Knockholt is expanded
- Facsimile intercepts by the British
- Teleprinter use increases at outstations
- Hut 4 redesignated Pembroke V
- BRUSA cooperation established between Britain and America
- American cryptanalyst visits Bletchley Park
- Hollerith data processing relocates to Drayton Parslow
- Battleship *Scharnhorst* sunk with intelligence aided by Bletchley Park
- Outstation Gayhurst remains after two country house stations closed
- Denniston visits codebreakers in America to dissuade them from building their version of the British Bombe
- Cobra developed to tackle four-wheel Enigma machines
- Swiss warning on Enigma goes unnoticed
- Robinson codebreaking machine is built
- Robinson delivered to Bletchley Park
- Wrens trained in operation of Robinson and later the Colossus machines
- SIGSALY used by Churchill for transatlantic communication
- America builds its Naval Bombe machine
- Newman approaches Flowers of PORES for assistance
- Tommy Flowers commences building Colossus
- Kursk
- Outstation Eastcote established
- Bombe No. 1 relocates to OSE
- Increased security at codebreaking outstations
- 6813th US Signals operates at Bletchley Park
- Colossus codebreaking machine delivered to Bletchley Park
- First Bombe machines delivered to Outstation Eastcote
- SIXTA established at Bletchley Park
- Bletchley Park intercepts intelligence on V2 rockets
- Double agent Garbo commences his build-up of false information reports leading up to D-Day
- Incendiary bomb hits Outstation Eastcote during an air raid
- American signals engineers arrive in Britain to operate codebreaking machines
- American signals engineers – details of ETOUSA orders
- Selected OSE Bombes given American names
- BTM builds the 'super-Bombe'

- V1 hits Stanmore at OSS
- Last Bombe machine allocated to Americans at Outstation Eastcote
- Enigma adapted to improve security
- Mark 2 Robinson is built
- Michie and Turing discuss advanced machines while playing chess
- Bletchley Park spy feeds Russians intelligence
- Speech encipherment project progressed by Turing
- Use of teleprinters at codebreaking outstations increases
- A lack of trust in the Nazi codebreaking sections
- British spying on captured German generals and senior officers while in captivity in England
- Luftwaffe intelligence withdraws
- End of the U-boat successes
- Germans listened to military police radio prior to D-Day
- 'Morrison Wall' intelligence at Bletchley prior to D-Day
- Colossus Mark 2 delivered to Bletchley Park
- Mark 2 Colossus modified by Michie
- D-Day assault at Normandy
- Enigma intercepted after D-Day referencing Army Group 'B'
- Garbo misleads the enemy via a message on D-Day
- Operational Bombe machines at end of 1944
- Meeting of trio of world leaders in Yalta
- President Roosevelt dies
- TICOM informed of Russian Fish intelligence
- Efficiency of codebreaking Bombes operationally reaches a peak
- Jewish personnel involved in codebreaking and intelligence
- Fish communication links after D-Day
- VE day
- VJ day and end of the Second World War
- Final Bombe count at Eastcote at end of the war
- Total codebreaking Bombe quantities by end of the war
- Milner-Barry writes to thank US signals detachments
- Churchill instructs destruction of codebreaking machines post-war
- Bombes retained at Eastcote
- Cantab dinner at BTM
- America and the race to build the first digital computer
- Turing goes to work at NPL
- Establishment of the Eastcote Association
- Post-war cynicism about Enigma and Lorenz weaknesses
- Bletchley Park closes post-war
- GCHQ Eastcote established
- Creation of UKUSA agreement
- Turing visits Eastcote as a consultant
- American presence at Eastcote post-war increases

LIST OF EVENTS

- Turing designs the ACE computer
- Crown purchases the Eastcote site
- Venona project established post-war by the West
- Russia changes its codes and ciphers post-war, blocking out the West
- GCHQ transfers to Cheltenham
- Eastcote GCHQ becomes RAF Eastcote
- Turing dies a tragic death
- Post-war hybrid decoding machine built and operational
- Two Colossus machines sent to Cheltenham GCHQ
- BTM Merges with others post-war
- Gary Powers' U-2 spy plane shot down by Russians
- Professor Michie leads on Artificial Intelligence
- Information released post-war on codebreaking
- CESG relocates from Eastcote to Cheltenham
- Northwood Hills support for GCHQ closes
- Bletchley Park establishes a memorial for the three pioneering Polish codebreakers
- Welchman writes *The Hut Six Story* and has it published
- Flowers passes a course in personal computing
- Bletchley Park established as a museum
- Replica Colossus built at Bletchley
- Enigma machine stolen and sent to media presenter
- Visit to Outstation Stanmore post-war for some Wrens
- GCHQ builds new premises in Cheltenham
- NSA decrypts and translates material relevant to the Holocaust
- TNMOC established
- Michie dies in a road accident
- Eastcote site demolished
- Bletchley Park Roll of Honour established
- Commemorative plaque unveiled at Pembroke Park
- HM the Queen unveils GCHQ plaque at Watergate House
- Enigma makes record sale at auction
- Enigma discovered by marine archaeologists in the Baltic
- Plaques commemorate Alan Turing, mathematician, codebreaker, and pioneer of computer science
- AI safety summit held at Bletchley Park

Endnotes

Introduction

1. GC&CS Government Code & Cipher School, the predecessor of the later GCHQ.
2. Non-Morse is a high-speed digital system using Vernam-Baudot codes usually on paper tape.

Events

1. Churchill honeymooned with his wife, Clementine at Highgrove House, Eastcote in 1908.
2. A horse and carriage accident resulted in Arthur Scherbius dying in his early 50s, and therefore never seeing the development of his Enigma machine in wartime.
3. The licence was seen as a start, but the aim of BTM would be to become independent of licensing to American companies and consequently increase profitability.
4. It would be the determination of the encoding machine's settings that would be crucial for the Allies. With the correct settings, the messages for that day and key could be read with the appropriate equipment.
5. The weight of the portable Enigma came down to roughly one eighth of the original after redesign, and that made it much more of a commercial opportunity.
6. The pairs of letters that would be connected by cable links would often be limited to sixteen, leaving several unconnected, even though the cabling connections would increase the security of Enigma significantly.
7. Two Dutch Naval officers, T. Van Hengel and RPC Spengler (de Leeuw), invented and designed a rotary machine in 1915. However, this was nothing like Enigma.
8. BT, the successor to the Post Office Engineering Research Station, now occupies Adastral Park, Martlesham, Ipswich, being a science and innovation research and engineering site, which also has a bust of Tommy Flowers and a plaque commemorating him. It is understood the Park sees more than 60,000 visitors per year. There is even a Tommy Flowers Network run by BT to encourage innovation in the modern world of communications and technology.

ENDNOTES

9. The Germans discovered an abandoned Typex machine in France in the early part of the war but it was not seen as a threat to the Nazis and was ignored.
10. The three Polish codebreakers and mathematicians would be commemorated with a monument for their wartime contribution at Bletchley Park after the war.
11. HW 8/97.
12. Official Monument record MDR13527.
13. PV is Pembroke V, the naval administrative designation for codebreaking outstations.
14. BTM became involved in modern machines and even computers after the war, helped by a number of mergers and expansion.
15. Names and numbers of codebreaking Bombes are held within the Bombe registers on loan at the National Archives in Kew, London. Several Bombes had their names changed over time and were sent to different codebreaking sites or for modification and repairs.
16. See The Valve museum online website.
17. By 1944 at the Mullard Blackburn factory, the number of staff would be 4,185. The factory in Blackburn escaped large-scale bombing, but the Mitcham site was not so fortunate.
18. Outstation Eastcote alone had 800 Wrens working shifts around the clock on Bombe machines.
19. Brush bounce was a symptom of an electro-mechanical machine using fine wire brushes on a revolving drum, and its limitations at speed.
20. HW 50/72 Dossier on Hollerith Machinery Historical Notes on use of Hollerith equipment under Mr Freeborn in Hut 7 at GC&CS, provided by BTM. HW 64/63 Involvement of the BTM Co Ltd with GC&CS 1/6/42 -3-/9/43.
21. The château is available for holiday and vacation stays in modern times. A Californian with knowledge of the wartime history of the area and the château has written a book on the subject.
22. Squadrons included 540, 541, 542, 543, 544 for photo reconnaissance work after October 1942.
23. This statement is more of an opinion by the author, and the reader is encouraged to research further into any interaction between photo reconnaissance evidence and of Bletchley Park's traffic analysis.
24. HW 14/9.
25. National Archives AIR 40/2650 1935-38; HW 2/69 1/9/41-31/3/44. Polish Y-stations WO 208/5092 1940. Lists of Y-stations : HW41/401 1/10/41 – 17/8/45 German Naval Y-stations ADM 223/6 1945.
26. HW 25/19 National Archives, Bombe Registers Volume 1. See Victory and Leo entry under Bombe No. 1.
27. The outer two wheels would be motor-driving wheels, leaving ten 'data' wheels as compared to the three or four wheels of the Enigma machines. Significantly higher permutations and security.
28. The Wrens would have some 74,000 personnel in the Second World War, and only a small proportion would be utilised on Special X codebreaking duties.

29. An account of her becoming a Wren and going to Gibraltar and being sunk by U-boats on the SS *Aguila*, losing her life, was found by the author in Eastcote library, a few hundred yards from the original Outstation Eastcote. She was brought up in Pinner, Middlesex. Eastcote is adjacent to Pinner geographically.
30. A sunken ship, *Arizona*, forms part of the National Memorial in Hawaii, with a designed walkway bridge at right angles to it where one is able to walk over the wreckage below the water and see the outline of it. The author has been there, and found the experience of visiting the war memorial over the USS *Arizona*, moving.
31. In July 2023, a number of British Hurricanes were discovered buried in Ukraine, and thought to have been supplied via the USA under the Lend-Lease process for Russia. It may have been the case that the Russians did not wish to have to pay for them after the war and buried them. Attempts may be now made to restore some of them.
32. Photo interpreter Constance Babington Smith was credited with the first confirmation of a V1 rocket missile, seen on an inclined launch pad and with a wingspan of less than 20ft.
33. Source: 'ENIGMA: On Cruise Missiles, Rockets and Superguns – First Time Round', technical paper, Dr Phil Judkins PhD MA (Cantab) MSc, chairman Defence Electronic History Society.
34. HW 14/43 11/7/42–20/7/42.
35. More detailed information about Midway and cipher work will be made available in book three of this series of the *Codebreaking Glossary*, subtitled *Systems, Equipment, and Deception*.
36. American Air Museum in Britain, www.airmuseum.com/archive/unit/ETOUSA
37. SIXTA, while established in 1944 at Bletchley Park, had been in existence in a different form for a number of years, and this new organisation was probably more of a formality in the organisation.
38. Jerry Roberts, *Lorenz*.
39. See HW14/57.
40. HW 14/60.
41. According to a Bletchley Park history on outstations (Bletchley Park Jewels) that OSS had forty-nine operational Bombe machines. The Bombe registers indicate that there were seventy-six at the end of the war.
42. HW 14/56.
43. Ivy Farm was around 30 acres but expanded later to some 160 acres to accommodate all the aerials, infrastructure and outbuildings to house the vast numbers of personnel operating on site at Knockholt.
44. When in London, look at the rail map and Knockholt appears in the bottom right-hand corner, inside the county of Kent.
45. The Newmanry and Testery would be a combined team effort in tackling decoding of the advanced Nazi encoding machines, using a combination of both manpower and machines.
46. HW 14/60.
47. HW 25/19 National Archives Bombe Registers Volume 1, Bombe No 1, Victory/Leo/London.

ENDNOTES

48. High-speed rotor Bombes were later designed and built by the Americans for their attack on the four-wheel Enigma machines, which increased the permutations of message settings considerably and made them much harder to decode. See WAVES and OP-20-G.
49. We are talking of using valve technology as digital switches instead of much slower relays used previously.
50. The public footpath still exists on the site although the codebreaking huts and wartime layout has since been demolished. The developers made a slight amendment to the line of the footpath at the western end of the site but it is possible to walk the path and gauge how large the wartime site was in terms of scale.
51. HW 25/19 National Archives Bombe No. 1 – Victory, Leo, London.
52. www.codesandciphers.org.uk. Tony Sale collection.
53. Source: ENIGMA: On Cruise Missiles, Rockets and Superguns – First Time Round, Dr Phil Judkins PhD MA (Cantab) MSc, chairman Defence Electronic History Society.
54. A blue commemorative plaque exists outside the house that agent Garbo used as a safe house in Hendon.
55. Stewart's name heads up the Christmas dinner listings of American signals personnel, source Bletchley Park online website.
56. For ETOUSA see www.americanairmuseum.com/archive/ETOUSA
57. Report on the Bombe by 6812th US Signals. www.codesandciphers.org.uk
58. HW 25/19 and HW 25/20 – Data from National Archives and the official Bombe registers, listing names and Bombe numbers together with dates and other pertinent information.
59. The history of the individual Bombe machines that made up Giant can be discovered in the volumes of the Bombe registers on loan to the National Archives at Kew. There would be a distribution of machines after it was dismantled as too unwieldy a project.
60. It is the case that any bombing of the codebreaking outstations was purely local random bombing and not targeted specifically against codebreaking sites as far as one can tell.
61. It is worth recalling that Bletchley Park had no faith in Colossus until the Mark 1 was delivered and tested at Bletchley Park. It would be mathematician and codebreaker Max Newman who had faith in Tommy Flowers of PORES. Without Newman, Colossus would probably not have been built.
62. First US Army Group, a completely fictitious army force, used for deception purposes.
63. The deception plan by MI5 and double agent Garbo was so successful that the Nazis believed the main assault from FUSAG in England would still be coming over to the Pas-de-Calais well into July 1944, holding back key resources as a defence.
64. Bletchley Park Jewels, Outstations, Brief History.
65. A map showing the reallocation of land in Europe post-war discussed with Churchill and Stalin can be viewed in the Westminster War Rooms in the

Churchill section. Any person or persons of Polish origin viewing the map must feel betrayed by such a proposal, and loss of sovereignty, discussed amongst world leaders without Poland being represented.
66. Source: Bletchley Park and D-Day, Author Dr David Kenyon.
67. At the end of the war, Eastcote, the largest outstation, had a total of 103 Bombe machines.
68. Some of the relays were installed in Bombes at both Outstation Stanmore and Outstation Eastcote.
69. Any Bombe machines seen by the reader at exhibitions or museums will be replicas and not original.
70. The Barclays Bank in Eastcote closed a few years ago and the building currently hosts a coffee shop and café at the crossroads of Eastcote.
71. It is reported that Victoria Principal, who starred in the 1970s US TV soap *Dallas*, attended the American school in Eastcote post-war.
72. A movie on the development of the atomic bomb under the Manhattan project was released in 2023, called *Oppenheimer*.
73. ICL would eventually become absorbed by the Fujitsu Company in the late 1990s.
74. Reference *Skunk Works* by Ben Rich and Leo Janos.
75. After thirty years classified documents are usually passed to the National Archives via the Public Records Act and the FOIA (Freedom of Information Act) except those that are considered too sensitive, when there is a formal review of the documents and a decision made after scrutinising them. The FOIA states that after thirty years the documents shall be released to the public unless a specific exemption applies.
76. One of the outputs of CESG was public key encryption, developed by James H. Ellis in 1969, and before that he had worked for CESD and CESG since 1965. Further advances were made by staff such as Clifford Cocks, on asymmetrical algorithms. Source Troodos Mountain website.
77. ERNIE was based on true random number technology and is checked frequently by actuaries.
78. Many of these people went on to important careers in post-war Britain. Michie became an expert in aspects of medical science with his wife, and an expert in Artificial Intelligence. Roy Jenkins became a successful politician in Government.
79. Robert J. Hanyok, *Eavesdropping on Hell, Historical Guide to Western Communications Intelligence 1939–1945*, 2005, Second Edition, Center for Cryptologic History, National Security Agency.
80. Bullet point listing extracted courtesy of Bletchley Park website, www.Bletchleypark.org.uk, Roll of Honour.
81. ERA News Autumn 2014. This also gives a listing of proposed road names and block names that had to be filtered down further to a final truncated list and used by the developer.
82. Susan Toms is a senior member of the RNELH Society and has written several articles on the Eastcote Outstation for the RNELHS journal. Some back numbers are available to read online.

ENDNOTES

83. A listing of some of the more significant Turing papers is within the appendices of the first volume of this glossary, subtitled 'People and Places'.
84. The Bletchley Park A.I. safety summit had not taken place when this draft glossary was prepared.

Links, Events and Sequencing

1. Early experimental electric cars were produced in the early twentieth century, so the concept of an electrically powered motor car is not new.
2. Not all the information on the E.H. website appears to be accurate as regards the quantity of Bombe machines listed. Read and study with caution.
3. The driver of the lorry had with him a letter signed by Churchill, which stated that anyone who dared to obstruct this man in delivering his goods would have to deal with the Prime Minister himself!
4. ICL developed the Post Office software system Horizon in 1996, which was later subject of a scandal involving a number of sub-postmasters, the Post Office accusing them incorrectly of fraud and false accounting, and compensation claims are still ongoing at time of writing. Fujitsu took over in 1999 from ICL.
5. For more detail see the paperback book *Our Uninvited Guests* by Julie Summers.
6. Sir Bernard Lovell worked at TRE and later became the director in charge at Jodrell Bank Radio Telescope, ironically sometimes used for listening in to other organisations when requested by Government agencies.
7. Around fifty machines were retained and of these some sixteen Bombes were kept operational at Eastcote after the war ended. Therefore, Churchill's instructions to dismantle all the codebreaking machines was not completely adhered to.

Commentary on Events

1. On the matter of power supplies and continuity during wartime, in London, the tube rail network arranged to construct underground, in tunnels and lift shafts, various electrical control centres to aid power distribution in case of enemy bombing knocking out systems above ground. One may have been at, or near, Brompton Road near Knightsbridge. This area is no longer accessible from street level, and was featured on the TV documentary *Secrets of the London Underground*, shown on the Yesterday Channel in 2024. Little remains, but a few maps do exist and the TFL Museum has an old drawing showing a cross-section through the various floors of the complex secret wartime control centre.
2. SIXTA log readers at Bletchley Park may have been an exception to this rule and many were told about Enigma machines to put into context their work and objectives to achieve.
3. The outer two wheels of Lorenz would be motor drive wheels, the remainder could be considered as 'data wheels'.
4. Source: *US Army Signals Intelligence in World War II, A Documentary History*, published Center of Military History United States Army, Washington D.C., edited by James L. Gilbert and John P. Finnegan.

5. The Germans would refer to Garbo/Pujol Garcia as 'Arabel', his code name working for the Nazis.
6. *The Imitation Game*, Black Bear Pictures.
7. Hanyok, Robert J., *Eavesdropping on Hell – Historical Guide to Western Communications Intelligence and the Holocaust 1939–1945* Series IV Volume 9 (Center for Cryptologic History, National Security Agency 2005, Second Edition. United States Cryptologic History/ADET).

Organisations

1. D. Mowry, *Cryptologic aspects of German Intelligence Activities in South America during World War Two*, National Security Agency, Series IV WW2, Volume 11. United States Cryptologic History.
2. Hut Six Ultra was one of many terms and phrases used at GC&CS by codebreakers and personnel.
3. Volume 1 of the Registers reference HW 25/19, National Archives.
4. One wonders why it took so long to get the mansion at Bletchley Park listed, although it would be dependent to a degree on the formal application from the site.
5. The Windrush scandal has highlighted the period of colonialism and the British Empire, in particular the unfairness and racism that sometimes occurred. However, the Empire had given Britain status, political strength, and economic wealth. It could not go on forever, and the British Commonwealth remains an adjunct to it, but even that is dwindling over time, with links to Britain being severed.
6. Source: Troodosmountain.org/GCHQ
7. Watergate House in The Strand, London, arguably the initial relevant building that now has a commemorative plaque outside for the centenary of GCHQ.
8. Officially the name used at the previous Outstation Eastcote in April 1946. Presently in Cheltenham, Gloucestershire.
9. Alan Turing also had an interest in speech synthesis and encoding speech, and worked on various projects elsewhere, but it was too late to be used in wartime.
10. Bending the Nazi Knickebein beam, constructing Oboe, and other advanced radio-based systems.
11. Various sources for this information, including people who worked at the base.
12. Source: Thames Valley Archaeological Services Site Code REH0742 Author of report –Steve Ford. Commissioned by George Wimpey (West London) Ltd.
13. Mr Cort-Wright of the RSGB has DVDs available of parts of the documentary on radio listening services and mentioning the role of amateur radio enthusiasts during the war. The origin of this material was shown years ago by the BBC. Sufficient material was filmed to cover two documentaries but due to limitations only one documentary was completed. Source of this information based on Paul Cort-Wright's email to the author on 11 July 2020.
14. Reference Bletchley Park Podcast E138 SIXTA.

ENDNOTES

15. A plaque exists outside the building commemorating the SOE planning of the attack on the heavy water plant in Norway that was going to be used for weapons of mass destruction by the Nazis.
16. The picture is within the Garden City Heritage Collection at Letchworth, Hertfordshire, but can also be viewed online on the website.
17. QinetiQ is also based in Malvern, which was the town that TRE was based near during the war.

Commentary on Organisations

1. There were rows of Ampex tape recorders within the basement of the American building in West Berlin, officially monitoring the nearby airport, but simultaneously secretly recording telephone conversations from the Russians, tapped in east Berlin. Further information on Russian spy *George Blake*, can be found within the first volume of this Glossary, subtitled 'People and Places', by the author.

Index

Abwehr 20, 73, 90, 108, 160, 161, 180, 201
Adstock 38, 55, 60, 72, 131, 132, 136, 200
Africa vi, 54, 63, 101, 137, 140, 141, 144, 168, 169, 174, 198, 203, 206, 219, 222
Alexander 37, 110, 122, 127, 162, 164, 166, 198
Algiers 11, 33, 58, 137, 138, 223
America vi, 1, 2, 3, 9-11, 16, 17, 22, 24, 25, 31, 42, 45-50, 52-56, 58, 59, 63, 69, 70, 72, 73, 75, 80, 84, 85, 87, 89, 96, 98, 101, 103, 106, 109-115, 117, 119, 120, 121, 133, 138, 142, 147, 149-152, 155, 156, 161, 164, 166, 170, 171, 174, 175, 179, 182-186, 188, 190-192, 194, 195, 197, 198, 201, 203-205, 207, 213, 222, 223-226, 228, 229, 230, 232, 233
Arabel 64, 232
Arizona 2, 228
Arlington Hall 112, 155
Army 7
Artificial Intelligence 117, 125, 129, 199, 225, 230
ATS 31, 42, 61, 140, 153, 162, 183, 199
Australia 43, 109, 112, 116, 150, 156, 168, 184, 206
Axis Powers viii, 6, 15, 33, 37, 48, 55, 63, 70, 81, 87, 91, 149, 162, 169, 193

Baker Street 182
Baltic 14, 52, 93, 128, 210, 211, 225
BAMS 52, 222
Barbarossa 14, 44, 109, 222
Barnet 185
Batey 34, 43, 44, 110, 210
Battle of Britain 179, 217
Baudot 57, 142, 201, 204, 222, 226
BBC 91, 117, 123, 180, 209, 215
Beaumanor 56, 81, 222
Bell Labs 150, 161
Benjamin 42
Bentley Priory 61, 86, 179, 208, 217
Berlin 10
Blagrove 127
Bletchley / Bletchley Park 1, 2, 8, 9, 12-38, 41, 43-46, 48-52, 54-63, 65, 68-74, 76-82, 84-90, 92-97, 99-106, 108-111, 115, 117-127, 129-150, 152-155, 158, 159, 161-172, 174, 178-184, 186-215, 217-225, 227-232
Blake 152
Block C Bletchley 71, 163, 166, 152
Block D Bletchley 163
Block E Bletchley 163
Block F 62, 163
Block G 163
Block H 164, 209
Blunt 201
Bodyguard 201
Bomba 11, 12, 20, 120, 138, 191, 220
Bombe ii,vii, 1, 3, 15, 16, 20, 21, 24-29, 34, 37-42, 50, 52-61, 64-70,

INDEX

72, 73, 75-77, 79-87, 93, 96, 97, 99, 102-106, 108, 114, 124, 126, 131-134, 138, 140, 141, 143, 144, 146, 147, 150, 153, 154, 158, 163-168, 170, 171, 174, 176, 178, 180, 182, 184, 186, 187, 188, 192, 195, 197, 198, 201, 203, 204, 206, 207, 213, 214, 216, 218, 221, 222, 223, 224, 227-231
British Empire 1, 3, 132, 134, 138, 165, 168, 169, 174, 232
BRUSA 69, 70, 80, 84, 85, 110, 220, 223
BTM 1, 3, 21, 24-27, 32, 33, 40, 59-61, 65, 66, 68, 70, 71, 73, 82, 86, 99, 103-106, 116, 131-135, 138, 140, 142, 144-146, 149, 163, 165, 166, 170, 171, 174, 182, 183, 188, 191, 192, 199, 201, 203, 213, 214, 218, 220, 221, 223-227
Burgess 113

Cairncross 88, 113, 149, 152, 201
Cabinet war rooms 11, 17, 18, 23, 113, 136, 140, 155, 169, 170, 204, 220
Cadix 33, 58, 201
Canada 109, 113, 140, 150, 156, 168, 184
Canaris 160
Cantab 24, 25, 105, 133, 134, 160, 201, 221, 224, 228, 229
CESD 119.171, 173, 193, 199, 230
CESG 119, 139, 171, 173, 193, 199, 225, 230
Ceylon 31, 102, 183, 187
Channel Islands 208, 212, 215
Chateau des Fouzès 33, 58, 137, 227
Cheltenham x, 2, 104, 105, 109, 114, 115, 116, 119, 120, 124, 127, 131, 139, 172, 173, 174, 195, 208, 225
Chicksands 31
China 106, 117, 152, 199
Churchill 1, 10, 11, 13, 14, 17, 18, 23, 26, 31, 33, 36, 37, 45, 47, 50, 70, 75, 83, 89, 98, 104, 105, 108, 111, 113, 122, 133, 135, 136, 143, 144, 147, 148, 155, 163, 165, 169, 170, 189, 196, 204, 208, 209, 211, 220, 221, 223, 224, 226, 229, 231
Churchill Rooms 18, 208
Cobra 29, 53, 73, 79, 103, 201, 223
Colossus vii, 8, 16, 18, 22, 28, 62, 73, 74, 76, 77, 78, 81, 87, 93, 94, 95, 97, 101, 105, 106, 108, 110, 115, 116, 117, 121, 122, 123, 124, 126, 131, 134, 136, 137, 141, 147, 148, 151, 154, 155, 158, 163, 164, 178, 180, 197, 198, 202, 210, 216, 218, 219, 223, 224, 225, 229
Cooper 170
COMINT 171, 181, 198, 199
Commonwealth 101, 126, 140, 190, 232
CSDIC 92, 171, 199
CSO 2, 171, 199

Dayton Ohio 50, 58, 75, 140, 176
D-Day 19, 22, 56, 64, 81, 82, 83, 90, 93-97, 100, 101, 106, 131, 137, 143, 144, 147-149, 151, 152, 180, 182, 187, 190, 194, 202, 203, 204, 211, 215, 223, 224, 230
Delilah 89
Denmark Hill 35, 40, 62, 127, 130, 131
Desch 58, 176
Denniston 14, 16, 37, 59, 72, 108, 162, 210, 220, 223
Diagonal Board 16, 20, 21, 27, 28, 37, 142, 221
Direction-finding 94, 199
Dönitz 65, 90, 93, 175
Dollis Hill 8, 17, 76, 81, 89, 94, 111, 126, 131, 132, 136, 137, 143, 178, 184, 190, 191, 204, 213
Dorset 53, 135, 149, 184
Drayton Parslow 70, 71, 82, 134, 149, 163, 166, 214, 223
Dunkirk 13, 170, 218, 219

Eastcote 1, 27, 28, 40, 49, 50, 54, 58, 60, 61, 64, 65, 67, 72, 73, 78, 79, 80, 81, 83-88, 99, 102-105, 107-116, 119, 123, 124, 125, 126, 127, 131-136, 139, 157, 158, 168, 172, 174, 175, 179, 188, 194-197, 200, 206, 208, 209, 210, 211-216, 223-228, 230, 231, 232
Eindhoven 27
Eisenhower 95, 97, 144, 147
ELINT 171, 199
English Channel 180
Enigma viii, 1-13, 16-24, 29-35, 37, 39, 43, 46, 47, 51-54, 57-59, 61, 63, 68, 70-73, 75, 77-79, 82-85, 87, 88, 90, 96, 97, 103, 108, 114, 120, 122, 123, 127, 128, 137, 142, 144-148, 150, 153, 154, 157, 160-167, 172, 174-179, 182, 183, 189, 190, 192, 195-198, 201-206, 210-214, 219-227, 229, 231
ETOUSA 54, 84, 85, 134, 141, 185, 195, 199, 222, 223, 228, 229

FISH 40, 62, 73, 74, 76, 98, 100, 101, 108, 128, 131, 147, 148, 202, 203, 206, 216, 224
Flowerdown 220
Flowers viii, 8, 18, 59, 73, 74, 76, 77, 78, 81, 87, 94, 95, 106, 110, 115, 121, 127, 131, 136, 137, 142, 148, 151, 152, 178, 221, 223, 225, 226, 229
Fortitude 64, 83, 152, 201, 203
Fortitude North 201, 203
Fortitude South 64, 83, 152, 201, 203
France 8, 11, 17, 31, 33, 34, 45, 53, 54, 58, 63, 64, 65, 81, 90, 93, 97, 100, 101, 135, 137, 138, 140, 141, 148, 149, 161, 168, 170, 189, 190, 198, 201, 203, 212, 219, 221, 227
Frankfurt Am Main 54
Freeborn 32, 33, 70, 71, 134, 138, 144, 145, 149, 163, 165, 166, 203, 227

Freebornery 203
FUSAG 93, 97, 199, 229

Garbo 64, 83, 97, 152, 194, 222, 223, 224, 229
Garcia 64, 83, 97, 152, 232
Gayhurst 38, 54, 60, 72, 131, 132, 136, 200, 222, 223
GC&CS X, 9, 12, 13, 14, 15, 16, 17, 42, 63, 85, 108, 109, 112, 114, 124, 126, 127, 131, 132, 134, 136, 137, 138, 139, 154, 155, 161, 162, 167, 172, 173, 180, 188, 193
GCHQ vi,ix,x, 1, 2, 11, 65, 80, 104, 105, 108-116, 119, 120, 124-127, 131, 132, 136, 139, 154, 155, 156, 161, 171-176, 179, 187, 193, 195, 199, 206, 208, 210, 211, 213, 215, 217, 220, 224-226, 232
Geheimschreiber 203
Germany 2, 4, 6, 7, 10, 11, 13, 14, 16, 17, 19, 35, 44, 48, 52, 54, 56, 64, 67, 87, 91, 93, 94, 98, 100, 105, 108, 110, 120, 139, 149, 168, 169171, 177, 178, 184, 205, 216, 220
Gibraltar 42, 187, 188, 228
Good 95, 100
Greece 161, 168
Green Hornet 203
Greenock 187
GRU 112, 113, 174, 189

Hall Place 85, 208
Hanslope Park 89
Harris 83
Harrow 135, 208
Hendon 64, 83, 121, 229
Hitler ix, 8, 10, 13, 14, 17, 31, 39, 40, 44, 45, 47, 65, 72, 74, 78, 82, 83, 90, 91, 93, 96, 97, 100, 108.109, 142, 143, 146, 148, 157, 168, 169, 170, 175, 177, 179, 193, 202, 221, 222

INDEX

HMS Broadway 29
HMS Bulldog 29
HMS Flowerdown 16, 220
HMS Formidable 43
HMS Gleamer 29
HMS Griffin 21
HMS Petard 51, 56, 222
HMS Pembroke V 28, 58, 65, 69, 78, 103, 114, 125, 127, 132, 134, 168, 178, 180, 203, 204, 205
Hollerith 1, 3, 24, 25, 32, 33, 37, 70, 71, 82, 116, 132, 133, 134, 138, 141, 144, 145, 149, 162, 163, 165, 166, 170, 174, 182, 191, 203, 220, 221, 223, 227
Hollingberry 215
Holocaust 91, 100, 101, 124, 156, 213, 224, 232
Hughes 215, 218
Hut One 26, 164
Hut Two 164
Hut Three 96, 164, 166, 167
Hut Four 69, 139, 164, 166, 223
Hut Six 16, 37, 60, 80, 88, 94, 119, 120, 163, 164, 165, 167, 182, 212, 225, 232
Hut Six story 119, 120, 164, 212, 225
Hut Seven 32, 33, 163, 165, 166, 227
Hut Eight 32, 43, 56, 71, 163, 166, 167
Hut Nine /9A 164, 166
Hut Eleven 96, 167
Hut 11A & 11B 60, 134, 167
Hut Fourteen 167
Hut Fifteen 167
Hut Sixteen 167
Hut Eighteen 167
Hut Twenty three 167

India 168, 183
Irvin 138
Italy 16, 17, 45, 91, 141, 168, 171, 218
Ivy Farm 61, 205, 228

Japan 10, 16, 17, 44, 45, 46, 47, 54, 69, 101, 102, 106, 134, 152, 155, 162, 163, 164, 166, 167, 169, 171, 177, 180, 187, 189, 192, 199, 204, 220, 222
Japanese 16, 17, 44, 45, 46, 47, 54, 69, 101, 102, 134, 155, 163, 164, 166, 167, 169, 177, 180, 187
Jellyfish 100, 203, 216
Jersey 208, 215
Jews 67, 91, 100
JSRU 174, 199
JTLS 173, 175, 199

Keen 20, 24, 25, 59, 66, 68, 99, 103, 104, 106, 133, 134, 138, 170, 199, 221
Kent 41, 61, 81, 84, 85, 95, 122, 149, 196, 205, 208, 228
Kesselring 40
Kew 87, 141, 165, 183, 209, 216, 227, 229
KGB 88, 112, 177, 189
Knockholt 41, 61, 62, 68, 69, 89, 95, 97, 196, 205, 222, 223, 228
Knox 34, 43, 44, 110, 199, 221
Kriegsmarine 19, 29, 31, 56, 72, 91, 92, 166, 175, 176, 204
Kursk 78, 89, 223

Laughton-Matthews 186
LCSA 173, 175, 199
Lend-Lease 47, 48, 150, 183, 185, 222, 228
Letchworth ii, 3, 21, 24, 25, 26, 27, 37, 40, 42, 59, 61, 66, 73, 79, 82, 86, 99, 102, 106, 131, 133, 134, 138, 140, 143, 144, 146, 165, 170, 171, 182, 191, 192, 201, 208, 212, 216, 218, 220, 221, 221, 233
Lever 34, 43, 44, 122
Lime Grove 125
Lisbon 64
Listening Stations 165

London 3, 8, 11, 17, 18, 21, 22, 25, 27, 29, 35, 38, 50, 54, 61, 64, 66, 76, 80, 82, 83, 89, 91, 92, 94, 97, 98, 107, 110, 111, 115, 119, 120, 126, 127, 128, 129, 133, 134, 136, 137, 138, 139, 152, 154, 161, 170, 172, 173, 175, 178-182, 186, 189, 190, 191, 194, 199, 204, 205, 208-213, 216, 217, 218, 222, 227, 228, 229, 231, 232
Lorenz 20, 39, 40, 41, 45, 46, 57, 61, 73, 74, 76, 81, 90, 94, 97, 100, 101, 105, 108, 113, 118, 122, 130, 131, 136, 142, 146, 147, 148, 150, 154, 191, 195, 202, 204, 206, 212, 219, 221, 222, 224, 228, 231
LSIC 175, 200
Luftwaffe 19, 27, 31, 35, 38, 50, 53, 55, 63, 83, 85, 91, 92, 136, 141, 166, 175, 179, 196, 204, 224

Maclean 113, 201
Magic 101, 204
Malvern 53, 135, 143, 179, 184, 222, 233
Mansion The 12, 13, 122, 162, 164, 167, 232
Maryland USA 75, 209
Matapan 34, 43, 44, 222
Mediterranean - 34, 43, 56, 63, 92, 101, 183, 204
Menzies 37
Menu 25, 28, 87, 89, 96, 99, 132, 164, 204, 214
Michie 88, 95, 117, 118, 122, 125, 129, 131, 162, 224, 225, 230
Midway 54, 143, 186, 221, 222
MI5 64, 83, 92, 95, 97, 152, 154, 162, 171, 176, 180, 185, 191, 194, 201, 215, 218, 229
MI6 12, 92, 176, 181, 182
Mill Hill 21, 29, 134
Milner-Barry 36, 37, 104, 164, 165, 224
Molotov 13, 14, 220
Morrison wall 93, 94, 224

Morse vii, 1, 2, 31, 35, 37, 39, 40, 41, 46, 57, 59, 61, 62, 68, 74, 76, 82, 85, 89, 95, 96, 98, 102, 103, 122, 130, 143, 157, 166
Mullard 27, 28, 227
Murray Hill 161
Museum 10, 11, 75, 105, 122, 124, 138, 153, 154, 164, 195, 200, 208, 209, 213, 214, 215, 216, 217, 228, 231
Mussolini 169, 170

National Archives 37, 68, 87, 91, 102, 112, 123, 124, 141, 165, 173, 183, 184, 209, 212, 213, 216, 227, 228, 229, 230, 232
National Physical Laboratory 107, 111
NATO 156, 169, 185, 200
Nazi Party 177, 178
NCR 58, 59, 75, 140, 176, 192
Netherlands 5, 27, 140, 141, 168, 170, 214, 221
Newman Viii, 15, 62, 76, 77, 78, 81, 94, 100, 131, 136, 137, 148, 178, 204, 206
Newmanry 62, 94, 100, 137, 204, 206, 222, 228
New York 86, 112
New Zealand 109
NKVD 30, 176, 177, 189
Non-Morse 130, 204, 226
Normandy 63, 82, 95, 96, 149, 151, 180, 190, 224
North Africa 54, 63, 137, 140, 141, 144, 168, 203, 206, 222
North Atlantic 175, 200
Northwood Hills 120, 215, 225
Norway 91, 203, 233
NSA x, 109, 114, 120, 124, 156, 161, 173, 200, 214, 225, 232

Official Secrets Act 24, 51, 79, 80, 105, 106, 107, 108, 115, 118, 133, 136, 137, 151, 186, 191, 196, 218, 219
OKH 177

INDEX

OKW 90, 160, 177, 200, 204
Operation Sealion 175
OP-20-G 55, 58, 59, 72, 75, 176, 186, 200, 229
OP-20-M 58, 59, 176
OSA Adstock 38, 132, 200
OSE Eastcote 79, 80, 85, 132, 200, 223
OSG Gayhurst 38, 54, 132, 200, 232
OSP Park 132, 200
OSS Stanmore 61, 64, 79, 86, 132, 200, 222, 224, 228
OSW Wavendon 38, 79, 132, 200
Outstations ii, 22, 27, 28, 37, 38, 40, 54, 58, 60, 61, 64, 67, 68, 72, 73, 78, 79, 80, 81, 83, 84, 85, 86, 87, 99, 102, 103, 104, 107, 109, 110, 111, 123, 125, 126, 132, 135, 139, 168, 179, 188, 195, 196, 197, 200, 211, 213, 214, 215, 222, 223, 224, 225, 227, 228, 229, 230, 232
Overlord 63, 204

Pacific 49, 54, 155, 190, 222
Paddock 17, 18, 136, 204
Page 211
Paris 19, 54, 96, 137, 203
Pas de Calais 83, 93, 97, 144, 229
Patton 97
Pearce E.T.W. 218, 219
Pearl Harbor 10, 16, 17, 47, 48, 54, 70, 168, 222
Peenemunde 36, 52, 82, 92, 222
Pembroke 22, 28, 58, 65, 69, 79, 103, 114, 115, 125, 126, 127, 132, 134, 168, 178, 180, 203, 204, 205, 209, 213, 223, 225, 227
Pers-Z 90, 178
Philpott 105, 106, 133, 134, 192, 212
Poland 7, 8.11, 14, 17, 30, 33, 65, 91, 98, 137, 138, 140, 177, 184, 189, 198, 212, 220, 230
Polish/Poles Vii, 6, 7, 8, 11, 12, 15, 17, 19, 20, 30, 33, 137, 189, 191, 198, 201, 220, 221

Portugal 64, 194
Pound The 61, 205
PORES 8, 18, 59, 74, 76, 77, 104, 132, 135, 136, 137, 140, 151, 178, 188, 190, 191, 200, 223, 229
Post Office Research Engineering Station 8, 18, 73, 74, 76, 81, 94, 178, 184, 191, 200, 218, 220
Prospect Farm 70, 71
Pujol 64, 83, 97, 152, 194, 232
Purple 47, 70, 101

Qinetiq 184, 185, 233

Radley 59, 76, 77, 78, 136, 148
RAF 9, 17, 26, 27, 29, 31, 36, 61, 64, 80, 86, 99, 104, 110, 114, 115, 123, 125, 126, 127, 140, 153, 162, 173, 175, 178, 179, 183, 188, 200
Rejewski 7, 11, 12, 33, 58, 65, 120, 137, 138, 223
Roberts 57, 202, 212, 228
Robinson vii, 22, 28, 73, 74, 81, 87, 88, 93, 94, 97, 108, 115, 131, 134, 136, 137, 141, 154, 158, 180, 184, 197, 202, 203, 205, 219, 223, 224
Roll of Honour 79, 122, 125, 126, 134, 158, 225, 230
Rommel 40
Roosevelt 10, 14, 45, 47, 48, 55, 70, 98, 113, 155, 169, 186, 224
Room 40 2, 124, 139, 161, 172, 173, 180, 205
Rotor 205, 206
Royal Navy 1, 9, 29, 34, 42, 51, 55, 58, 65, 103, 132, 134, 140, 153, 169, 178, 180, 186, 187, 188, 200, 205, 209, 222
Rozycki 12, 58, 120, 137, 138, 222
RSGB 180, 185, 209, 216, 232
RSS 180, 185
Ruislip 84, 110, 127, 155, 158, 179, 200, 209, 210, 212, 213, 214, 215

Russia vi, 13, 14, 16, 17, 30, 31, 44, 45, 58, 63, 65, 67, 78, 88, 91, 98, 99, 102, 104, 105, 109, 111, 112, 113, 114, 117, 136, 139, 140, 147, 149, 150, 152, 156, 168, 171, 174, 176, 177, 178, 183, 184, 189, 191, 195, 206, 214, 218, 221, 222, 224, 225, 228, 233

Sale 105, 122, 124, 213, 214, 216, 229
SCAG 110, 161, 181, 200
Scarborough 1, 2, 42, 173, 220
SCDU 120, 181, 200
Scherbius 2-6, 10, 46, 202, 220, 226
Schmidt 7, 8
Scharnhorst 71, 72, 223
Science Museum 11, 154, 209, 215
Scotland 21, 133, 134, 135, 179, 186, 187, 188, 203
Secret Writer 67, 205
Selfridges 11, 75, 89, 98, 189
Settings 205
SHARK 35
SHAEF 54, 200
Sicily 63, 78, 141, 144, 168
Siemens 205
SIGABA 205
SIGINT 1, 2, 35, 36, 53, 62, 114, 139, 171, 181, 200, 211, 221
Signal City 187, 213
SIGSALY 11, 50, 75, 89, 136, 150, 161, 189, 200, 203, 223
SIM 181
SIS 181, 200
SIXTA 56, 82, 94, 167, 181, 182, 188, 189, 190, 223, 228, 231, 232
SLU 200
SOE 200
Spain 16, 33, 58, 65, 138, 194, 212
Special X 21, 22, 42, 103, 126, 134, 141, 168, 180, 186, 227
Speech Synthesis 75, 150, 174, 175, 232
Spirella 25, 65, 66, 99, 134, 138, 140, 143, 170, 182, 183, 188, 192

SS 52, 90, 91
SS Aguila 42, 187, 222, 228
Stalin 14, 17, 30, 44, 45, 78, 98, 109, 148, 174, 229
Stanmore 27, 28, 38, 40, 50, 60, 61, 64, 68, 72, 73, 79, 80, 96, 97, 102, 103, 123, 124, 131, 132, 136, 139, 157, 158, 188, 194, 195, 200, 208, 216, 217, 222, 223, 224, 225, 230
Stowe 49, 50, 60, 131, 132, 222
Sturgeon 206
Sweden 110
Switzerland 4, 5, 10, 19, 20, 30, 73, 128, 221, 223

Teleprinter 69, 71, 131, 206, 223
Testery 62, 77, 101, 137, 147, 206, 222, 228
Tiltman 16, 220
TNMOC 88, 105, 124, 125, 133, 158, 164, 195, 200, 217, 225
Tokyo 44, 69, 222
Tower of London 92
Traffic Analysis 56, 82, 94, 149, 163, 195, 222
TRE 53, 59, 66, 68, 73, 104, 135, 140, 143, 179, 184, 185, 197, 200, 222, 231, 233
Triton 35, 51, 52, 166, 205, 206
Truman 98, 155, 169
Turing viii, 3, 15, 16, 20, 24, 25, 27, 37, 43, 50, 55, 67, 70, 75, 76, 80, 88, 89, 96, 106, 107, 110, 111, 115, 117, 118, 120, 122, 125, 128, 129, 132, 133, 134, 136, 137, 138, 142, 151, 153, 154, 159, 161, 162, 164, 166, 197, 201, 210, 212, 213, 220, 221, 222, 224, 225, 231, 232
Tutte 20, 35, 39, 46, 57, 62, 122, 130, 131, 142, 143, 148, 162, 222
Tunny 40, 57, 62, 74, 76, 97, 108, 130, 131, 136, 137, 143, 148, 163, 164, 206
Typex 9, 29, 34, 35, 96, 145, 147, 154, 162, 163, 203, 214, 220, 221, 227

INDEX

U-Boats 31, 32, 35, 51, 52, 56, 59, 63, 65, 93, 141, 146, 147, 153, 163, 176, 180, 188, 202, 203, 204, 206, 221, 228

Ukraine 48, 218, 228

UKUSA 109, 155, 224

ULTRA 53, 63, 64, 119, 144, 150, 163, 182, 206, 210, 222

United States of America 10, 47, 50, 52, 54, 57, 69, 70, 75, 80, 84, 85, 93, 97, 105, 106, 109, 110, 111, 113, 120, 134, 140, 141, 155, 169, 173, 185, 195, 199, 200, 209, 210, 222, 223, 224, 228, 229

US Signals 29, 54, 80, 81, 84, 85, 87, 99, 103, 104, 126, 134, 141, 149, 183, 185, 195, 197, 198, 223, 224, 229

Valves 18, 22, 27, 59, 73, 74, 76, 81, 94, 106, 121, 136, 141, 161, 178, 197, 202

VE Day 101, 102, 134, 224

Venona 109, 111, 112, 113, 139, 155, 156, 206, 216, 225

Vernam-Baudot 57, 222, 226

Voluntary Interceptors 180, 183, 185, 206

Von Rundstedt 40, 97

Vowles ii, 215

V1 27, 36, 82, 83, 86, 184, 224, 228

V2 27, 36, 82, 83, 86, 184, 224, 228

WAAF 31, 42, 58, 140, 153, 187, 200, 231

Warsaw 6, 7, 33, 58

Washington 30, 45, 49, 50, 75, 84, 112, 114, 133, 150, 166, 170, 186, 192, 195, 198, 213, 231

Watergate House 14, 124, 127, 139, 154, 162, 172, 225, 232

WATU 214, 200

Wavendon 27, 37, 38, 55, 60, 61, 64, 72, 79, 131, 132, 136, 200

WAVES 55, 59, 75, 134, 140, 176, 185, 186, 192, 195, 200, 207, 222, 229

Welchman 3, 16, 20, 25, 27, 28, 37, 55, 56, 59, 77, 119, 120, 121, 122, 133, 134, 136, 137, 138, 142, 162, 163, 164, 165, 182, 190, 211, 212, 220, 221, 225

Woburn 21, 22, 38, 207, 221

Wrens viii, 21, 22, 23, 26, 27, 28, 29, 38, 39, 41, 42, 55, 58, 60, 61, 62, 64, 69, 73, 74, 77, 79, 80, 83, 84, 86, 87, 95, 99, 101, 102, 103, 104, 107, 114, 115, 122, 123, 126, 132, 134, 141, 142, 153, 158, 162, 165, 166, 168, 178, 180, 186, 187, 188, 194, 198, 202, 205, 207, 208, 215, 221, 223, 225, 227

WRNS viii, 2, 21, 26, 31, 37, 41, 55, 58, 60, 61, 69, 75, 79, 81, 89, 102, 104, 114, 126, 132, 134, 140, 152, 154, 155, 162, 178, 186, 187, 188, 200, 202, 203, 205, 207, 209, 212, 215, 216, 222

Wynn-Williams 59, 66, 68, 73, 104, 135, 184

Y-Stations 16, 27, 31, 37, 48, 63, 70, 80, 92, 94, 96, 103, 118, 119, 122, 131, 134, 143, 144, 146, 165, 166, 168, 179, 181, 183, 185, 187, 190, 206, 215, 218, 219, 227

Zimmerman 2, 220

Zygalski 12, 33, 65, 120, 137, 138, 223

6811th US signals 80, 85, 104, 185

6812th US signals 80, 84, 85, 87, 99, 104, 134, 185, 195, 197, 214, 229

6813th US signals 80, 84, 85, 104, 185, 213, 223